A
Writing Guide
for
IT Professionals

Dawn Henwood

OXFORD
UNIVERSITY PRESS

OXFORD
UNIVERSITY PRESS

70 Wynford Drive, Don Mills, Ontario M3C 1J9
www.oup.com/ca

Oxford University Press is a department of the University of Oxford.
It furthers the University's objective of excellence in research, scholarship,
and education by publishing worldwide in

Oxford New York
Auckland   Cape Town   Dar es Salaam   Hong Kong   Karachi
Kuala Lumpur Madrid   Melbourne   Mexico City   Nairobi
New Delhi   Shanghai   Taipei   Toronto

With offices in
Argentina   Austria   Brazil   Chile   Czech Republic   France   Greece
Guatemala   Hungary   Italy   Japan   Poland   Portugal   Singapore
South Korea   Switzerland   Thailand   Turkey   Ukraine   Vietnam

Oxford is a trade mark of Oxford University Press
in the UK and in certain other countries

Published in Canada
by Oxford University Press

Copyright © Oxford University Press Canada 2007

Library and Archives Canada Cataloguing in Publication

Henwood, Dawn E., 1969–
A writing guide for IT professionals / Dawn Henwood.

Includes bibliographical references and index.
ISBN-13: 978-0-19-541997-9
ISBN-10: 0-19-541997-9

1. Information technology—Authorship. 2. Technical writing.
I. Title.
T11.H46 2006   808'.066004   C2006-903779-5

1 2 3 4 - 10 09 08 07

Cover and Text Design: Hye Kyong Son
Cover image: digitalvision/First Light
This book is printed on permanent (acid-free) paper ♾.
Printed in Canada

Contents

A Word for the Instructor

Dear Colleague:

You have probably already noticed, just by glancing through the Table of Contents, that *A Writer's Guide for IT Professionals* is not a conventional writing textbook. That's because our students—whether they're headed for jobs as computer programmers, network administrators, web developers, or computer technicians—will participate in fast-paced work environments where communication happens outside the box of traditional genres of business or technical writing. In their chosen careers, they'll have to adapt, with the reflexes of professional tennis players, to new writing technologies, new modes of composing and collaborating, and new genre expectations. This book will enable them to cultivate the fundamental skills they'll need to function successfully in writing contexts shaped by various, ever-changing technological and social pressures.

As I've interviewed and interacted with both supervisors and lower-level workers in the IT world, the need for flexible writing skills has echoed as a recurrent theme. It serves, therefore, as the central principle of this guidebook. This text resists the temptation to provide ready-to-use templates for students to copy in the workplace. Instead, it leads readers through the process of analyzing and responding to each writing situation they encounter. The method is student-centred and future-oriented.

This book has emerged by way of my teaching writing and speaking skills to hundreds of undergraduate computer science students, conducting technical writing classes for working IT professionals, interviewing dozens more, and working as a freelancer with high-tech companies. Undergirding the pedagogy are a few key lessons I've learned through these experiences:

1. **In technology-oriented careers, writing requirements can fluctuate as rapidly as a new stock on the NASDAQ market.** Maybe last month the boss wanted a two-page report submitted as a Word attachment to an email message; this month a writer might be expected to produce a similar report as a series of PowerPoint slides. We have to equip our student writers so they can move beyond the speed of current conventions to master and create new ones.

2. **Teaching students preparing for IT careers is not the same as teaching students headed for the general world of business.** Neither is it the same as teaching students in traditional technical writing courses, typically designed for engineers-to-be. As students get ready to enter the IT work environment, they're learning a unique professional discourse, and their jargon runs more than skin deep. "Geek speak"

reflects cultural, not just lexical, peculiarities. The more relevant we can make our teaching and assignments to IT contexts, the more likely we are to engage students in writing tasks.

3. **A process-based approach to writing is far more effective than a product-oriented approach that teaches students to memorize and replicate set patterns and forms.** This isn't old news, by any means—a solid body of research going back thirty years or so reiterates the point over and over again. It can still be disconcerting, though, to realize that focusing on the "how" rather than the "what" means you're covering less material.

   When you give students the chance to experiment in class with various composition techniques and to revise their work, the number of assignments inevitably shrinks. However, the degree of student empowerment increases. Knowing that I'm preparing learners to tackle any writing situation they'll encounter, not just those I can imagine, frees me from worrying over the fact that I haven't managed to expose them to reports and instructions and proposals and white papers in a single term. Focusing on process rather than on a strict agenda of particular genres also frees me to teach responsively, adjusting to the needs in a particular class.

4. **Writing is always personal.** It doesn't matter whether we're producing a piece of poetry or a routine email, forming thought into printed words means putting forward a piece of ourselves. In the classroom, I help my students overcome their nervousness about sharing their written thoughts by presenting myself as a coach or mentor rather than as the absolute authority figure standing between them and their ideal GPA. Likewise, I've chosen to use the first-person voice throughout this book so that I can speak to your students in a similar tone. Because writing is both an art and a science, I don't pretend to pontificate in absolutes. Rather, I hope that my personalized approach will promote clarifying and creative discussion—and the development of more self-assured, intentional writers.

So there you have, in a zip file, the philosophy and pedagogy behind this book. You know enough about my assumptions to understand some of the key choices I've made and to integrate this text successfully into your own teaching style and course requirements. Thank you for allowing me to accompany you and your students along the road to better writing.

Dawn Henwood

Dawn Henwood

A Welcome from the Author

The news has been so consistent over the past thirty years that it's really not even news any more. Everyone knows that so-called "soft skills," those abilities that enable us to interact with others in positive and effective ways, show up as hot commodities on the IT job market. Just open up today's newspaper and you'll see the proof. Whether you're reading the *Montreal Gazette*, the *Edmonton Sun*, or the *New Brunswick Telegraph Journal*, you'll notice that the classified ads for IT professionals inevitably name "communication skills" as one of the important hiring criteria used to rank job applicants.

What the job ads don't always tell you, however, is what employers really mean by that very broad term, "communication." Do they want a person with strong presentation skills or someone who can relate well to colleagues as individuals? Do they want a person who can create accurate, efficient emails or someone who can facilitate discussion in a team meeting? Do they want someone who can work with live teams or virtual teams? Do they want someone who's a thoughtful listener or a polished speaker? Just what kind of effective "communicator" do today's recruiters have in mind?

Chances are your future employer will want it all. As the roles of IT professionals continue to broaden, so does the range of communication tasks they need to perform. You can see this by examining changes in job titles over the years. Yesterday's "programmer" or "software developer" is often now a "business analyst." The additional responsibilities implied by this label entail interacting directly with clients as well as with other employees (perhaps from Sales, Marketing, and Finance).

You can also appreciate the increasing demands on the IT professional's communication skills by looking at today's range of employment contexts. Even though the credentials you're earning are "technical," you'll have the opportunity to use those credentials in a variety of non-technical environments. You could work in a hospital, a school, a government office, a university, a navy ship, a grocery store, a bank, an airport, a law office, or maybe in a company you own yourself. In each of these situations, whether you're dealing with clients or colleagues, you'll need to use verbal and non-verbal means of communication to explain your ideas, express your emotions, and interpret the ideas and emotions of others.

The report on an extensive 2005 survey conducted for Canada's Software Human Resource Council (SHRC) indicates that Canadian employers and employees rate the following skills as being exceptionally important:

#1   analytical skills
#2   communication skills
#3   design skills

(Gunderson, Jacobs, and Vaillancourt 2005, p. 91).

It's significant that communication skills appear sandwiched in the middle of this list. Communication—especially those skills we practise when we communicate in written language—forms the heart of the suite of skills demanded by today's employers. To become an effective writer, you need to cultivate a critical mind so that you can confidently analyze a communication situation, assess its risks, and design different strategies for reaching your goals. Those strategies involve a complex matrix of interrelated choices. What's the best verb to capture my meaning here? What's the best sentence structure to use to make my thought clear? Which paragraph form should I follow? Which page layout? Which font? Which voice?

As you'll see, the parallels between the writing process and the software development process are striking. Both processes require detailed planning along with the flexibility to adapt and reshape the plan. They also require a person to work in both panoramic and close-up mode; to succeed, the "designer" needs to keep the big picture and the grainy details in focus. Most importantly, software developers and writers alike need to shape their materials (code language or human language) to fit the needs of a particular end user (the program's operator or the reader).

Although we've tended to think of them separately, the supposedly "soft" skill of writing and the so-called "hard" skills (such as programming, maintenance, and system operation) actively reinforce each other. Employers recognize this; that's why they're demanding what another recent SHRC report refers to as a "'package' of capabilities and personal characteristics" (Rifkin, p. 5). According to SHRC's research, it's a "seller's market" for IT job-seekers who can demonstrate a set of such "relatively intangible" skills as creativity, initiative, the ability to multi-task, and the ability to learn rapidly. It's a "buyer's market," on the other hand, for those whose skills fall mainly into the "technical" category.

By simply picking up this book, you've taken the first step towards putting yourself squarely in the "seller's" job market. As you consciously work to develop your writing process, you'll also find yourself progressing in many of the other skills employers desire. As you engage with the theory, examples, and exercises in the following pages, you'll learn to unleash your brain's creative powers, overcome personal inertia, meet multiple goals at once, and reflect on your own work so that you can continue to upgrade your performance. Who knew a writing textbook could involve all this?

Here, I should perhaps warn you that what you're about to read is not a typical writing textbook. Rather than create an all-encompassing instruction manual on how to write, I've composed a kind of letter of advice to you, sharing the insights I've accumulated through my experience as a writer, researcher, and teacher. My purpose is to act as your personal guide on a journey through the writing process and through some of the document types common to IT workplaces.

The material in this book divides into three sections. The chapters will likely make the most sense if you work through them in order.

Part I: Developing a writing process that works for you guides you through the various aspects of an audience-oriented writing process, inviting you to assess your current writing practices and try on some new ones for size.

Part II: Creating effective electronic text leads you through some of the complexities of producing writing that must deliver its meaning onscreen.

Part III: Adapting to professional forms introduces you to some of the most common categories of workplace writing and provides helpful tips for using them effectively as vehicles for your ideas.

You may find that this book raises as many questions as it asks. I actually hope it does. I'd hate for you to think I was offering *The Writing Bible for IT Professionals*. I suggest you keep a reading log as you complete the chapters your instructor assigns so that you can raise your questions as issues for class discussion. One of the most helpful strategies for improving your writing is to talk about writing with other writers, both experienced and inexperienced. In your journal, you can also talk about writing with yourself, which is another very useful practice.

As you work your way through this book, I'd like you to keep in mind two thoughts:

1. You know more than you think you know about how to write.
2. You'll never, even if you live to be 177, know half-enough about how to write.

With respect to the first point, this book takes a personal, reflective approach that enables you to assess and improve your writing skills. Allowing for the second point, it avoids delivering cookie-cutter approaches for dealing with specific forms, or *genres*, of writing. Learning to modify your writing to suit various audiences and formats will be an ongoing task for you as long as you're in the workforce.

Programmers come into the workforce having learned a number of programming languages in the classroom. But ask a programmer which of those languages is now used most on the job, and the reply will likely be "None." Because coding languages seem to become outdated almost as soon as they're written down, successful programmers learn how to learn new things quickly. In the same way, successful IT writers must adjust rapidly to ever-shifting writing contexts. What one company calls a "report" another may call a "whitepaper"; what one supervisor considers "wordiness," another considers "power-talk"; what one colleague considers an obvious document structure, another complains is confusing. Flexibility and an evolving self-awareness are the keys to surviving.

Consider this guidebook not as a comprehensive atlas but instead as a rough map, one you will draw in more detail as your career develops. I'd be interested to hear what you find most and least useful in *A Writer's Guide for IT Professionals*. Please forward your comments to Oxford University Press; I'll be grateful for them.

Dawn Henwood

Dawn Henwood

Acknowledgements

This book draws its life from the industry supervisors, employees, and entrepreneurs who generously shared with me their own observations about communicating in IT environments. I want to thank in particular the following people: Alan Parslow, Allison MacDonald, Ann Dent, Bart Daniel, Bruce MacDougall, David McCurdy, Derek Anderson, Garth Smedley, Gwyneth Edwards, Jim Mullen, John Harbarenko, John Leahy, Karen Heffell, Karen Spaulding, Lysia Taylor, Mark Pettigrew, Mignona Cote, Mike Musial, Nancy Holland, Patrick Welsh, Robert Levings, Ron MacCormick, Sandy Walsh, Sylvie Thibault, Tanya Shaw Weeks, Tommy Yeomans, Wayne Bussey, and Ron McLeod.

During the writing of this book, I've been blessed with supportive colleagues. Lyn Bennett provided invaluable research assistance—and encouragement when my stamina for the project was lagging. Keith Lawson offered expert advice about writing for the Web, and Jill Manderson was a kindly second reader.

Throughout the project, I've also appreciated developmental editor Paula Druzga's patience in coping with delays caused by illness and in handling the jitters of a first-time author. Tom Howell's sensitive editing has taught me more about the craft of pruning than I've learned from all the research and advice I've read.

If it takes a village to raise a child, it takes a family to produce a manuscript. Thank you to my parents, Gwen and Hayden Henwood, and to my parents-in-law, Bruce and Myrna Nauss, for providing childcare, meals, and moral support while I was at my computer. Love and endless thanks to Mom especially, for keeping me afloat. And to my husband, Ken, for repeatedly reminding me that when the going gets tough, the tough get writing.

For my parents, who gave me wings,
and for Ken, who pushes me to use them.

Part 1

Developing a Writing Process That Works for You

Chapter 1

Putting the End Reader First

Who's at fault for faulty communication?

Terry realizes too late that he's in a real pickle. He's the team leader of a project to create web-based training software to teach oil-rig workers about emergency evacuation procedures. The client is expecting to receive a mock-up of the first module in two weeks, but the team is so far behind that this deadline will be impossible. He knows he needs to break the bad news, but gently.

After chewing through a pencil eraser, gulping two diet Cokes, and cleaning out all the drawers in his desk, Terry finally sits down to his difficult task. He takes a deep breath and tells himself: "Just bite the bullet, Terry. You'd better just get it over with." Then, hunched over his keyboard and frowning deeply, he pecks at the keys non-stop for ten intense minutes. Here is Terry's email message:

From: Terry Montague [mailto:tmontague@ccconsulting.com]
Sent: May 5, 2004 11:55 AM
To: Ravi Sood
Subject: Candlewave project

> Hi Ravi,
>
> Things are going great on the first module. I'm sorry to have to tell you that we're a little behind where we thought we'd be on the project by this time. We'll have the prototype to you no later than June 15th.
>
> Hope this isn't too much of an inconvenience.
>
> Please don't hesitate to contact me, if you require any additional information.
>
> Terry

As far as Terry is concerned, once he clicks the *Send* button, he has solved his problem. "Phew!" he mutters to himself. "That's one nasty job taken care of." However, he hasn't taken into account Ravi's reaction.

Had he paused to reflect upon the context of his message, Terry would have found it ripe with anxiety-producing factors. To begin with, Ravi is a new middle manager at Candlewave, and this is the first training project he has coordinated for his boss, Alfred. In addition, this is Candlewave's very first venture into web-based training. Terry's audience is already half-nervous about the project. The fact that neither Alfred nor Ravi has ever contracted CC Consulting before adds to their feelings of uncertainty. Terry is a relative stranger to them, and they're not yet sure if they can trust him.

As Terry is patting himself on the back, telling his boss he just sent an "upbeat note" to inform the client of the new deadline, let's look over Ravi's shoulder as he reads the message. The text in brackets indicates what's going through his mind as he processes the words on the screen:

From: Terry Montague [mailto:tmontague@ccconsulting.com]
[Oh good, finally a message from Terry. Now I'll have something to report to Alfred when he asks about the project in today's meeting.]
Sent: May 5, 2004 11:55 AM
To: Ravi Sood
Subject: First module of Candlewave project
[I can't wait to see the first module. It should be ready any day now.]

Hi Ravi,

Things are going great on the first module. [I'm relieved to hear that—I wasn't sure what to make of Terry. Seems like he's going to pull through for us after all.]

I'm sorry to have to tell you that we're a little behind where we thought we'd be on the project by this time. [Hey—what's this? I thought things were going great... I'm confused. Well, I guess we can cope with a slight delay.]

We'll have the prototype to you no later than June 15th. [Yikes! That's nearly a month off schedule. How am I going to explain this to Alfred? He didn't believe in these guys from the beginning. Last time there was a goof-up like this with a contractor, he went through the roof. Is he going to want to pull the plug and start over? This is one giant headache.]

Hope this isn't too much of an inconvenience. [Who do these people think they are, acting so casual about this? Oh, no, not much of an inconvenience at all. Just throws off our entire production plan for the next six months! The people in marketing are going to be livid—they were expecting to show the prototype to the sales reps at the spring sales conference.]

Please don't hesitate to contact me, if you require any additional information. [You're darn right I need some additional information, and I'll give Terry an earful of some information of my own. Now if I could only find his phone number. I really don't have time to dig for it. Why isn't it in his signature?]

Terry

By the time he's finished reading Terry's message, Ravi is in a thoroughly sour mood. Although Terry believed he'd created a simple solution to his problem, his words exacerbated an already difficult situation. Who's to blame for this, Terry or his reader?

Ahh, now we're in the realm of philosophy. This question is one we could endlessly ponder, something like the age-old riddle of the chicken and the egg. To speak practically, however, the short answer is that both Terry and Ravi are to blame, but Terry more than Ravi. A longer answer—well, that's the rest of this chapter.

This chapter introduces the wise writer's secret weapon of self-defence: audience analysis. We'll expand on the question of whether Terry or Ravi should bear responsibility for the unfortunate effect of this email by exploring the way readers and writers work together to create virtual meaning from a piece of writing. Then we'll examine two practical tools you can use to prevent your own written messages from misfiring.

Understanding writing as hypertext

A piece of software can contain a marvelously elaborate universe in potential, but until someone logs on and activates the program, it's just lines of code. Likewise, you may author a technically flawless, beautifully coherent document, but, unless your reader engages with it and brings it to life as you expect, you have not successfully communicated your message. Words on the page or screen take on meaning only when they're interpreted by active readers, who bring to a text their own background understanding, assumptions, and emotions. It's difficult, however, to adjust our mental framework to consider reading and writing as two halves of a virtual reality game because modern North American society still cultivates a reverence for the written word, even in this age of hypertext. Our culture encourages us to value writing because it appears intact and immobile. When we're closing a business deal, we say, "Put it in writing." We confer special rights on couples who have a written marriage certificate as opposed to those who live together under a verbal agreement. We further stress the ability of writing to nail down meaning by paying high fees to the scribes with specialized knowledge (i.e. lawyers) who know how to use writing to safeguard our interests before the law.

Despite such assumptions, written language is in many ways less exact than spoken language. To grasp this point, try the following experiment. Say aloud three times this sentence from Terry's email to Ravi, changing your tone each time: "Things are going great on the first module."

Most likely, you varied the tone of the sentence by altering vocal qualities, such as your pitch, pace, and volume. Had you tried the exercise in front of a mirror, you probably would have noticed additional changes to your posture and facial expression. Had Terry delivered his message face-to-face, such elements would have enabled him to soften the blow of his bad news. By delivering his initial sentence slowly, for instance, he could have given Ravi a hint that, contrary to his words, things weren't actually going great. The hesitation in Terry's voice would have allowed Ravi time to prepare himself for the negative information to follow. In the written medium, however, the transition from the positive opening to the bad news is so abrupt that it startles and angers Ravi.

If a picture is worth a thousand words, a vocal cue or a raised eyebrow is worth at least a hundred. The problem is that, when we communicate in writing, none of us has eyebrows. The page or screen projects an image of us as a writer, but, without the aid of bodily signals, we have to work extremely hard to generate the voice and the personality we want the reader to receive.

Unlike the machine languages that tell a computer how to behave, natural (human) languages are full of riddles. In a computer language, for instance, "run" can have only one meaning; the *Oxford English Dictionary*, however, lists more than a hundred. Programmers sometimes tell me that the easiest way for them to find a solution to a coding dilemma is to communicate with their peers in pure code, rather than explaining their thoughts about the code in English. The practice of pair programming derives from this belief that machine language is, in some situations, more straightforward and accurate than human language.

Even though Machine may be a highly efficient language under certain conditions, its range proves, of course, to be severely limited. Ambiguity is the price we pay for the more elastic, subtle functionality of English. Fortunately, there are steps you can take to steer a reader's reaction to the text, and control—as much as possible—the virtual reality he or she helps construct from your words.

The most important step toward producing the reader response you want is to analyze your anticipated audience. In this chapter, you'll learn a method for analyzing an audience composed of readers whom you can identify and get to know personally. The next chapter will deal with the more complex situation of writing for an audience or multiple audiences consisting of people you can't meet in person, or even name.

Thinking like a defensive driver

It's often said that the key to becoming a good interpersonal communicator is first becoming a good listener. This is also the key to becoming a good writer. Clear writers learn to listen in advance to the needs and attitudes of the audience that will receive the writing. They learn to adapt their content, organization, and presentation to suit the preferences of the readers who will partner with them in creating meaning from written sentences.

To write well, you need the skills of a defensive driver, that sixth sense that enables you to predict when the car in front is suddenly going to brake or swerve into another lane. That mysterious sense isn't magical, and it's not something you can develop by studying the driver's handbook from the Department of Motor Vehicles. It's an acquired skill you master through experience. You begin by training yourself to practise defensive habits, such as looking both ways as you cross an intersection on a green light, and maintaining a generous braking distance between your car and the car in front of you. Then, as you gain more traffic exposure, you build up a memory bank of typical situations you encounter. This roster of past experiences becomes a filter you use to assess new situations.

If you've ever been involved in a car accident then you know that the law and the insurance industry hold you legally accountable to drive defensively. A woman I know learned this the hard way the day she slammed into the rear bumper of a car driven by an elderly nun, who abruptly stopped in the middle of the road for no apparent reason. As apologetic as the nun was, the woman behind her was the one responsible for the accident, in the eyes of her insurance company. The rules of the road say that the driver in the rear is always to blame, even if the driver in front behaves carelessly.

The rules of written communication say that the writer bears at least partial responsibility for the way a piece of writing is received by its intended audience, even when that audience reads carelessly. This rule is particularly strict in the workplace; if the mantra of retail business is "the customer is always right," the mantra of effective writers is "the audience is always right."

Writing with action in mind

Defensive audience analysis forms the foundation of all business and technical writing because workplace writing is *transactional*. It aims to transact business of one sort or another by gaining the cooperation of the audience. That "business" might be winning a contract, informing a colleague of a change in procedure, or gaining an extra week of vacation. Whatever the situation, workplace writing moves audiences to get things done.

Workplace writing differs dramatically from what poets or students produce. Both poets and students write for very narrow audiences. Poets, unless they're commissioned to compose a piece for a formal occasion, usually write first of all for themselves. They engage in *expressive* writing, the main goal of which is to allow authors to pour out thoughts and feelings. Students also write for an exclusive audience, which is also artificial—the instructor. No matter how clouded the writing is, an instructor must read and evaluate the entire text. On the job, on the other hand, workplace readers are so pressed for time that they're likely to skim through your documents, if they even get past the first few paragraphs.

In the workplace, no one will give you a grade A or B for effective writing. Instead, what you write will be judged by the extent to which it makes its audience hear, understand, and do. These are tough standards. We've already established that no writer has total control over the meaning an audience extracts from a message, yet authors are held accountable for the audience's reactions. Workplace writers need a powerful strategy to cope with this challenge: audience analysis.

Analyzing your audience

Researchers tell us that the background knowledge readers bring to a piece of writing has a greater influence on their comprehension of the writing than the coherence of the writing itself (Faris & Smeltzer). The proven importance of a reader's prior understanding means that savvy writers should consider audience analysis the foundation of each and every piece of writing they produce in the workplace. Taking the time to reflect on your audience's characteristics and assumptions isn't an activity you can reserve for large projects with a generous timeline. If you're not writing directly to your audience, then why bother writing at all?

For each writing task, plan to spend as much or more time thinking about your audience's background as you do thinking about the presentation of your ideas. If you're accurate in the first part of your planning, you'll find the second part will evolve naturally and easily. If, on the other hand, you skip over audience analysis, you'll lack the framework you need for making intelligent choices in the other writing decisions you need to make. It's hard to decide, for instance, whether to use acronyms or spell out technical concepts in full, if you don't have a clear picture of your audience's technical knowledge. In the same way, it's nearly impossible to choose the most effective method of persuasion without knowing whether your readers tend to make judgments based primarily on emotion or logic.

Analyzing your audience means, first of all, putting the audience first. It seems a natural human tendency to begin a writing task by thinking, "Now, what do I want to say?" or "What ground do I need to cover?" Such questions, though, put the cart before the horse. Before you can decide what to say, you need to have a clear picture of the person you're addressing.

Thinking about your audience is not necessarily the same as analyzing it. When you analyze something—whether it's a chemical compound or a screenplay—you break it into components in order to study it systematically. Audience analysis, then, requires a deliberate system, especially because it's easy to fall prey to one of two common fallacies: (1) to assume your audience is very similar to you, or (2) to assume your audience is totally dissimilar.

Imagine that you're creating a user manual for an upgrade to a piece of software that you have created. The first fallacy might lead you to assume that readers want to know the ins and outs of every feature you've added or improved, whereas most readers may be interested in only a handful of features they use to perform a limited number of daily tasks. If, on the other hand, your instinct leads you to the opposite fallacy, you could end up frustrating people by over-generalizing or over-simplifying the technical information. As Allison MacDonald, an experienced freelance programmer, says: "Just because people don't know what you know doesn't mean they're stupid."

Adopting a systematic method for considering your audience ensures that you make intelligent and persuasive writing decisions. Figure 1.1 lists just some of the elements of writing that are affected by the way you define your audience (or audiences) for a document.

Audience analysis is as important to the writing process as design is to the software development process. In fact, reflecting on how software developers work gives us insight into how effective writers move their audiences to do what they want done.

Figure 1.1 Elements of writing affected by the way you define your audience		
tone	word count	organization
amount of jargon	paragraph length	spelling
content	format	sentence structure
word choice	use of acronyms	font

As we'll explore in detail in Chapters 3 and 4, building a piece of software and writing a document are both complex exercises in designing. In the software market, the successful products are those that most effectively meet the needs and whims of the end user. As a discipline, then, software engineering has developed a number of methods for creating a portrait of the target consumer. Skilled writers adopt parallel strategies to sell their ideas in print.

Both software developers and writers often find it tempting to skip the critical step of end-user or audience analysis. Naturally, it's much easier to create something to satisfy your own preferences than it is to guess at someone else's. Moreover, in the absence of an analytical method, the end user can seem more like a mythical construct of the imagination than a real person.

Admittedly, unless you're custom-building a program for an individual whom you know well, you have to use a certain amount of imaginative guesswork to flesh out the user profile. However, by following an analytical method, you can make informed inferences rather than random guesses. In the end, you are far better off designing for a slightly warped vision of the end user than for an anonymous, faceless user. As many a military strategist will tell you, any plan is always better than no plan at all.

Creating a writer's profile

Before you begin to describe your audience, it's a good idea to create a self-portrait of yourself as a writer. Only once you understand the position from which you approach a writing task can you think strategically about how to communicate your perspective to someone else. Figure 1.2 provides a short list of questions you can use to improve your understanding of yourself as a writer, along with brief explanations of why each of the questions matters. A blank copy of the form appears at the end of this chapter.

You'll find the questions in the Writer's Profile particularly helpful when you need to create a long, complex document or one that needs to be especially persuasive. You probably won't need to revisit each of these questions each time you sit down to craft a document, but I recommend you take the time to write out answers to the questions at least once. (Why not try it now?) As you develop professionally, you'll also want to update your writer's profile periodically to make yourself conscious of the way new knowledge and experiences are shaping your view of the world.

Figure 1.2 Writer's Profile

1. **How would you rank your level of technical knowledge in general? (5 = expert, 1 = novice)**

   Your ranking here should reflect your familiarity with the field in which you're working and with the specific technology in question.

2. **List the specific areas in which you have technical knowledge (e.g. C++, Java, networking, business management, accounting).**

   Itemizing your expertise enables you to understand accurately how it relates to your audience's knowledge level.

3. **Are you a direct or indirect communicator?**

   Direct communicators value clarity, sometimes at the expense of politeness, They present information in a straightforward, even blunt way and tend to use direct commands when they want something ("Close that window, please").

   Indirect communicators value social sensitivity, sometimes at the expense of clarity. They preface information with polite preambles and tend to use questions rather than commands when they want something ("Would you mind closing that window?").

4. **What are your likes and dislikes as a reader?**

   Identifying your likes and dislikes allows you to analyze your writing style and to adapt it to suit your audience's preferences. If you know you're a reader who favours long, chatty introductions, you'll have to put aside your personal preferences when writing for a supervisor who says, "Just cut to the chase."

5. **How do you typically read a document?**

   Once you understand your reading practices, you can develop strategies that suit habits different from your own. If you're a person who reads reports from cover to cover, for instance, it's important to recognize that you're likely in the minority of most professional audiences. Once you realize that your way of reading is not your audience's way, you can design a document that consciously accommodates readers who skim or forage for information.

6. **What factors have most influenced your opinion on the topic you're writing about?**

   In almost every piece of workplace writing you create, you'll need to express an opinion or recommendation. It's important to recognize where your conclusions come from so that you can offer adequate supporting evidence. Scrutinizing the roots of your opinions also enables you to look for loopholes in your logic and to anticipate objections.

Creating an audience profile

Once you're confident you've fulfilled the first law of good writing—"Know Thyself"—you're ready to get to know your audience. Because each writing task has its own context and priorities, there is no single best method for analyzing your audience. As you experiment with various methods, you may find one that works well for you most of the time, or you may discover that you have to blend elements of different methods in order to get the results you need. When you can identify at least some of your individual readers, the simplest approach is to create an audience profile by gathering information you can readily access through personal channels.

I think of this method as the James Bond approach. Every great spy adventure begins with a briefing to inform the secret agent about the environment of the assignment and the enemy's history and personality—not just height and weight, but also education, age, work history, and personal foibles. I'm not suggesting that you consider your audience as an enemy (although it's always safer to assume a resistant rather than a sympathetic reader), but I do think writers can take a key lesson from the domain of espionage. In order to earn someone's trust, you need to know as much as possible about what makes that person tick.

For some documents, you'll be lucky enough to know your reader or readers personally, so generating an audience profile will be straightforward. In many cases, though, you'll face the challenge of trying to reach readers you know only vaguely or have never even met. In such cases, you'll likely need to allow yourself time for some research, which may mean conducting an interview, surfing the web, or visiting the library.

If you find your fingers itching to skip this background work and just start typing, fight the urge. Yes, audience analysis is time-consuming. However, the more information you have about the people to whom you're writing, the greater the likelihood that they'll respond positively. If you think audience analysis costs too much time, consider the possible alternative costs: having to rewrite a misdirected message, calm down an angry reader, or make embarrassing explanations. I recently interviewed an IT consultant who confessed to having written emails that "set a project back three days." Audience analysis up front can save you from having to do painful back-pedaling later on.

To help you formally define your audience, I've created an Audience Profile Sheet. As you work through the form, you'll discover that seemingly trivial details about a person can significantly influence attitudes toward your writing. Figure 1.3 explains how each item on the form affects your decisions as you plan and compose your document. A blank copy of the form appears at the end of this chapter.

Figure 1.3 Audience Profile Sheet

Supply the following information to describe your reader(s). If your document addresses more than one reader or group of readers, profile each of these on a separate form.

Audience Information

Name

A misspelled name gives your readers the impression that you don't really care about them. If your document will address your reader(s) personally, as in a letter or email message, always double-check the spelling of names and the appropriate title to use (e.g. Ms., Mr., Dr.). Unless you know for a certain that a married woman calls herself "Mrs.," use "Ms."

Gender

Communication research has uncovered significant differences in the ways men and women typically communicate. One of the main distinctions is that women tend to be indirect communicators, whereas men tend to communicate more directly. Given that men still outnumber women in the IT sector, gender colours opinions on organizational and managerial issues, too.

The trouble is that a person's name does not necessarily indicate gender. (Consider these examples: Tracy King, Toni Hurley, B. C. Jupp.) If you can, try to determine a person's gender by discreet inquiry (by reaching her or his voice mail, for instance, or contacting an associate).

For insight into the significant role gender plays in workplace communication, read Deborah Tannen's book, *Talking from 9 to 5: Women and Men at Work* (1994).

First language

Try to obtain accurate information about your reader's level of English comprehension. (To find out, you could perhaps initiate a phone conversation.) To reach ESL (English as a Second Language) readers most effectively, keep your sentence structure straightforward, use simple vocabulary, eliminate slang expressions, and avoid complex cultural or humorous references.

Age

Beware of making the ageist assumption that older readers know little about technology. On the other hand, also be aware that an age gap can create certain barriers relating to language usage. Play it safe by avoiding slang, which often makes sense only within a certain age group.

Figure 1.3 Audience Profile Sheet (continued)

Job title

Determining a person's rank within the organization enables you to judge how formal your written message needs to be. However, depending on the size of the organization, a job title can tell you a lot or a little about a person's real status. It's not uncommon for a small start-up company to have three Directors and a Vice-President, for instance, but no other employees. In such a situation, the company culture is likely very informal, so it would make little sense to begin a letter proposal to the Director of Operations with the salutation, "Dear Mr. Robinson." If you're addressing a similar document to a Vice-President of a multinational consulting firm, on the other hand, "Mr. Landry" may be more appropriate than "Dear Bob," depending on the context.

As with personal names, always verify the spelling of official job titles.

Position in organization relative to me

It's important to compare your own status to the status of the reader(s) you're addressing so that you can pitch your tone appropriately. This isn't always easy if you work in a large company and need to communicate with someone outside the company or in another division. In Canada, professionals normally deal with each other on a first-name basis, but that doesn't make the bantering tone you use in an email message to a peer suitable for a message to your boss. In most cases, it's better to err on the side of formality.

Education

When considering your audience's educational background, remember to take into account the date that formal education was completed. A person who completed an M.B.A. in 1963 could have a very different business vocabulary and overall frame of reference (not to mention computer knowledge) than a recent M.B.A. graduate.

Length of time with organization

One of the easiest ways to frustrate your audience is to provide either too much or too little background information. To assess just how much of this to include, find out about the audience's previous involvement with the topic or project. Suppose you're writing a completion report for a senior executive, for example. If that person has been with the organization longer than you have, he or she might require less background information about a project than you did when you started it.

Previous work history

If you have access to other biographical material, check it for information about the person's work history, which can help you judge how much industry-specific terminology or technical jargon to use. If Faizel, the new software engineer, spent several years in the army reserves, then he is likely fluent in military acronyms, so you can save time and space by using them to describe the project you're working on for the Department of National Defence.

Level of technical knowledge in this writing context

What matters most is not the audience's knowledge level on an absolute scale but the audience's status as compared with yours in a very particular context. You may find it useful to give both yourself and your audience a numerical score on a sliding scale of technical expertise, using Figure 1.4 as a guide.

To give you some idea of what it means to consider technical expertise within the context of a specific writing situation, let's pretend you're a programmer writing a proposal to create a database for a credit union to manage its mortgage clients. Your document will likely have several readers, but you know for certain that one of the most important readers will be John Khan, the regional manager of personal lending.

Speaking generally, we might describe John as highly technically literate. In terms of computer use among the general population, he might be a 4 on our scale of technical expertise. He's a whiz with Excel and project management software and is working on developing a family web page with Microsoft Front Page in his spare time. However, he understands next to nothing about how a database works from the inside. In terms of the program you need to describe, his knowledge is at the level of 1 or 2.

You, on the other hand, have only been out of school a brief time and still think of yourself as an apprentice programmer (you give yourself a 3 in terms of general programming expertise). Compared to John, though, you are highly expert regarding the construction of databases (5). Therefore, in this specific writing situation, your document will need to close a significant gap between your knowledge base (5) and John's (1–2).

Now consider a different scenario. Let's say you're a technical writer preparing a user manual for software to be used by testing technicians at a power station. Your educational background includes a Bachelor of Computer Science and a Masters degree in English. You didn't create the software you're documenting, but you've worked along with the development team as a writer from the beginning of the project. You score yourself as a 5 in general programming knowledge and a 4 in your knowledge of this particular program.

From your research, you know that a typical technician at this power station has the equivalent of a Grade 10 education. Scored on general knowledge about how software functions, your end user ranks a 1. From one point of view, then, it seems that a wide gulf separates you from your audience. In this particular writing context, however, you are actually closer to your readers than you may think.

You know a lot about how the testing software works, but your readers know much more than you do about how the testing process itself works. Who is really the greater technical expert, you or your reader? Within the narrow context of the particular computer application you're describing, the technical expertise

Figure 1.3 Audience Profile Sheet (continued)

of your audience might be as high as a 4, even higher if your readers have had previous experience with similar software.

Familiarity with topic

There's a vast difference between sending an unsolicited proposal and responding to a published Request for Proposals. There's also a big difference between submitting an informal progress report to your supervisor (after you've already provided a brief update over lunch) and writing a more formal report for your supervisor's supervisor, who may know very little about the nuts and bolts of the project.

Purpose in reading my document

Why is your audience reading your document? Here are some common reasons:

- to make a decision
- to justify a decision
- to receive information
- to give information to someone else.

Once you recognize your audience's purpose, you're ready to consider another question: what information does your reader primarily want?

You need to answer this important question in order to choose the best way of organizing your material. The order that makes the most sense to you may not be the order that makes the most sense to your audience. If you're mapping out a new project for your boss, for instance, you may get so caught up in design details that you bury the schedule and budget deep in the document. Those items likely contain, however, exactly the information your boss would like to extract first.

Amount of time available for reading my document

The world of business is one of fast-paced reading, and time-stressed readers respond most positively to streamlined documents that are easy to navigate.

Interest in reading my document

The first question to ask is, "Does my audience expect this document?" The next question is "Does my audience look forward to reading my document?" If the answer to both of these questions is "yes," then you can use a direct approach to your topic. You don't need to spend a lot of time thinking about how to grab your reader's attention.

If the answer to either question is "no," then you should invest time thinking about how to engage your audience. Keep in mind that, in the world of work, there are very few documents that audiences actually look forward to reading. Most of us are so strapped for time that any kind of written communication carries a built-in irritation factor.

Pre-formed opinions about my ideas

What is your audience's perspective on the topic you address? In some situations, it may be appropriate to arrange a telephone chat or an in-person meeting before you put your ideas on paper. In other cases, you may be able to raise a few pointed questions in an email message.

When writing to someone outside the company, don't overlook the resources of the Internet. Company websites often feature biographical blurbs about key team players. Internet search engines could uncover further personal information, such as online articles authored by your reader or contributions made to newsgroups or blogs.

Preferred writing style

Experts who study interpersonal communication tell us that people react most favourably to people who mirror their own communication styles. This piece of wisdom is at least as old as the Roman empire: when in Rome, do as the Romans do. To put a more modern spin on the concept, if a Texas cowboy says "Howdy, y'all!", say "Howdy!" back.

If your readers are well-known to you, you can maximize the impact of your message by adapting your writing style to theirs. That doesn't mean that if your boss writes cryptically short, misspelled emails you need to do the same. It does mean, though, that you should probably eliminate lengthy introductions, save space by using jargon and abbreviations wherever appropriate, and avoid small talk.

Favourite jargon

Using jargon enables us to take shortcuts by compressing complex technical concepts into a few syllables. Using your reader's favourite jargon creates an instant rapport. You show that you belong to the same group as your audience and therefore suggest that you also share common interests. If you use jargon appropriately and correctly, you create a sympathetic and authoritative voice.

Hot-button words

Just as readers have favourite jargon words, they also have hot-button words that trigger negative emotions such as anxiety or anger. These could be, for instance, words that bring back memories of a project gone bad or buzzwords promoting unpopular policies imposed by management. Whenever possible, make yourself popular with your readers by avoiding negative language.

For female readers, gender-exclusive language often has a hot-button effect. To avoid alienating the women in your audience, revise sexist terms such as "chairman," "policeman," or "man-hours." Wherever possible, steer clear of using gendered pronouns to refer to both men and women.

For example, consider how you could rewrite the following sentence: "Each employee will receive his new user name on Tuesday."

Figure 1.3 Audience Profile Sheet (continued)

Here's an inclusive, but wordy, revision: "Each employee will receive his or her new user name on Tuesday."

Here's an inclusive revision created by pluralizing the subject: "Employees will receive their new user names on Tuesday."

Here's a revision that removes the pronoun completely: "Employees will receive new user names on Tuesday."

Pet peeves

If you have intimate knowledge of your readers, use that information to your advantage. If your supervisor harps constantly on the need to improve productivity, then pitch a proposal to institute flexible work hours to that theme. You might emphasize, for instance, that workers who are able to balance work with family commitments experience less job stress and therefore take fewer sick days. If, on the other hand, the company president's main complaint is the lack of innovative thinking in the organization, you might sell the same proposal to her by pointing out that employees who are able to work to their own rhythms are more likely to produce creative ideas.

Figure 1.4 Scale ranking technical expertise

As you consider each element in the Audience Profile Sheet, keep in mind that you need always to consider your audience's profile in relation to your own profile.

5	4	3	2	1
Expert		*Competent*		*Novice*
Has thorough, detailed understanding of how a technical object or process works from the inside out.		Has a surface understanding of how a technical object or process works in very general terms.		Has little or no understanding of how a technical object or process works; is unfamiliar with the most basic functions and terms.

Now, let's pretend that you are a software team leader crafting an email proposal for the company's Chief Financial Officer, Lana Jupp, urging her to increase your division's budget so that you can purchase a new network drive. Here's how you might use the Audience Profile Sheet to present your arguments in the most convincing light.

Audience Information	Notes
Name E. Lana Jupp	Everyone calls her Lana.
Gender Female	
First language English (U.K.)	Moved to Canada within the last two years. Avoid North American slang.
Age 45–50	The few times we've met in person, she's been very formal and polite.
Job title Chief Financial Officer	Reports directly to the President. Has the authority to decide whether to act on my request.
Position in organization relative to me Superior	Lana is not only way up the corporate totem pole, but she also has a very reserved, formal manner. I'll have to make sure I mind my p's and q's, even though I'm only sending an email.
Education She's a C.A., I assume. Educated in the U.K.	
Length of time with organization Eighteen months.	The operations budget has been pretty tight for a couple of years, so we've been discouraged from making requests for major equipment purchases. That means she hasn't really had to think through equipment issues before now. Since she wasn't around when we bought the current drive, I'll have to explain the criteria for choosing a new one.
Previous work history Not sure. Manufacturing?	I'll have to do some digging about this. I'm not sure how familiar she is with what we do on a day-to-day basis, how much knowledge she has about backup options, in particular.

Audience Information	Notes
Level of technical knowledge in this writing context Suspect minimal.	See above.
Familiarity with topic I think Peter has mentioned this to her in passing.	Check with Peter to get gist of his conversation with Lana. How positive was she about entertaining a request for new equipment?
Purpose in reading my document To make a decision.	Lana will need really clear numbers. Consider putting various drives in price grid.
Amount of time available for reading my document Very little. My request represents a major expenditure for our division but a minor expenditure in terms of the company's overall budget. She'll not likely give it much attention.	I'll have to be super-compelling up front. I'll need to show how desperate our situation is, how badly we need a new drive. (The old one is costing us in repairs and unproductive down-time, and we're almost out of space.)
Interest in reading my document Probably the last thing Lana wants is another purchase this close to the end of the fiscal year.	Accountants tend to be risk-averse. I'll grab her attention and hold it by emphasizing the risks of maintaining the status quo.
Pre-formed opinions about my ideas Not sure.	Ask Peter.
Preferred writing style Any emails I've seen from Lana have been crisp and to the point. Few social pleasantries.	

Audience Information	Notes
Favourite jargon I've often heard her use the phrase "close-to-the-bone budgeting." Two of her last company emails talk about maintaining "fiscal responsibility."	Emphasize that the drive I'm recommending offers real value. It's more expensive than the others but should be more reliable over time. It's suitable for our "close-to-the bone" budget because it will save us headaches and repair bills in the long run.
Hot-button words Lana speaks so precisely that I suspect sloppy grammar is a hot button for her.	Ask Joe if he'll proof my email this afternoon.
Pet peeves I haven't had enough to do with Lana to find out about these.	Jocelyn was recently turned down when she asked for 3 new laptops for her team. I'll try to find out why her request was rejected. That way I can anticipate—and refute—Lana's objections before she raises them.

As you can see, completing the Audience Profile Sheet for your email message to Lana raises several questions. To finish your background research, you're going to have to find out a bit more about her work history, as well as ask Peter and Jocelyn some specific questions about their interaction with her. Fortunately, because Lana and you work for the same organization, it shouldn't be difficult for you to fill in the gaps in the profile. Thanks to the detailed information you have about your specific audience, you'll be able to begin planning your email message from a position of strength.

What happens, though, when you have multiple audiences, or when you're not sure exactly who might receive your message? If you know the various individuals who will be reading your document, you can complete an Audience Profile Sheet for each of them. You'll then have the information you need to design a document that plays to their shared interests, while allowing readers to access the information that's most important to them.

In many cases, however, you won't be able to put names or faces to the people who will be reading your document. When you submit a proposal to a client, for instance, you can't be certain how widely that document will circulate in the client's organization. When you write a letter of inquiry or a cover letter for a job application, you are often writing to a complete stranger. How, then, can you tailor your writing to a wide or unknown audience?

Take heart. With a little detective work, you can devise effective strategies for reaching unfamiliar audiences. In the next chapter, we'll examine how you can create a broad audience profile by researching a "community of practice" and applying the TACT method of document planning.

Exercises

1. You are a software engineer for Voxa, a small company that designs voice-recognition software. Currently, your product is being used by General Electric to create a line of small kitchen appliances designed especially for people with physical disabilities.

   Now that the contract with General Electric is nearing completion, Voxa is looking for a new project and a new partner. You have been asked to collaborate with the Director of Marketing to create a proposal for the Ford Motor Company. Voxa would like to design software that will turn its Windstar minivan into a "smart" van with voice-activated controls.

   Your challenge is to create a document that will serve more than one audience. Your proposal will be read by at least the following people, about whom you have minimal information:

   - Jacquelyn Doherty, Director of Marketing, Minivan Division. Jacquelyn graduated in 1976.

   - Sam Ashraf, Director of Finance, Minivan Division. Sam is new to Ford.

   - Yusin Lao, Senior Engineer, Minivan Division. Yusin leads the team that develops the electronic equipment and controls in the current Windstar. He is an electrical engineer. His two-year-old twins have been featured in recent ads for the Windstar.

   Tasks:

   (i)   Create audience profiles for Jacquelyn, Sam, and Yusin, inferring as much as you can from the information you have been provided.
   (ii) Make a list of the key questions you need to answer before you begin to write.
   (iii) Determine how you would go about finding out the answers to your key questions.

2. Imagine you are constructing a website for the provincial division of the Canadian Cancer Foundation. Write a one-page letter to your eighty-year-old grandmother describing the site you are creating. (Use your imagination to fill in the details of the site's features.) Your grandmother is a survivor of breast cancer. She has never used a computer and has no understanding of how the Internet works.

3. Write a "Getting Started" module to introduce the email browser you use to someone who has never used email before. Then write a "Quickstart" guide for someone who has used email for several years but never with the particular browser you use.

4. Imagine that you would like to ask for an extra week's vacation to go climbing in the Rockies. Write two versions of an email to your supervisor to make your request, one suited to a direct communicator, and the

other suited to an indirect communicator. Use your imagination to paint the scenario surrounding your request.

5. Imagine that you are delivering a proposal, using presentation software, to a Vice-President of one of the major Canadian software companies. Using Internet and library resources, complete an audience profile sheet for him or her. You must choose a real company and a real person. Here are some suggested companies: Geac Comptuer; Cognos; Hummingbird; Corel; Open Text; STS Systems; Algorithmics Incorporated; JetForm; Constellation Software; MDSI-Mobile Data Solutions; Hyprotech.

Writer's Profile

1. How would you rank your level of technical knowledge in general? (5 = expert, 1 = novice)

2. List below the specific areas in which you have technical knowledge (e.g. C++, Java, networking, business management, accounting).

3. Are you a direct or indirect communicator?

4. What are your likes and dislikes as a reader?

5. How do you typically read a document?

6. What factors have most influenced your opinion on the topic you're writing about?

Audience Profile Sheet

Supply the following information to describe your reader(s). If your document addresses more than one reader or group of readers, profile each of these on a separate form.

Audience Information	Notes
Name	
Gender	
First language	
Age	
Job title	
Position in organization relative to me	
Education	
Length of time with organization	

Audience Information	Notes
Previous work history	
Level of technical knowledge in this writing context	
Familiarity with topic	

Audience Information	Notes
Purpose in reading my document	
Amount of time available for reading my document	
Interest in reading my document	
Pre-formed opinions about my ideas	

Audience Information	Notes
Preferred writing style	
Favourite jargon	
Hot-button words	
Pet peeves	

Chapter 2

Using the TACT Method to Reach Your Audience

Old-fashioned manners for the new-fangled workplace

Ling works in Calgary as the office assistant/receptionist/bookkeeper for a small computer consulting firm with branches in London and Munich. Besides monitoring the phone lines for the local office, she handles much of the routine correspondence with the overseas offices.

Yesterday, Ling took the day off to get a tooth pulled. That means that today she's facing a pile of email messages in her inbox, three of which are flagged as high priority. The phones have been ringing nonstop, and she's developing a headache to complement the ache in her jaw.

One of the urgent email messages comes from Gerald, an employee in the Munich office. Although Ling doesn't know it, Gerald tried to reach her by phone three times yesterday. He wants her to send him the updated phone list for the London office, which he needs so he can coordinate a conference call later this afternoon.

When Ling opens the red-flagged message from Gerald, this is what she reads:

Ling,

I need the London phone list right now.

Thx,
Gerald

Now Ling's whole head starts to throb. What phone list, she wonders? Why does Gerald sound so angry?

Ling has never met Gerald in person, but she worries that she's unwittingly done something to offend him. Anxiously, she searches for the list in the filing cabinet, but her head hurts so much and the phones are ringing so frequently that it's hard to concentrate on the files in front of her.

What would your reaction be, I wonder, if you were standing in Ling's shoes? Would you feel irritated or worried by Gerald's message? Would you perceive him as someone with whom you'd like to cultivate a relationship? Would his tone make you answer his request promptly or reluctantly?

Although new technologies often require us to write in great haste, Ling's situation demonstrates how risky it is to sacrifice politeness for speed. Ironically, the faster workplace communication moves, the more important the old-fashioned quality of tact becomes. Polite manners may slightly increase your word count, but without them your words may not be received accurately or even heard at all.

To cope with the communication challenges of the digital age, we need to take lessons from generations past. When Canada was a nation of pioneers, our forebears recognized how important diplomacy is to the success of the written word. When they were writing a letter to someone halfway across the continent, they couldn't count on a follow-up phone call to clear up misunderstandings, so they did all they could to avoid misinterpretations and hurt feelings.

These days, we can send a message through multiple media, but the potential for creating friction between ourselves and our readers seems to multiply with each new channel added, especially as the size of audiences increases. Thus, tact is now—more than ever—an essential survival skill for writers.

But it's not enough to be merely mannerly. With due respect to Miss Manners, just following various formulas of etiquette will only get you so far. In today's global workplace, you need a more comprehensive strategy for becoming a tactful and a tactical writer, especially when you don't know your readers personally. For these situations, the four-phase TACT process described in this chapter enables you to analyze your audience and write clear, personable messages.

Recognizing communities of practice

You don't have to be a fan of science fiction to appreciate that parallel universes exist, at least in the world of work. In fact, a more accurate phrase is the "worlds" of work, since each occupation generates its own social system, with its unique practices, values, and language or languages. Even within one occupation, significant cultural differences can occur from organization to organization.

For instance, Toni is the systems administrator for an employment services association that hires mentally challenged adults to make custom-built pine furniture. Her former college classmate, Kevin, holds a position with a similar title for a mid-sized networking company. Although the two friends have similar credentials (they even graduated from the same college), their work experiences are dramatically different. Toni works in isolation as the only IT person in her organization. Her physical environment is a small office in the building that houses the woodworking shop and showroom. The employment agency operates as a not-for-profit organization, so its core values emphasize community service rather than aggressive growth. Kevin, on the other hand, works for a branch office that's part of a larger American company. At his location, he manages other network installers, who form part of a division of twelve people. Customer service, rather than community service, is the driving value, since customers are bringing in the profits. As similar as Toni and Kevin look on paper, then, they operate in separate galaxies in their day-to-day working lives.

Researchers describe a particular workplace culture as producing a peculiar *community of practice*, a group of writers who share common beliefs about how written communication works, how it should be practised, and how it should be packaged. It takes time and personal interaction to integrate into a community of writing practice, just as it takes time to become part of a neighbourhood, a mosque, a club, or any other community. Because the group habits of a writing community are not always directly explained, it can take years for a novice professional to master them.

Nonetheless, simply recognizing that all workplace writing takes place within the context of a community takes you one huge step closer to addressing your audience with tactful skill. By examining your audience's community of practice, you can tailor your writing strategy to its particular customs and expectations.

In an ideal world, every community of practice would have a clubhouse on the Internet, where it would list its official rules and regulations. Every company, or cultural subgroup within a company, would post a list something like the following:

> Hi! Welcome to Fred Smithers and Associates Computer Consulting. Here are some of the most important conventions we follow in our writing:
>
> - We favour an informal style of written communication. We like first names, contractions, and bulleted points wherever possible.
>
> - We use only email for internal communication, and Fred won't read anything longer than ten lines.
>
> - We don't use any forms or templates.
>
> - We never use red ink, even on sticky notes. (Because Fred used to be a military pilot, he is very superstitious about red pens. The only time a pilot uses red ink is to make the final entry in the flight log of a dead pilot.)
>
> - We require that a proposal be read by at least one other person besides the author before Fred reads it.
>
> - We don't have a set format for proposals, but most of us include the following sections:
>
>   1. Background
>   2. Work to be completed
>   3. Work schedule
>   4. Costs
>   5. Benefits
>   6. Qualifications
>   7. Conclusions

- We include an Executive Summary for any document longer than five pages.
- We use *The Chicago Manual of Style*, 15th edition, as our style guide. For matters of spelling, we refer to *The Canadian Oxford Dictionary*.

In the real world, however, such lists of club rules rarely exist. Community members often follow their conventions unconsciously. Even the above guidelines contain several loopholes that could confuse a new writer. How casual is "an informal style of written communication"? (Is it okay to start an email to the boss with a simple "Hey there"?) Who normally functions as a second reader of a draft proposal? (Would a boyfriend or girlfriend count?) If there are standard elements for a proposal, are there also standard design requirements? (What is the normal font size, for instance?) If you're addressing a document to Fred Smithers and Associates—either from within the organization or outside it—you'll need to have clearer answers to these questions and others like them.

Given that communities of practice seldom spell out their conventions, sharp-witted writers approach each writing task with the mindset of a private eye. With some detective work, you can infer the preferences of a community, even if you can't picture the individual faces in it.

Using the TACT method

The TACT method gives you a procedure for decoding the hidden assumptions a community of practice makes about written communication. It means considering the following:

1. the **type** of document you need to create;
2. the demographic profile of your **audience**;
3. the social and historical **context** of the writing task;
4. the best **translation** strategy for accomplishing your writing goals.

T = Type

Like any academic or technical field, the discipline of communication studies has its own jargon (i.e. a specialized technical vocabulary). The term that scholars use to discuss different types of business documents (such as letters, memos, and reports) is *genre*. You're probably familiar with the concept of genres from high-school literature courses. Most of us can readily distinguish between the three major literary genres of poetry, prose (e.g. novels and essays), and drama. We naturally try to orient ourselves in a text by looking for signals to show us which of these genres we are dealing with, so that we know how to interpret the language. Sometimes, the answer is not immediately obvious. Consider the following example:

A 26-year-old Milltown man has been
hospitalized after an ATV accident
late last night on Route 7

a 19-year-old woman escaped the
accident
with minor cuts and bruises

witnesses
say they suspect alcohol was involved,
although a
police
    breathalyzer
      was negative.

If we interpret the above text as prose, we can treat it as we would a news bulletin, accepting it as an objective report of the facts relating to an all-terrain vehicle crash. If, on the other hand, the text is really a poem, we should treat it as an imaginative piece of writing; we might extract from it some meaningful ideas or emotions, but we would be misguided to take the words as describing a real occurrence.

In business and technical writing, the notion of genre refers to both the purpose and the form of a piece of writing. Generally speaking, you can identify documents as belonging to the same genre because they look similar and attempt to achieve similar goals. We recognize a proposal, for instance, as a document that proposes a specific project and asks for permission (and funding) to undertake the work. Many formal proposals exhibit a similar "look and feel," as web designers would say. They contain the standard elements included in the proposals at Fred Smithers and Associates.

However, a formal proposal can also resemble a different document called a "feasibility report." Both types of documents can be lengthy (up to several hundred pages); both include elaborate front and back matter (such as a table of contents and appendices); and both make use of similar headings (such as Introduction, Background, Description of the Work, Costs, and Conclusions). Form alone, then, may not give our audience enough clues that a writer intends a document to be read as a proposal, not a report.

To prevent an audience from mistaking a proposal for a report, writers may have to emphasize that they're not merely describing a situation for description's sake but are asking for permission and financing to make the situation happen. In other words, to clarify the genre, they may have to draw attention to the document's purpose rather than rely on its structure and formatting to get the point across.

We can use our knowledge of how genre works to gain insight into the expectations and values of readers whom we don't know. Suppose you're new to your job as a software analyst and the Director of Marketing has asked you to write a product description of the software you've been working on for the past two months. This description could eventually be circulated to sales representatives, customers, potential customers, and investors. Where do you begin?

The first step is to consider the *type* of document you've been asked to create. You might seek out examples of previous product descriptions other analysts have written. It would also be worthwhile to see other types of written communication that go out to the same audiences, so that you can more clearly define your document type by comparing its features with other types. Is a product description the same thing as an entry in the company sales catalogue, for instance? How is it similar? How is it different? Is it the same as the descriptions that the company business plan lists?

Genre signals give us direct clues about how a particular community sees the world. For instance, an organization that uses elaborate forms for even the most basic requests, such as taking a vacation day, is probably a large operation with a substantial bureaucracy. A group that prefers to read and produce documents written in impersonal, highly technical language (such as the scientific research community) likely values objectivity and logic over subjectivity and emotion. A work environment where friendly, even bantering emails set the tone for corporate communication reflects a decentralized, informal culture.

To help you recognize and describe genre indicators, I've created list of questions to ask about document type, which forms the first section of the TACT Worksheet at the end of this chapter.

A = Audience

Although you can use the method we examined in Chapter 1 to size up an audience of strangers, there are a two other kinds of analysis that you may find more effective: demographic profiling and the creation of audience personas.

Demographic profiling

"Demographics" refers to the characteristics of specific population groups. When you use demographic information to profile your audience, you're thinking like a social scientist, making generalizations about human behaviour based on information collected through public censuses and private polls. The Internet and print libraries provide resources that enable writers to paint a reasonably accurate group portrait of an audience.

Begin your demographic research by listing all the communities to which your readers belong, not just the community of practice in which they participate as on-the-job writers. You might find it useful to list this information in chart form. Let's say, for instance, that Ben is a software analyst outlining project specifications to create new patient management software for a regional hospital. He predicts that his proposal will circulate to at least six people in the hospital. Using information gathered from the Internet and other sources, Ben creates the following chart listing readers and their communities:

Head of IT support, Bert Luckyj	Have met Bert personally. His communities: 1. Men 30–40 years old 2. Computer programmers 3. Hospital administrators
Head of human resources	Sonia Fitzgerald. Hospital website gives brief bio and shows her photo. Her communities: 1. Women 40–50 years old 2. Human resources professionals 3. Bankers (she worked for the Royal Bank for ten years) 4. Hospital administrators
Comptroller, Gus Mitchell	Have spoken with him on the phone once. His communities: 1. Men over 45 (guessing by the sound of his voice) 2. Accountants 3. Hospital administrators 4. Squash players
Head of client services, name unknown	Communities: 1. Hospital administrators 2. Marketers (?)
Head nurse, name unknown	Communities: 1. Hospital administrators 2. Nurses 3. Front-line workers
Admissions supervisor, name unknown	Communities: 1. Hospital administrators 2. Clerical workers 3. Front-line workers

After completing his chart, Ben can see that he shares a sense of community with only two of the people on the list: Bert Luckyj, because he shares a similar technical background, and Gus Mitchell, because he, like Ben, is an avid squash player. Ben makes a marginal note to connect personally with Gus by mentioning squash in the informal email he'll send to him as a preface to the official project specs. Now, how can Ben connect personally with the rest of his audience?

Fortunately, all of the readers in Ben's chart share membership in one group: hospital administrators. We can call this the "dominant community." To begin, Ben could find out about what hospital administrators, as a group, are like. He could scour the web for sites of relevant professional associations, or ask a reference librarian to help him locate a newsletter or trade journal for the community. He could examine his list of contacts for possible personal connections whom he could approach with a few well-chosen questions. (Didn't Ben's girlfriend's older brother marry a hospital administrator in Saskatoon?)

Just by Googling "hospital administrators," Ben comes up with some insights. The U.S. Department of Labor website provides him with details describing what a career in hospital administration involves, including the required education and a summary of daily working conditions and challenges. Knowing the educational background of his audience enables Ben to choose the appropriate vocabulary level. He immediately realizes that he'll have to couch the technical information in layperson's terms, since most hospital administrators seem to have a background in management or human resources, not information management. Another Google hit takes Ben to an e-zine called *Health.IT World*, which contains an article entitled "Getting Hospital Administrators Over the Technology Hump." Quickly, he scans the piece and learns that hospital administrators are notorious penny-pinchers. Whereas he had previously planned to stress the ability of his software to reduce errors and improve patient safety, he now realizes that he'll need to emphasize how it will increase efficiency and save money.

With a little thoughtful sleuthing, Ben has made substantial progress in creating a community portrait of the audience he needs to address, even though he lacks many individual details. This will help him determine the best tone and techniques for encouraging his various readers to endorse his proposal.

Using audience personas

The broad demographic picture has many benefits, but it can also cause you to lose sight of the real individuals with whom you need to communicate. If you find this is the case, you may want to try a method suggested by interface-design guru Alan Cooper (1999). This entails creating fictional characters, which Cooper calls "personas," to guide the software development process from start to finish. Rather than trying to sift through piles of demographic data, his project teams compile representative impersonations of the data—real people with real lives.

Cooper's personas are not universal composites but rather lifelike individuals. One of the dangers of using demographic information, he realizes, is that it can be tempting to try to design a product (or, in our case, a piece of writing) to accommodate such a wide variety of characteristics that it satisfies no one. Sometimes it's better to focus on a handful of characters you can address as persons, not abstract compilations of data.

It's key, Cooper says, to give your persona a name so that you treat him or her as a real person. Once you've named your character, add as many personal details as you can imagine. The more flourishes you're able to add to your portrait, the more likely you'll have a realistic picture of your persona's representative needs and preferences. For instance, to return to our patient-management software example, once Ben has learned all he can about supervisors of hospital admissions departments in general—their typical education, working conditions, and pet peeves—he decides to craft a persona called Wei Chan. Here are his notes on Wei's profile:

Wei Chan, Head of Admissions, Ardmore County Regional Hospital

- Forty-five years old.

- Has been at hospital fifteen years (started as admissions clerk and worked his way up).

- University education in China (in mechanical engineering).

- Supervises eleven people.

- Married. Three kids.

- Lives in the city and commutes to Ardmore County because his wife has a job downtown.

- Fluent in Mandarin. Stronger in spoken than written English.

- Sometimes has to work in very hectic environment because ACRH has only emergency room in radius of 100 km.

- Injured his wrist playing tennis last year—sometimes bothered by keyboarding for long periods.

- A whiz with previous patient database. Not very easygoing with those who aren't as quick to catch on.

- Avid golfer. Leaves at 4:30 p.m. sharp in the summer so he can get in nine holes at the local course before he heads back to the city.

By creating a detailed character sketch of Wei, Ben gains insight about how to approach both his specifications and the actual software he's designing. For instance, recognizing that Wei commutes from the city challenges Ben's earlier assumption that the admissions staff at a regional hospital work under less time pressure than their urban counterparts. Another eye-opener is that just because Wei is a supervisor doesn't mean he has any inclination for training. Clearly, Ben realizes, both his document and his computer program will have to be straightforward and easy to use.

In terms of Ben's writing task, it doesn't matter that there is no real Wei Chan. If he is scientifically accurate in the demographic data he collects, he can trust his imagination to flesh them out with the appropriate details. As part of his pre-writing thinking about the admissions staff members who could read his document, Ben might construct three or four additional personas. By visualizing these realistic characters in his unknown audience, he's able to focus on usability, which is a key characteristic of quality writing as well as quality software.

The second section of the TACT worksheet helps you with your demographic audience analysis. Once you're satisfied that you've thoroughly examined your audience from the demographic perspective, consider constructing two or more personas to complement your demographic profile. Then you'll be ready to move on to the third phase of the TACT process, in which you evaluate the historical and cultural context of your document.

C = Context

You know what type of document you need to craft and the audiences for whom you're crafting it. If your task was to tell a story, we might say that you've selected the form and sketched out the characters. Now you need to determine the details of your setting—the history, social structures, ethnic influences, religious beliefs, and organizational attitudes that form the background of your communication task.

In order to speak to your audience's interests, you'll need to become a corporate historian. Sometimes knowing the personal history of your readers is not sufficient. You may have to consult company archives, visit the library, or surf the web to examine an organization's general history and perhaps the historical thread of the topic you're addressing. For example, if you're writing a cover letter to accompany an unsolicited resumé, you'll want to search the company website and local newspapers to find out what the company's areas of growth, and its challenges, have been in the past year. Here's another example: let's say you're writing a letter to offer computer repair services to an organization. Find out all you can about what kind of computer problems typically occur in the organization and how they've been handled in the past. A brief phone call to the right person could give you the details that make the difference between a bland sales letter that goes directly to the wastebasket and a targeted, solution-oriented letter that causes the reader to take positive action (pick up the phone and call to request your services).

Just as important as the history of your topic is its social context. Many, if not all, workplace documents promote an underlying social function. For instance, consider the routine status report. Let's imagine you work in a small company, where there are two teams of half-a-dozen programmers each. Every Friday, you're required to send your project manager an email describing the progress you've made on the project since the previous weekend. We might say that the basic function of your status report is to inform—you're simply telling your supervisor what you've done and what you have left to do. On another level, however, your report serves various social functions: (1) it offers your boss reassurance; (2) it enables you to assert your competence; and (3) it fosters a sense of teamwork.

You need to have a firm grasp on your document's social (and sometimes political) context in order to strike the right tone and project the most positive self-image you can. If, for example, you overlook the status report's role in reassuring your boss, you could produce a message as abrupt and cryptic as the following email from a web developer, Sam, to his supervisor, Jed:

From: Sam [mailto:swebb@teamxyz.com]
Sent: May 5, 2004 11:55 AM
To: Jed
Subject: Status report

Done this week: Specs for new home page for Ceylon Enterprises; XML coding for contact form for MKJ Fisheries Inc.; Javascript complete for Red Apple Barn Restaurant site

To do next week: Meet with designer for Ceylon Enterprises site; XML coding for various sites

Later,

Sam

Put yourself in Jed's shoes. Is there enough information in Sam's message to create a feeling of confidence in his work? Do you have all the details you need to confirm that the work has been done thoroughly and precisely? I suspect not. The document fulfills its minimal obligation of listing the tasks that Sam has accomplished, but it completely bypasses its social obligations, which, in this situation, are equally as important. Sam's message is really only half-written because it uses such an abrupt style that it borders on being rude. The email is so terse that it fails to promote rapport between Sam and his boss—in fact, it could even damage their relationship.

Besides tailoring your writing to the historical and social situation, there is one last element you need to consider before you begin drafting: the cultural context. When we talk about the writing habits of a community of practice, we're dealing with one aspect of workplace culture. There are many other cultural influences that people bring into their working environments, and you need to pay equally close attention to those.

In addition to considering the company culture, writers must think about such things as the religion and ethnicity of the reader. If you fail to take notice of your own cultural context and also the culture with which you're communicating, you risk a sensational gaffe. Over the course of a long career in international marketing, Roger Axtell noticed so many intercultural communication blunders that he compiled them into the book, *Do's and Taboos Around the World*. As Axtell's examples illustrate, developing cultural awareness as a communicator means paying attention to even the smallest gesture. For instance, use your hand to wave a friendly, American-style "hello" in Germany and you'll actually be indicating "no." Do the same thing in Greece and you'll deliver an accidental insult (Axtell, p. 43).

To avoid unwittingly offending an audience from a different cultural background, whether that person is across the plant floor or across the globe, take the time to educate yourself about standard greetings and closings in that culture. What works in North America could be considered rude elsewhere. A German client who has never met you would probably not interpret your "Dear Fritz" kindly; he'd probably prefer "Dear Herr Vogelbacher." By the same token, a company colleague in Jordan might not appreciate an email with the following ending:

Hope to see the results ASAP.

Fred

Two potential problems exist with the above closing. First, the acronym "ASAP" may not be intelligible to a reader whose first language is not English. Second, many Middle Eastern (as well as Latin) cultures do not share North American attitudes concerning time. Whereas North Americans dissect the clock into five-minute segments and count every tick, most business people from the Middle East don't like to be rushed. Even though Fred perceives his "ASAP" comment as little more than a routine closing, his Jordanian colleague may read it as conveying a pushy, "do-it-now" attitude. No matter how graceful or diplomatic the rest of Fred's email, those four letters could alienate his reader.

Besides thinking carefully about the salutation you choose and the formality of your language, make sure you also weigh cultural considerations when choosing document structure and style. Although North American business communication privileges a direct communication style, other cultures, particularly Asian and Latin cultures, favour a more indirect approach. The short, straightforward sentences you've spent so much time pruning for a sales letter pitched at the Singapore market may fall terribly flat on the other side of the Pacific.

You'll find questions to help you analyze the context of your writing task in the third section of the TACT Worksheet.

T = Translation

Writing for readers who do not share your language or nationality is, in one way, a straightforward task. The differences are so obvious that they beg to be addressed. If you want to form a strategic partnership with a firm in Belgium, it's plain that, unless you're fluent in written French, you'll have to hire a translator to complete the contract forms. In a sense, though, whenever you write for an audience from an educational or cultural background different from your own, you are engaged in an act of translation. Thus the final phase of the TACT process involves choosing the best strategy for translating your technical knowledge into terms your audience can readily comprehend.

The value of analogy

I recently interviewed Ann Dent, a computer scientist and instructor who has developed effective translation techniques through two very different work experiences. Since 1981, she's worked for Defence Research and Development Canada (DRDC), where she's had to collaborate with highly specialized physicists and engineers. Since 1999, she has also worked as a part-time community college instructor, teaching a course called Internet for Surfing Seniors. In both situations, Ann has consciously taken on what a biologist would call "adaptive behaviours." She has learned to derive the mental models and the vocabulary she uses from the communication context, not the technology itself.

Ann got the idea for introducing seniors to the web from her mother. She recalls how one telephone conversation "had them both in stitches" as Ann tried to explain, without being able to point to a keyboard, what the tilde key (~) was. When she's teaching seniors, Ann has to revisit even the most basic assumptions. Once common question is: "Which part of the machine is 'the computer'?" (Is it the monitor? Is it the tower?) Ann says she can relate to the urban myth about the new computer user who thought his CD drive was a handy cup holder. With her students, many of whom have never handled a computer mouse before, she can take no prior knowledge for granted.

By the end of Ann's course, however, her students are able send email messages to one another, scan photos, use search engines, and download sound files. The secret to their success is Ann's ability to relate web technology to familiar experiences. "I try to teach by analogy to the real world," she says. For instance, some students find it hard to understand why they have to click the *Send* button in their email browser. Ann compares email to regular mail by stressing that writing a letter is not the same as mailing it; clicking *Send* is like walking to the mailbox and dropping your letter in. She finds it helpful to ask herself, "What do I do unconsciously?"

That's the challenge of translating technical knowledge so that it will reach a non-technical audience: to find words for concepts that are so familiar to you that they seem intuitive or innate. Ann is fortunate because she's been on the other side of the knowledge divide. She remembers very clearly what it's like to be a non-expert trying to make sense of technical jargon. When she started her first project with DRDC, she had to collect technical information from the experts who would eventually use the acoustic classification system she was developing. These people were scientists, not computer programmers, so she had to figure out how to extract the information from them step by step, detail by detail, so that she could understand and record it. Recalling that experience enables her to translate her own technical knowledge for her students.

Using analogy—direct comparisons—is one of the most effective strategies you can use to translate a technical concept for non-technical readers. Try finishing the following sentence: "A router is like..." How many different comparisons can you find? Is a router like a telephone switchboard? Like a central post office? Like a bridge? Like the axle at the centre of spokes?

The more familiar and vivid the concept to which you compare the technology you're defining, the more likely your audience is to understand.

Prime examples

Another very simple way to translate technical information for non-experts is to use concrete examples. Punctuate your technical description or product presentation with frequent instances of "for example" or "let's say you need to. . ." To be a truly effective translator of technical information, you need to enable your readers to stand in the shoes of someone who is using the technology. Remember the old saying, "actions speak louder than words," and dramatize your meaning by enabling your audience to see the technology in action.

For instance, as part of the research for this book, I interviewed the vice-president of a company that makes embedded software. After reading through all the online product information, I had only the foggiest notion of what the company made. Only when the vice-president gave me specific examples of appliances that use embedded software—such as microwaves and VCRs—was I able to understand what the company actually produced and why it mattered.

If you're writing for non-experts and you're worried that examples will take up too much space in your document, then perhaps you need to condense some of your other material. Lay readers will depend on your examples more than any other part of your technical descriptions. Leaving examples out would be like a budget-strapped television ad executive deciding to cut the video component of a commercial and run the sound only. Give your readers as many pictures as you can so that they'll truly be able to say, "I see what you mean."

Putting translation into practice

Nerds On Site is an Ontario-based computer services company that realizes just how valuable a skill it is to be able to translate technical knowledge into plain, ordinary English. The mobile "nerds," who make house and office calls to fix all kinds of hardware and software problems, are distinct because they drive around in bright red Volkswagen beetles with the company name emblazoned on the side. What really distinguishes them, though, is their ability to deal with customers in what they call "NORMALspeak," rather than the "NERDspeak" they use with one another. Their ability to translate technical information for end-users answers a widespread need. The company is growing rapidly, and today has more than two hundred independent Nerd contractors across Canada. You don't have to wear the official red "Nerd" T-shirt to make yourself stand out as someone who can translate technical know-how into everyday language, however. Keep in mind that many of the non-experts in your audience may feel resentful, fearful, or anxious about technology. The more explicit translation strategies you can use—the more analogies, examples, and definitions you incorporate—the more you will inspire your audience's trust and confidence.

The final section of the TACT worksheet provides space for you to identify the kinds of technical information your audience will need you to translate for them. After completing a TACT analysis, you will have a good sense of the *who* involved in your writing task. You're ready to start thinking about *what* to say.

Figure 2.1 TACT Worksheet

T = TYPE

1. How long is the document?
2. What is the vocabulary level in the document?
3. What kind of sentence structure is most prevalent in the document?
4. Does the document use abbreviations and jargon? If so, are these defined?
5. Does the document incorporate diagrams, charts, or tables?
6. Does the document use topical or descriptive headings (*Background* or *Why we need a new server*)?
7. Does the document use a personal or impersonal style? (Does the writer use *we* or *I*; does the document address the reader directly as *you*?)
8. Does the document make use of any boilerplate (text borrowed from another company document)?
9. Does the document include any special layout or design features (such as columns, horizontal lines, or company logo)?
10. Does the document overtly refer to its purpose ("This report describes...")?

A = AUDIENCE

Note: Depending on the make-up of your audience, you may have to complete more than one version of this section of the worksheet.

1. What is the dominant occupational group for your audience?
2. What are the chief job duties for your readers?
3. What challenges do your readers face on the job?
4. To which age group do most of your readers belong?
5. What is your readers' educational background?
6. What is your readers' income level?
7. What is your readers' first language?
8. Where do you readers live?

C = CONTEXT

1. Is this the first document to deal with the matter in question?
2. What other documents have been generated on the subject?

Figure 2.1 TACT Worksheet (continued)

3. Does the audience expect your document?
4. Does the audience have strong opinions on the document's subject?
5. Where do your opinions on the subject come from?
6. What social functions does your document need to serve?
7. Are you dealing with any politically "hot" or controversial issues?
8. How would you describe your audience's organizational culture?
9. Does anyone in your audience have a different ethnic background than you?
10. How does your audience's cultural background differ from yours?
11. What specific adjustments do you need to make to your thinking and your writing in order to accommodate cultural differences between you and your audience?

T = TRANSLATION

1. How does your audience's technical knowledge differ from yours?
2. Which technical terms can you be certain your audience will know?
3. Which technical terms will you need to describe or define?
4. What is the main technical concept you need to communicate?
5. Are you able to create a definition of your main technical concept relying only on vocabulary you know your audience will understand?

Exercises

1. For each of the following passages, name the genre of writing and try to guess at the probable source. Identify specific features in the writing that serve as genre markers. (How do you know the writing belongs to a particular genre?) Consider such elements as the following: word choice, sentence structure, organization, tone, imagery, and format.

   a. As a churchgoer, Rowlandson would have been accustomed to hearing psalms read or sung both before and after every sermon she attended (Hambrick-Stowe *iii*). She would have sung psalms in family devotions and incorporated them in her private meditations. Moreover, she would have recognized in David's collection of spiritual songs a Biblical precedent for the public conversion narratives required for church membership (Swaim 36). If, as Patricia Caldwell has suggested, the first New England authors were able to move "through the Bible, almost as through a physical space" (Caldwell 31), the Psalms provided one of the most familiar and trustworthy Puritan paths through the scriptural landscape.

   b. Everyone has a favourite villain whom they like to blame for our current state of social decay. Bill Gates takes a lot of heat on this score. So—depending on whom you talk to—do Pierre Trudeau, Gloria Steinem, and the Pope. As for me, as I consider the frayed and tattered condition of our social fabric, I put the blame squarely on the shoulders of Alexander Pope, the eighteenth-century satirical poet who was as controversial a celebrity in his day as Madonna has been in ours.

c. *Raising the Bar for Software Success*

Agile Methods: The Quiet Revolution

More and more software teams worldwide are turning to <u>Agile</u> software development methods like <u>XP</u>. They are meeting deadlines, delivering the features customers really want, lowering defect rates, and producing <u>better code</u>. After decades of <u>Waterfall</u> failures, the Agile business case is pretty compelling.

2. Imagine a colleague from another country is coming to Canada to deliver a business presentation. What cultural considerations should she keep in mind?

   Try the same exercise with reference to the distinct culture of your province. Suppose a colleague from another province is coming to deliver a presentation in your province. What regional differences should he keep in mind?

3. Imagine that you work for a cable company that provides high-speed Internet access. You have been asked to help write the user's guide for new subscribers. The marketing department tells you that your audience is very broad. There seems to be no "typical" subscriber; the Internet service is mostly used by men and women between the ages of ten and sixty. About 40 per cent of the subscribers own home-based businesses or use the Internet at least some of the time for work.

   Using Alan Cooper's method, construct three personas to help you focus on the usability needs of your diverse audience.

4. For each of the following technical terms, provide at least two different analogies (e.g. "A mouse is like . . .").
   a. a mouse
   b. an applet
   c. a motherboard

5. If you are employed, list the writing conventions you are aware of on the job. Give as many specific examples as you can.

   If you are not employed, list the writing conventions you are aware of in one of your courses. (Choose a writing-intensive course.) Give as many specific examples as you can.

Chapter 3

Coping with Writing Resistance

Anya chews on her lower lip as she gazes at the calendar posted on her cubicle wall. Her boss wants the report tomorrow, and she feels her stomach twist into knots just thinking about the all-nighter she's going to have to pull to get it done. This is the third afternoon in a row that she's tried to start the dreaded document, and she's still stuck in the first paragraph. The ideas, she tells herself, are there—somewhere in the back of her brain—but she just can't make them come out the end of her pen. As if to make the ink flow, she shakes her pen, taps it on the blank page, and starts to doodle in the empty margin . . .

If this scenario sounds familiar, you're not alone. It's a common belief that writer's block plagues only novice writers, but that's just as much a myth as the notion that stage fright happens only to inexperienced actors. (Just ask British hypnotist Paul McKenna about that. Some of Hollywood's leading lights have sought his advice for help conquering their persistent fears about performing in public.) For most writers, the complex physics of turning thoughts into print involves a certain amount of creative friction.

In this chapter, we'll explore several methods you can use to help you extract those ideas from the back of your brain and break through the seeming barrier between you and the empty page or screen. As we'll see, this resistance surfaces quite normally as a regular phase of the writing process. By learning to tap into your emotional brain and practising idea-generating techniques, you can overcome the resistance and perhaps even appreciate it.

Writing and emotional intelligence

When I was in grade school, IQ tests were all the fashion. It seemed that we took one every couple of years. As children, we never saw the numerical scores, which were for parents' eyes only, but the results were apparent enough when we were sorted into streamed classes. We knew, without being told, who was in the "smart" class.

Thank goodness that public schools have now moved past the idea of treating a high IQ score as a badge of intelligence. We know now that rational intelligence is not the only kind of "smarts" a person can have, especially when it comes to writing. Writing is such a complex activity that it requires more than one kind of mental capability. Harvard University professor Howard Gardner distinguishes between eight different kinds of intelligence, including *interpersonal* (intelligence regarding other people) and *intrapersonal* (intelligence regarding self). Today, watchers of business trends tell us that the people who are most successful in their careers cultivate these two intelligences, commonly lumped together as Emotional Intelligence (EI for short). A strong EI and strong writing ability go hand-in-hand.

Having a high EI score means being able to tune into your own emotions as well as the emotions of the people around you. People with advanced EI are self-aware and empathetic; they know how to manage themselves and other people because they're flexible, tolerant, and positive. In terms of writing, people with well-developed EI perceptively tune into their readers so the message doesn't get tuned out. In our wired world, where so many of our working relationships are forged via emails and faxes, EI has become a particularly valuable component of effective business writing. Emotional intelligence plays an important role in the writing process, from the very beginning. It isn't just useful for persuading audiences to act as you want them to; flexing your emotional brain will also empower you to break through the inertia you are bound to confront at some point in the writing process.

Two brains are better than one

Using your EI to picture real readers requires the use of both hemispheres of your brain: the creative, imaginative right hemisphere as well as the rational, organizing left hemisphere. You need to recognize your multi-lateral intelligence and make it work for you. Thus, before you begin the sorting and reflecting process of composing (arranging your thoughts into the most effective order), it's crucial to let loose the exploratory energy of your right-brain. As you'll discover, the best way to "boot up" for writing is to think of yourself as having two brains rather than one.

Although writing is an art, science has provided extensive insight into how that art happens. Researchers have managed to document, albeit with fairly broad strokes, what happens in the writing brain. They've now studied the mental activities of enough expert and novice writers that we can confidently make assertions about what the most productive writing behaviours are. Consistently, studies have confirmed the point about drawing on both brain hemispheres throughout the various phases of the writing process. One of the best practices of expert writers is the ability to draw on both brain hemispheres as they move through the various phases of the writing process. Mike Sharples (1999), a computer scientist who specializes in artificial intelligence, describes writing as a "cycle of engagement and reflection" (p. 7) that happens as writers move between phases of contemplation, interpretation, organization, and production. This cycle doesn't function algorithmically—there's no best place to begin and no preset order for the phases. The distinguishing characteristic of effective writers, though, is that they proceed through *all* the phases of the writing process, drawing alternately on the two sides of the brain. Composition theorist Gabrielle Rico refers to these as "Sign Mind" (the left hemisphere) and "Design Mind" (the right hemisphere) (1983).

In *Writing the Natural Way* (1983), Rico posits that most of us primarily use our Sign Mind. That's the mental region where our formal education develops, through emphasizing reason and logic. When we approach a writing task, though, we need to engage our Design Mind, that part of the brain that "thinks" in emotions and non-verbal patterns. Only by stepping outside the familiar groove of linear, rational thinking can we generate the creative ideas we need to solve problems, which is what writing is all about.

If this sounds to you like rich philosophy that only poets can afford, you may need to reorient your own perspective on writing to allow for creative wastefulness. Most of us, in this environmentally conscious era, are familiar with the expression, "Waste not, want not." The programming world emphasizes this proverb by encouraging developers to reuse or recycle chunks of code whenever possible. However, as far as the writing process is concerned, a more helpful motto would be "Waste plenty, produce plenty." Writing requires selecting and organizing ideas, but first it involves producing them. The more fertile your invention stage, the more choice you have when it comes to choosing the ideas you want to express. The more creative wastage, in other words, the better the quality of your final product.

The challenge for most of us is to give Design Mind free rein when we tackle a writing task. Writing seems to involve so many restrictions, including rules for punctuation, grammar, word usage, formatting, paragraph organization, and sentence structure. The list of dos and don'ts can seem endless and formidable. Peter Elbow, who has spent more than twenty years helping students become more fluid writers, speaks of the need to escape temporarily the harsh, overseeing gaze of the internal critic:

> The editor is, as it were, constantly looking over the shoulder of the producer and constantly fiddling with what he's doing while he's in the middle of trying to do it. No wonder the producer gets nervous, jumpy, inhibited, and finally can't be coherent. It's an unnecessary burden to try to think of words and also worry at the same time whether they're the right words. (Elbow, *Writing Without Teachers*, p. 5)

Like Rico, Elbow believes that only by unleashing our creative side can we tap into the kind of deep, double-minded thinking that makes it possible to articulate our thoughts in writing.

The Sign Mind isn't a resource that's special to so-called creative writers such as playwrights and novelists. Whether you're producing a technical report, a white paper, an abstract, a journal article, a press release, or a website, you need to make your Design Mind a conscious partner in the writing process. It acts as your strongest ally in the struggle with that dreadful sense of mental impasse that all writers experience at one time or another.

Overcoming writing resistance

To cope with so-called "writer's block," try thinking of it not as a negative obstacle but rather as positive *writing resistance* that can actually help you express your ideas. Bear in mind that the resistance is often most intense when we're closest to capturing in language our most innovative, groundbreaking thoughts. We're far more likely, for instance, to feel stuck when we're wrestling with complex or abstract ideas (completing a feasibility study, for example) than when we're simply relating a series of chronological events (writing an email describing what happened at last night's party).

Sharples points out the paradoxical benefits of the resistance we encounter in such situations. The sense of restriction that seems temporarily to paralyze us actually kickstarts creativity. It's feeling trapped in a box that spurs us to think "outside the box." Writer's block, we might say, is really a good sign, if we view it as a constructive stage we encounter en route to developing and expressing our ideas.

Each writer develops her or his own way of working through writing resistance, so I have no magic solution with a money-back guarantee. What I do have are several suggestions, supported by the testimony of generations of writers (famous and ordinary) as well as by empirical research.

1. Brainstorming

Quick! You have to write an email to your boss suggesting a theme for this summer's annual office party, but you haven't a clue what to recommend. The all-you-can eat Hawaiin buffet has been done. Ditto dinner theatre and a Chinese banquet. How are you ever going to find a fresh idea?

Chances are, if you find yourself in the above situation, you'll probably begin with some unstructured "brainstorming," either on your own or with a colleague. If you're working on your own, this will likely mean taking out a fresh sheet of paper and rapidly scratching down ideas as they come to you. As your list grows, you may see a pattern emerge and start to group similar ideas together, until one central idea comes into focus. Or you may suddenly find one idea that leaps off the page because it strikes you as more original and worthwhile than the rest. Your brainstorming session might be over in thirty seconds, or it might still be rolling after ten minutes.

That's the best scenario. You could also find, however, that your "brainstorming" leads to mental gridlock and finds you still struggling for inspiration half an hour later. When unstructured brainstorming works, ideas can come gushing forth as if from a miraculous spring. What happens, though, when the faucet of invention just doesn't seem to turn on? One tactic is to follow the example of professional facilitators, who begin group brainstorming sessions by establishing a fundamental ground rule: no censoring allowed. For experimental thinking to flow unchecked, you need to create a safety zone where untested, even bizarre, thoughts can freely float. It's important simply to record each idea as it comes, without commenting on its value or evaluating it in any way.

Since we're often our own worst critics, you may have to fight against habit to avoid self-censoring. You may even have to turn to devious methods to restrain your inner critic. You might, for instance, need to choose a writing implement that makes it difficult for you to erase your words (a pen instead of a pencil or a keyboard). You should also work as rapidly as you can and establish a time limit for your brainstorming, perhaps even set an alarm so you'll keep it. Another technique is to aim for a target number of ideas, regardless of their quality.

Working with such boundaries as time periods and idea quotas makes the difference between self-censorship and productive innovation. Such limits on brainstorming encourage you to work quickly and to explore the outlandish, the improbable, and the unpopular. They free you to play devil's advocate and embrace unconventional points of view. There are now a number of brain-storming software packages available, and you might also find these provide useful structures for liberating your thinking.

If, despite some of the above tactics, your brainstorming session proves to be unproductive, you might have to put your paper (or keyboard) away and let your unconscious mull over the problem for a while. You can try again later. If you're facing a tight deadline, you might switch to another technique for finding ideas: free-writing.

2. Free-writing

Free-writing means writing for a sustained period of time, without stopping. If you're writing longhand, your pen or pencil should never leave the paper; if you're typing at a keyboard, your fingers should never stop moving. When you free-write, you take an idea and run with it, without looking back. You don't stop to change a word, insert a comma, or re-read what you've written. Neither do you pause to consider what you'll write next. If you run out of ideas, you can keep the free-writing process moving by repeating your last word or reflecting on what you're doing and thinking ("I don't know what to write next. I feel really stuck. What should I do now? I wonder why I'm so hung up on this idea. . .") Eventually—this I can personally guarantee—a new idea will come.

For some, free-writing comes as easily as rolling out of bed in the morn-ing. I'll confess that I'm not one of those lucky writers. I fall into that camp for whom free-writing is scary and difficult. But, precisely for those reasons, I force myself to do it regularly, in my journal and as part of other writing tasks. Regular free-writing is the best technique I know for diminishing writer's resistance. I think of practising free-writing as giving my writing muscles a workout. It helps me stay in shape, so to speak, so that when I have to produce a public document I'm confident that I'll be able to find the ideas I need to solve the writing problem and come up with the words to express them. Although you can free-write by hand or at a computer, many writers find that scratching across the page with a pen or pencil somehow stimulates creativity. I recommend you experiment with both methods several times to discover which works best for you.

To experience free-writing for yourself, try this simple exercise. Take out a clean, lined piece of paper and write at the top of the page: "Network." Then set a timer for ten minutes and write, without stopping, whatever thoughts occur to you on your topic. When I tried this, here's what my free-write looked like:

> Cables. Wires of all different colours tangled together. The cable repair person who came last week to hook up the television for us. Now we're officially networked to the world—we actually have cable. Network is kind of a misnomer (is that the word?) for what the television conglomerates really are or do, though. They pretend to connect us, link us together by plugging us into a web of information. But what television "networks" really do is allow us to tune each other out. We watch "Friends" instead of spending time with our real friends. Television has such a tranquillizing effect. The Internet, though, I truly believe that's different different different I'm not sure how it differs because it actually disconnects a lot of people at the moment—all those who can't afford computers and an Internet provider—but that will change. I like the fact I can email a friend's friend in China to find out about work opportunities there. That I can log on to a forum and find like minds from around the world. Ooh my hand is starting to hurt, where was I going with this? But what does that do to my local connections? When I think about it, I'm tuning them out by spending my leisure time in front of a box. I may be connecting with someone across the globe, but I have little sense of what my neighbours do. But what does all this have to do with the idea of a "network," which is where I started out? Maybe I've gone down a blind alley. OK how's this: Is the idea of a "network" replacing the old-fashioned idea of a neighbourhood? And then there's the more skeptical—or or or rather business-oriented definition of "networking." It means stringing wires, but also trying to pull wires. Self-interested socializing. I truly am skeptical today, aren't I?

Not very engaging or very polished, is it? But even though there is nothing sparkling about this mental meandering, it did produce the germ of an idea that I find interesting and could pursue in an article about new media and evolving social patterns. I wouldn't want to use any of the above sentences in that article, but free-writing isn't about producing ready-to-go copy. Rather, it shows that only once you accept all the warts and pimples of a first draft are you free to see the truly valuable parts of it, those flashes of insight worth developing. Free-writing teaches us to "satisfice," as researcher Linda Flower says (1981, p. 39). Satisficing means making do with an inferior choice for the sake of expediency—in this case, grabbing the first word that comes to you rather than holding out for the perfect phrase to appear.

If you have any perfectionist tendencies (and most of us do), satisficing while writing can be very hard to do. Some people's fingers and stomach tense at the very thought of free-writing, and they find it helpful to experiment with "invisible writing." Here's how to do it: open up a blank document in your word processing program, then turn your monitor off and free-write for five to fifteen minutes. The exercise will likely seem strange at first, and you may have to try it several times until you're able to type without interruption.

Free-writing is like panning for gold. I feel as if I've hit pay dirt if, for every page or two of rambling drivel, I find a tiny nugget of an interesting idea worth exploring. The activity proves the point that mining for new ideas involves a lot of creative waste. A few lucky prospectors hit gold the first time they break ground, but most of us have to shovel a lot of dirt before we spot the rare glint of an original thought. The more you dig, though, the stronger and more productive you become.

Free-writing makes us more self-aware as writers because sometimes the only thoughts that keep the pen moving are thoughts about the act of writing itself, which allows us to analyze our own thinking as it evolves. Re-reading a passage of free-writing is like watching the slow-motion replay of a sports moment. Just as athletes watch videotapes to understand and improve their performance, we can use free-writing to generate more original and incisive thinking. Look again at my free-write on "network," and you'll see that my process-related passages address a range of issues: word choice, the direction of my thoughts, the physical discomfort of writing. As I look back on my free-writing, I can observe myself arguing with myself. This ability to conduct an internal debate on paper is one of the most worthwhile reasons to free-write, since dialogue is a highly productive technique for discovering and clarifying ideas.

If I should choose to explore further the connection between network-ing and changing concepts of community, I might decide to produce another free-write, using a nugget from the first passage as my point of departure. This might lead to the discovery of more nuggets, and then further free-writes, until I have a solid framework of an idea, with supporting ideas holding it up. By using a progressive series of free-writes, you can zero in on an idea and take your creative thinking to a deeper and deeper level.

3. Clustering

Gabriele Rico presents a method that stimulates creative thinking by activat-ing the visually oriented Design Mind (the right brain). It's called "cluster-ing," and it works by representing thoughts as movable objects on a page. This graphic approach enables writers to explore previously unseen connections between ideas, and form new ones. Although the theory behind clustering is scientifically sophisticated, the technique is very simple. (Many people find, however, that it takes some practice before it feels natural.) Creating a cluster is like playing a word association game with yourself on paper. You can begin with any word—an object, an action, or an abstract concept. To start with, let's try a concrete noun: "robot."

Take a clean sheet of paper and turn it to the landscape orientation (long sides of the rectangle at top and bottom). In the centre of the page, write the word "robot" and circle it. This will be the core of your cluster. Then take the first idea that occurs to you, write it down, circle it, and draw a line con-necting it to "robot." Repeat this until you've created a web of associations spanning out from the core.

As your cluster develops, it will likely sprout sub-branches, mini-webs shooting out from associated ideas rather than the core. Don't expect your cluster to be perfectly symmetrical. If you find yourself creating an elaborate sub-branch that wants to sprawl off the page, that's probably a sign that you've found a rich vein of thought worth pursuing. When you start to see such a pattern emerging, it might be time to move to the next phase of the writing process. Since the Design Mind perceives the world holistically, by making sense of impressions through association rather than logic, it has the ability to recognize patterns, even before Sign Mind can rationally describe them.

Figure 3.1 shows how my version of a cluster developed around "robot." As you can see, although the first association that occurred to me was the word "helpful," the cluster soon took off in a very different direction. I began to picture robots I'd seen in movies, first Robbie from *The Forbidden Planet*, then HAL from *2001: A Space Odyssey*. Then I thought of a robot I heard about on the news today who, as I write this, is serving as a go-between in a local stand-off with police. Then my mind made a long leap to a magazine article I read several years ago about "nanobots." This leap, however, soon brought me full circle, back to the idea of imaginary robots from science fiction. Once I sensed this repetition, I felt my cluster was complete.

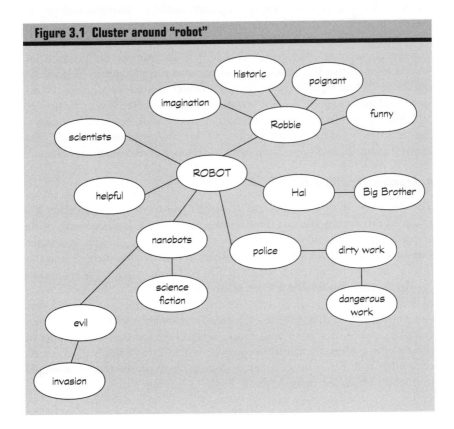

Figure 3.1 Cluster around "robot"

Take a close look at your own cluster around "robot." Do any of your associations seem to group themselves together in your mind? Does any sub-branch stand out as particularly dense in ideas? As soon as you sense your ideas starting to form a definite shape, it's important to get them into words as soon as you can, before you have time to second-guess yourself.

At this point, Sign Mind may press for a formal outline or a step-by-step introduction, but I join Rico in recommending that you use free-writing to complete the clustering process. Free-writing provides an intermediate stage between free association and formal structure. By allowing you to pursue your most original ideas further, without letting them become too rigid in their definition, it offers a way of interpreting your cluster diagram by going deeper into it.

As with free-writing, clustering only really works if you can temporarily silence your inner critic (Sign Mind) and turn your creative side loose. For this reason, try to work as rapidly as you can, without pausing to evaluate ideas. Above all, don't forget to circle the associations you record; the circles speak as strong visual cues to your pattern-oriented Design Mind.

Clustering, like free-writing, is a technique that can help you overcome writing resistance, no matter what your writing context. You can create a cluster around a concept (say "productivity" or "user ID") just as easily as you can around an object. Clustering is particularly useful for forming analogies to describe technical concepts in everyday terms a layperson can understand. Take Joe's situation. He works as Business Developer for a small software company that sells a graphing program for Pocket PCs. To promote the product, Joe wanted to stress that it is much easier to use than the alternative—a graphing calculator. To find an analogy, he created a cluster around "easy." After producing the cluster in Figure 3.2, Joe saw that the aspect of the software he needed to emphasize was its transparent interface. Consequently, he created a marketing campaign based on the metaphor of an "invisible graphing calculator" that allows students to focus purely on math problems, not technology problems.

4. Creating a graffiti wall

The advantage of clustering is that it enables you to make connections you might otherwise miss. Because there is no set format for a cluster, you can create as many lines, loops, and squiggles as you need to link one thought to another. But some writers prefer even more flexibility in playing with their ideas. If this is your case, you might try creating a graffiti wall from sticky notes.

To do this, you'll need a large, blank surface such as a table top, a piece of bristol board, or an empty wall. Conduct a brainstorming session the way you normally would, but write each idea on a separate sticky note. As you complete a note, stick it on your blank surface. Don't worry about trying to decide which ideas are worth keeping or which ideas belong together. As with other techniques for generating ideas, the goal of this process is simply to uncover ideas, not evaluate them. Figure 3.3 shows a sample graffiti wall

Figure 3.2 Cluster around "easy"

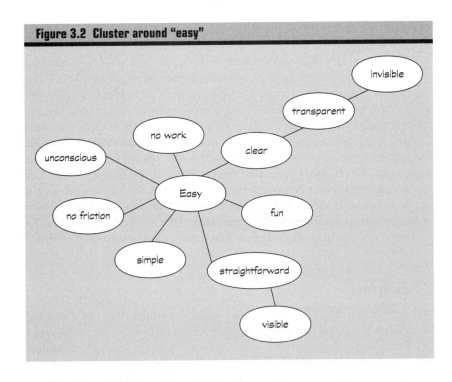

Figure 3.3 Graffiti wall on "entrepreneurship"

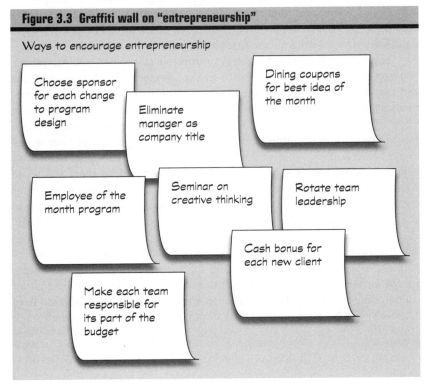

provided by a writer creating a report on ways to encourage entrepreneur-ship in a company.

Once your surface is covered with sticky notes (or once you've used up your allotted brainstorming time or reached your quota of ideas), you can move them around to try out new combinations of ideas. If at first you don't see any clear pattern or theme showing, you might try grouping ideas that are opposite rather than similar. Or you might pick two or three ideas that seem half-promising and use them as the start of another brainstorming session. As with other techniques for creating ideas, this one tends to be most fruitful when used in a series of trials rather than as a one-shot solution.

Trying out various combinations of ideas is not the same as creating a map of them, with a clear hierarchy of thoughts. That process is the province of Sign Mind and belongs to the organizing phase of the writing cycle. An advantage of a graffiti wall, though, is that it eases the transition to the struc-turing stage.

5. Paraphrasing

Writing resistance is often most extreme in the initial stages of a writing project, but it can crop up at any time. Any of the techniques we've discussed so far can help you get unstuck when you find yourself suddenly flounder-ing in quicksand, whether you're writing the beginning, middle, or end of your document. Free-writing can be a particularly helpful technique for overcoming writing resistance that you encounter in the midst of composing because, as we've seen, it permits a kind of self-talk that can help you under-stand how you got stuck in the first place.

Paraphrasing focuses deliberately on this self-talk. When you paraphrase, you step temporarily out of the voice you've adopted to reach your audience and talk directly to yourself on paper as if thinking out loud. This is some-times necessary because it's easy to lose your train of thought when you're using an impersonal style of writing, especially if you're used to talking in a manner much different from the one you're expected to use in your docu-ment. If this happens, one way to find your voice and thoughts again is to have a frank chat with yourself on paper. Take out a clean sheet and write what you really intend to say, in your own words, for your eyes only. Start your conversation with an intentional introduction, such as "What I really mean is. . ." or "What I'm trying to say here is. . ." (Flower calls this the "WIRMI" strategy (1981, p. 39).)

If your formal writing is filled with multi-syllabic words, strings of jar-gon, or empty phrases that just take up space, then paraphrasing can restore you to a more clear, direct approach to your subject. Here's an example of paraphrasing in action. Halfway through a proposal to install a Wireless Area Network (WAN) for a mid-sized accounting firm, Marc finds himself stuck at the following passage:

In all probability, by installing and initiating the new wireless networking technology under consideration, it is to be expected that Consulting Technology Associates will be able to assist Apple Accounting in rendering their employees more effective.

Marc knows he needs to expand on this idea, but he can't seem to find anything more to say. The problem is that the above sentence is so wordy, convoluted, and general that it gives only a foggy impression of an idea, rather than a platform on which he can build. Marc turns to paraphrasing to try to get out of the dead end he's created. On a separate piece of paper, he writes the following note to himself:

What I'm trying to say is that the WAN will make the accountants more productive. With a network, there will be less time required for photocopying, since it will be easy for the accountants to share information. Backup will also be simplified and take less time than it did when each computer had to be backed up individually.

As you can see, simply stepping out of the artificial style he'd assumed enables Marc to regain his momentum and generate the supporting ideas he needs to complete his proposal. In fact, in his self-talk, his thoughts are so clearly expressed that they will require little editing.

Following through

After you break through the barricade of writing resistance, what do you do next? Coaxing original thoughts from your mind onto paper is only one phase of the writing process. Many novice writers mistake free-writing for composing, but these are actually two completely distinct phases of the writing cycle. In contrast to the idea-generating stage, composing requires you to evaluate and sort the raw material you've compiled. In the next chapter, we'll discuss how to give Sign Mind its turn to further the creative process.

Exercises

1. Invisible writing

    (i) Open a blank document in your word-processor, then turn off your monitor. Free-write for ten minutes on one of following topics:

    - my ideal job
    - why I chose my major
    - summer
    - cloning
    - "Only the strong survive"
    - friendship

- my favourite thing about my college/university
- Earth Day

(ii) Write a paragraph describing your experience with invisible writing. Consider such questions as the following:

- Did you find it easier or harder to write without seeing the words?
- What kind of thoughts or emotions passed through your brain as you wrote?
- Does the quality of your invisible writing differ from the quality of other free-writing you've produced?
- Do you think invisible writing would be a helpful strategy for overcoming writing resistance?

2. Free-writing

(i) Free-write for ten minutes on one of the following topics:

- pirates
- hockey
- home
- jazz
- surf
- arcade

(ii) Review your free-writing. Underline words and phrases that are examples of process writing. What insights do these give you into the way you work as a writer? Do they help you pinpoint any original ideas worthy of further thought?

3. Clustering

(i) Create a cluster for one of the following topics:

- mud
- rainbow
- fear
- bee
- shell
- purple

(ii) Once your cluster is complete, circle the main idea you would like to explore further. Create a second cluster around this idea.

4. Clustering and free-writing

Produce a cluster and ten minutes' worth of free-writing on one of the following topics:

- wireless communication
- blogging
- spam
- telecommuting
- bug
- interface

Chapter 4

Organizing Your Thoughts

Saul's brainstorming session to generate ideas for the trade-show brochure has been highly productive—too productive, it would appear. His graffiti wall of sticky notes has grown so large that he's had to move from his cubicle to the boardroom.

But now he has come to an abrupt standstill. How can he possibly fit all those great ideas into two pages of copy?

Staring from the boardroom table are two sheets of paper, clean except for the skeletal structure of a formal outline waiting to be fleshed out with selections from Saul's fruitful chaos. They've been doing that for the better part of an hour, but Saul still can't find the right place to start. The ticking of the clock on the wall reminds him that the Research and Development group has booked the board room for a meeting that will start in forty minutes. Aaargh!

Organizing your ideas doesn't have to become this sort of painful, anxiety-producing task. You can experiment with various ways to evaluate and arrange ideas until you find one (or more) that suits your personal style.

Finding a successful personal approach to organizing

One of the most striking differences between inexperienced and expert writers is that the experts spend far more time planning their work. They might do this before they start to compose, during the composition process, or after they've completed a first draft (or during all three stages). Whatever their individual approach, seasoned writers have a mature vision of the writing process; they've come to terms with the role that organizing plays in helping them fathom and shape their ideas. They see organizing tools, such as outlines, as creative props that help clarify and develop their thinking, rather than as fences that imprison their ideas.

Although the formal outline is the "textbook" model for organizing a piece of writing, it doesn't suit everyone. There is no single best formula. Writers need instead to be flexible and adaptable, ready to craft their writing into shape rather than force it into a prefabricated mould. Throw away, then, whatever rules you've learned about the three-point thesis, the five-point essay, or the funnel paragraph. Listen instead to a suggestion from Peter Elbow: imagine yourself as a sculptor discovering the hidden form emerging from a block of written expression (1998, p. 41). I suggest that you try out multiple ways of getting organized so that you'll have a range of methods available for forming your words into paragraphs, sections, and, eventually, complete documents.

Let's begin by being clear about the difference between the *process* of organizing your thoughts and the finished *product*, an organized piece of writing. As we'll see, there are many different routes you can take to get organized, and most of this chapter will be devoted to exploring these. However, as the final result of your organizing activity, you need to lay down a clear pathway for your reader to follow. You'll know you've created an efficient system of organization when your audience is able to follow the path of your thinking with ease. In the end, only you know the best way to sort your ideas, but only your readers can judge the success of your sorting.

Finding the best route to organization is often a matter of trial and error. Julie Morgenstern, a frequent talk-show guest and a regular contributor to *The Oprah Magazine*, has gained near-celebrity status by visiting homes and offices to help the helplessly disorganized rearrange their space and their time. In *Organizing from the Inside Out*, she points out that organizing is a very personal matter for which there is no one-size-fits-all method:

> There are people whose homes and offices appear neat as a pin on the surface. Yet, inside their desk drawers and kitchen cabinets, there is no real system, and things are terribly out of control. By contrast, there are many people who live or work in a physical mess, yet feel very comfortable in this environment and can always put their hands on whatever they need in a second. Could they be considered organized? Absolutely. (Morgenstern, p. 9)

Morgenstern goes on to say: "Being organized has less to do with the way an environment *looks* than how it *functions*" (p. 9).

To determine the best pattern for arranging your ideas, then, you first need to determine how the various parts and sub-parts of your writing fit together like cogs in a set of gears. Some ideas are bigger than others and only some are directly connected to the pistons that drive the mechanism, but all are interconnected and must be properly aligned to communicate your message. There is, however, more than one way of arriving at a working arrangement of cogs, wheels, and chains.

Picture three engineers sitting down with three separate boxes of gear parts to assemble a mechanism. The first engineer begins by sorting the parts into piles by type: large cogs, small cogs, chains, and pins. The second engineer quickly surveys the contents of the box and starts making a rough sketch on a piece of paper. The third engineer picks up pieces randomly and starts toying with them, seeing which pieces seem to interlock most readily. Which engineer has taken the right approach? The answer, of course, is the one who creates a working mechanism within the allotted time. The first step toward learning the craft of organizing your writing is determining what kind of engineer you are.

Understanding your writing personality

British researcher Ali Wyllie (1993) conducted a survey of academic writers (students and professors) that asked them to describe their writing process. From her results, she proposed five different writing personalities, as paraphrased in Figure 4.1.

Figure 4.1 Writing Personalities	
Watercolourist	Performs no advance planning on paper. Writes steadily and speedily, from start to finish, with little revision.
Architect	Performs advance planning on paper, including scratch outlines. Doesn't necessarily compose sections in final order. Writes steadily, with few pauses, saving revision for after the draft is complete.
Bricklayer	Performs little overall planning. Writes slowly, pausing frequently to revise sentence by sentence.
Sketcher	Performs advance planning on paper (such as a scratch outline), but often deviates from it as writing progresses. Doesn't necessarily compose sections in final order. Sometimes writes continuously; sometimes stops frequently to revise at the sentence and paragraph level. Revises more thoroughly once draft is complete.
Oil Painter	Performs planning in midst of composing. Tackles a writing project by engaging in a repeated cycle of free-writing and revising.

How do your writing habits fit into the above scheme? You can answer this with the help of the Writing Profile Questionnaire in Figure 4.2, which is based on Wyllie's descriptors. Completing this will make it easier for you to develop writing rituals to organize your work.

Developing a writing ritual

We normally think of rituals occurring in a religious context, but we also regularly practise them as habitual actions that provide stability and structure to our days. For example, most of us have some sort of morning ritual, such as reading the sports pages over a cup of coffee or brushing our teeth before getting dressed. Doctors often treat insomnia by advising patients to adopt a bedtime ritual, such as taking a hot bath or eating a bowl of yogourt.

Most expert writers follow a writing ritual of some sort. It might be as simple as sharpening a fresh pencil each morning, or as complex as the super-

Figure 4.2 Writing Profile Questionnaire

Imagine you have to produce a four-page essay for one of your classes. The deadline is five days away.

For each of the following questions, choose one response from the list, then compare your responses to the profiles described in the chart on page 60.

How would you begin your writing task?

___ I would brainstorm a list of ideas.

___ I would free-write to find ideas.

___ I would free-write an entire draft.

___ I would use clustering to find ideas.

___ I would create a scratch outline or list of headings.

___ I would create a flowchart or other diagram of my ideas.

Where would you begin your writing task?

___ I would start with the easiest part.

___ I would start with the introduction.

___ I would start with the longest part.

How would you compose your essay?

___ I would write with few pauses.

___ I would write with occasional pauses.

___ I would write with frequent pauses.

___ I would write with frequent stops, over several sittings.

How would you revise your essay?

___ I would review and revise sentence by sentence, not writing a new sentence until I was satisfied with the one before.

___ I would review and revise at periodic intervals as I wrote, rereading and sometimes rearranging entire paragraphs as well as sentences.

___ I would write the entire first draft and then revise at the end.

stitious charade that the hero, a sports writer, acts out in Mordecai Richler's *Joshua, Then and Now*. Before Joshua can force himself to sit down at the typewriter for the day, he scrubs the keys with a toothbrush, watches out the window until he spots a car with seven as the final digit on its license plate, and touches his cheek to his father's lucky boxing gloves.

What does it take to get your writing engine started? Over the years, I've used a variety of catalysts, involving such aids as music, gum, pencil sharpeners, and popcorn. The trouble, I've discovered, is that not all of these are suitable in a public environment. In the privacy of one's basement office, it's fine to snap your gum as accompaniment to blaring rock music; it's not, shall we say, good manners to do so at the workplace.

Lysia Taylor works as a technical writer for Vemco, a small company that produces electronic equipment for tracking fish in the wild. She knows how difficult it can be to establish and maintain writing rituals in a workplace environment because she writes user manuals by working side-by-side (literally) with colleagues who are building the products. The advantage is that Lysia has good relations with the production staff; she knows how they work and is free to ask them questions at any time. On the downside, however, she must cope with ever-present background noise and constant interruptions. In her distracting environment, Lysia finds that she has to write her manuals in bits and pieces. Creating lengthy documents is challenging, she says, because she often loses the flow.

Most on-the-job writing environments are more like Lysia's noisy workshop than Joshua's solitary study. If you're writing school assignments in the quiet of the campus library or during uninterrupted blocks of time (such as in the wee hours of the morning), you'll likely have to develop new writing habits in order to succeed as a workplace writer. Making a method of organizing part of your writing ritual can build your confidence and your productivity. It enables you to hang on to the "flow" of your ideas, even in the midst of surrounding turbulence.

Finding your Big Idea

The first step in getting organized is to identify your main idea and the key supporting ideas. This requires some sorting criteria to deal with the grab bag of possible ideas you produced at the idea-generating stage.

If we compare the structure of a document to the frame of a house, the abstract and more general ideas tend to serve as load-bearing walls, the ones that prop up the weight of the house rather than simply dividing the internal space. So what do these abstract "Big Ideas" look like? First of all, they tend to recur. Check your pre-writing notes for words that seem to be synonyms. Chances are these words point to a common, central thought, which you can sum up with a more general term. For instance, let's say that you need to write an email to your boss that will convince her to allow employees to set their own flexible schedules. You brainstorm the following list of the advantages of flextime:

1. employees don't have to take time off for doctor's appointments

2. employees don't have to use company phone or Internet to take care of personal affairs

3. improved morale

4. increased loyalty to the company

5. people can work during their most productive time (follow their own biorhythms)

6. reduced stress for employees trying to balance work and child care

As you review your list, you notice that all of the reasons for adopting flextime point, either directly or indirectly, to an increase in employee productivity. Employees who don't have to worry about having time to take care of personal business, for instance, can concentrate more effectively on their job during their time at the office. Employees who are under less stress feel better about their jobs and their employer, so they don't waste energy griping and complaining. The results of your brainstorming suggest that, however you look at the situation, flextime will make people more productive, which will benefit the employer as much as the employee.

We could sum up the gist of your brainstorming efforts by writing the following sentence: "Flextime improves employee productivity." This is the Big Idea. It will function as the theme of this piece of writing. You might want to write it at the top of your page or on a note you can stick to your computer. Do whatever you need to do to maintain your focus. In particularly difficult circumstances, I've considered tattooing my main point on my left forearm, but, of course, you need to find the strategy that works best for you.

Using free-writing to clarify your Big Idea

Some writers find their Big Idea almost as soon as they start thinking about their topic, whereas others find it through free-writing or reviewing a complete draft. If you find free-writing a fruitful way to generate ideas, you may also find it useful for identifying your central point. In *Writing with Power*, Elbow advocates a process he calls "loop writing," which involves circling over, under, around, and through a topic by drafting a series of free-writes, each of which approaches the subject from a slightly different direction. (Elbow suggests such imaginative techniques as creating a dialogue of opinions, writing as if you lived in a different time period, or sketching individual scenes related to the topic (1981, pp. 59–77).)

My students have also found a more directed form of cyclical free-writing helpful in identifying and scrutinizing main ideas. I call it "freecycling." You start by free-writing for a set period (perhaps ten minutes) on your chosen subject. Then you read what you've written and pick out what seems to be the most striking idea. In other words, you invite your inner critic to step into the idea-generating process and momentarily direct it. Once you've evaluated the various ideas and made your selection, you send the critic away again. Then, you use your core idea as the prompt for another free-writing session. You can keep up the freecycling rhythm of free-writing and evaluation until you have the clarity you need to begin composing.

Testing your Big Idea

Once you think you've identified your abstract Big Idea, you can test it by asking yourself, "Is this an idea that takes a specific, defensible position?" Ideas that are simply general or vague fail the test because they contain too many undefined quantities. Big Ideas stand up for themselves and stake a claim. They can be expressed as complete statements that answer the questions "how?" or "why?"

The general idea, "Flextime helps employees," leaves us wondering, "How does it help?" and "Why should the company care?" The more precise idea, "Flextime improves employee productivity," establishes the foundation of an argument (i.e. the company should introduce flextime because it will benefit from increased productivity). We can easily build on this base by listing the examples of more productive attitudes and behaviours that we discovered through brainstorming.

The notion of taking a stance can be difficult to be absorb because so much academic writing favours description. When you write a lab report, a short-answer exam question, or a case study, for example, your objective is to show how much you know about the subject. Assignment instructions often ask you to "describe," "explain," or "discuss." Because your instructors want you to demonstrate the breadth of your knowledge, their favourite assignments require you to compare and contrast ideas. Such exercises may produce no clear answer, and ambiguity is completely acceptable—even sometimes desirable—in the academic environment.

For example, if you're writing a paper discussing causes of the greenhouse effect, you might examine our dependence on cars, our use of industrial chemicals, and our lack of policies regulating air pollution. Since you're just analyzing the causes, not making policy, you don't necessarily need to recommend a workable course of action in order to get a passing grade on the essay. In this academic context, your Big Idea might simply be that there are multiple, interrelated causes of the greenhouse effect which are difficult to disentangle.

In the workplace, on the other hand, readers want you to express a firm, and firmly supported, opinion. If your boss asks you to write a report investigating the feasibility of outsourcing some programming work, he does *not* want a thorough but inconclusive discussion of the pros and cons—he wants your specific recommendation. If, out of respect for his authority, you decide to leave the conclusion open, you'll disappoint and frustrate him. Your Big Idea for this writing situation must clearly indicate whether you think it's in the company's best interest to go ahead with the outsourcing.

Understanding relationships between ideas

Imagine you're facing a table where the following items are laid out:

- a baseball
- a metal bat
- an orange
- a wooden spoon
- a polyester baseball uniform

Your task is to sort the items. Take a piece of blank paper and list the objects in groups. How many different categories can you use to perform your sorting? How many different arrangements can you create?

Even with such a small group of objects, the possibilities are many. You could, for instance, sort the objects according to the activity with which they're associated:

Baseball   bat, ball, uniform
Eating   orange, spoon

You could sort the items according to material:

Natural   baseball (leather and cork), orange, wooden spoon
Synthetic   metal bat, polyester uniform

You could arrange some of the items by shape:

Globe   orange, baseball
Stick   spoon, bat

If you knew the price, age, or weight of the objects, you could also use these as sorting categories. Given the range of choices, we can't say that there is a right or wrong way to group the items. The criteria you use to organize them depends on the particular quality you want to emphasize.

In one way, organizing your thoughts in writing is no different than organizing objects on a table. By arranging sentences into paragraphs and sections, we're grouping together "like" things (in this case, written thoughts) to create points of emphasis. The arrangement you choose depends on your audience and context. Let's suppose that you're drafting two proposals to create custom-built databases. The first is for a medium-sized investment banking firm that is upgrading its current database. The second is for a small, privately owned bookstore, which has never had a database before. The basic software development cycle is the same in both cases, but the way your organize your ideas will likely be very different. For the investment bankers, you'll naturally want to emphasize the financial information and stress the return-on-investment in terms of improved productivity and efficiency. For the bookstore owner, on the other hand, you'll probably want to stress how easy it will be to use the database and how it will improve customer service.

We can see the principles of document organization at work on a micro level by examining how paragraphs work. Contrary to what you may have been told, there are no hard and fast rules governing paragraph structure. While we often find a topic sentence (main idea) at the beginning of a paragraph, it doesn't necessarily belong there. A paragraph that features the topic sentence in the middle or the end could be equally effective. Moreover, in business writing, unlike academic writing, it's common to see a one-sentence paragraph, where the topic sentence is the only sentence.

Writing specialist Ann Berthoff reminds us that paragraphs are not pre-shaped containers into which we pour meaning. Rather, they're arrangements of ideas that grow to suit the concepts they assemble. Berthoff uses the metaphor of a "gathering hand" to describe how paragraphs function. The hand that gathers, she notes, works differently, depending on the matter it holds:

> [T]he hand that holds a couple of eggs or tennis balls works differently from the hand that holds a bridle or a motorbike handle. When you measure out spaghetti by the handful, scoop up water by the handful, hold a load of books on your hip, knead bread, shape a stack of papers, build a sandcastle, your hands move in different planes and in different motions, according to the nature of the material being gathered. (Berthoff, p.6)

Berthoff suggests that we can best understand paragraph form by thinking of the topic sentence as the verbal equivalent of "the opposable thumb" (p. 6). How can an idea work as a thumb? The analogy hinges on the concept of opposition. The human hand is capable of sophisticated movement because the thumb can move against the fingers. In a similar way, a paragraph is capable of organizing and shaping thought because it positions a main idea against the explanations, evidence, and opinions that support it. The meaning of the paragraph is thus shaped by the relationship among the ideas it contains rather than by a pre-established model imposed from without.

Let's look at an example. Can you find the "opposable thumb"—that is, the central idea—in the following paragraph?

> First it was "technical experts," then it was "knowledge workers." Now there's a new buzzword to describe the ideal employee desired by the information-technology economy: "enthusiast." An enthusiast combines technical skill with "soft" interpersonal skills and the personality of an entrepreneur. In show-business terms, such a person would be known as a "triple threat." In today's IT job market, it seems that acting talent alone (mere technical knowledge) won't cut it anymore; you have to know how to sing and dance, too. Enthusiasts are expected to be able to communicate clearly, manage projects efficiently, and present a solid business case. They're also expected to learn quickly, adapt to tasks outside their area of expertise, think creatively, and take initiative. In short, whether they want to work for Nortel or for a three-person shop, recent graduates will need entrepreneurial vision as well as technical competence in order to be among the fittest who survive.

The main idea above is *not* the one expressed in the first sentence. It is instead that the ideal employee desired by the information technology economy is now the "enthusiast." This idea, Berthoff would say, acts as the paragraph's opposable thumb. It stands over and against the rest of the paragraph, which goes on to define what an "enthusiast" is and the kinds of traits such a person is expected to exhibit.

We can see the relationship among these ideas even more clearly by using a graphical means of representation developed by Richard Coe. Coe calls his system a "discourse matrix" (1988), but it is not really the complex array this label would suggest. Actually, it's a very simple way of charting the way ideas in a paragraph interconnect in a hierarchy of dependence.

In order to create a discourse matrix of a paragraph, you need to identify how the ideas in it operate on different levels of meaning. We begin by numbering each thought (not each sentence) in the paragraph. Then we write the number of the main thought at the top of the matrix. Now we're ready to sort the rest of the thoughts into levels of meaning:

- Ideas that are *subordinate* to the main idea (i.e. that have a dependent relationship to it) appear on the level below. Such ideas may define, explain, qualify, or draw conclusions.
- Ideas that are *coordinate* with the main one (i.e. that are equal in importance) appear on the same level. Such ideas may repeat, join with, or contradict.
- Ideas that are *superordinate* (that operate at a higher level of generality) appear on the level above. Such ideas may take the form of a general comment that functions as background to the main idea.

Figure 4.3 shows how a matrix of our sample paragraph would look:

Figure 4.3 Sample Discourse Matrix

(1) First it was "technical experts,"
(2) then it was "knowledge workers."
(3) Now there's a new buzzword to describe the ideal employee desired by the information-technology economy: "enthusiast."
(4) According to the Software Human Resource Council, an Ottawa-based nonprofit industry organization, an enthusiast combines technical skill with "soft" interpersonal skills and the personality of an entrepreneur.
(5) In show-business terms, such a person would be known as a "triple threat."
(6) In today's IT job market, it seems that acting talent alone (mere technical knowledge) won't cut it anymore; you have to know how to sing and dance, too.
(7) Enthusiasts are expected to be able to communicate clearly, manage projects efficiently, and present a solid business case.
(8) They're also expected to learn quickly, adapt to tasks outside their area of expertise, think creatively, and take initiative.
(9) In short, whether they want to work for Nortel or for a three-person shop, recent graduates will need entrepreneurial vision as well as technical competence in order to be among the fittest who survive.

Coe's matrix technique shows that the order of thoughts in a paragraph does not necessarily reflect the order of their importance. This is a key distinction and one that can be difficult to grasp, especially if you've been taught rigid formulas for paragraphing, such as "the topic sentence always comes first."

Working with an outline

Like the matrix, an outline places ideas in a hierarchy so that you can clearly see how they function in relationship with one another. Whereas Coe's matrix is useful for understanding the way your organization works after you've developed a draft, an outline is a helpful tool for both planning and revising. An outline functions as a blueprint you can use to assess document structure before and after construction. (We'll explore post-construction uses of outlines in the next chapter, which looks at the process of revising.)

Julie Morgenstern's strategy of household "containerizing" provides a helpful metaphor for how outlining works. Morgenstern urges us to "containerize" household clutter by grouping objects that belong together into boxes, baskets, or bins so that items are arranged in a clear, logical order. There is no recommended size, shape, or colour of container; lifestyle and aesthetic preference determine these. Neither is there any pre-established position for arranging containers. Morgenstern suggests that people integrate the containers into their lifestyle. Someone who frequently performs bicycle repairs might place a box of bicycle tools by the back door, but someone else who rarely tinkers with a bicycle might place the box on a remote shelf in the basement. In either case, Morgenstern emphasizes, the box should be well labelled and large enough to accommodate all the tools .

When you create an outline, you're essentially "containerizing" the ideas into a set of nesting boxes, with larger, more general ideas containing the more specific, supporting ideas. Like Coe's discourse matrix, an outline provides a visual image of a document's organization, often using numbers, letters, and indentation to distinguish between different layers of generality. Figure 4.4 shows the evolution of a brainstorming session into a loosely structured outline.

When you're creating an informal outline for yourself, you can group ideas into levels of generality using any system that's meaningful to you. You might use letters, numbers, or contrasting colours of ink to indicate the various levels of thought. Or you might simply use indentation to distinguish between main and supporting ideas, as the writer in Figure 4.2 does. To generate an outline that others will read, however, you'll need to become familiar with certain established conventions that your reader will expect. A *formal* outline follows a standard configuration that uses letters, numbers, and indentation to indicate the different layers of thinking (the nesting containers) of a document. (Most word-processing programs have an outlining tool that provides automatic formatting.)

Figure 4.4 From Brainstorming List to Outline

Topic: why the company needs a WAN (Wireless Area Network)

<u>Brainstorming list</u>

- cheaper in the long run than wired network
- sales reps from out of town use office space
- members of project teams move around in building
- presentation software used in several areas
- easier to add new computers
- lower maintenance costs
- state-of-the-art — why invest in outdated technology?
- could use Blackberry technology to improve communication with colleagues and clients

<u>Outline</u>

WAN cheaper in the long run than wired network
- lower maintenance costs
- easier to add new computers

WAN accommodates mobility of workers
- sales reps can easily hook up to the network when they're visiting the office
- members of project teams can access the network when they're working in different areas of the building
- presentation software can be easily used in different rooms in the building

WAN allows for future improvements to communications
- implementing current Blackberry technology could improve communication within the company as well as with clients
- investing in state-of-the-art technology will make it easier to take advantage of future technological developments

---

The category of formal outline includes two variations on the basic structure: topic outlines and sentence outlines. A topic outline, as the name indicates, simply lists the main points or ideas the document will discuss. In terms of our containerizing metaphor, the various nesting boxes of a topic outline feature general labels that are short phrases or even single words. In a sentence outline, however, the nesting boxes are labelled with full statements that indicate the function or purpose of the containers' contents. Such a detailed document plan can be very valuable for assessing the viability of your ideas, since it requires you to articulate a defensible position on each topic and sub-topic. If you're having trouble generating a sentence description for a topic, your difficulty may indicate that the idea you're planning to discuss is too weak or flawed to be developed properly.

Figure 4.5 converts the informal topic outline of Figure 4.4 into a formal sentence outline.

Even if outlining does not feel at first like a natural way of organizing your ideas, I encourage you to experiment with the method because it's a key competency you'll need in the workplace. Most workplace writing nowadays involves collaborating with other people, so you'll need to be able to outline

---

Figure 4.5 Investing in a WAN will improve company profitability and productivity

I. Investing in a WAN will result in long-term cost savings.
   A. It's cheaper to maintain a WAN than a conventional network.
      1. Less hardware is required.
      2. All maintenance tasks can be handled in-house.
   B. It's inexpensive to add new computers to a WAN.
      1. Wireless routers can handle up to 10 computers each.
      2. Most new computers come ready-made for WAN hook-up.

II. Investing in a WAN will better accommodate worker needs for mobility.
   A. Visitors will be able to access the network easily.
      1. Visiting sales reps can easily tap into databases housed in the network.
      2. Subcontractors who need the Internet to conduct research can easily connect to the web.
      3. Subcontractors and trainers can easily conduct web-based presentations.
   B. Workers will be able to communicate more effectively with each other in-house.
      1. Project team members can access the network when they're working in different areas of the building.
      2. Team leaders and managers can easily conduct presentations from different areas of the building.

III. Investing in a WAN will facilitate future improvements to communications.
   A. A WAN will make it easy and inexpensive to adapt current technologies to improve productivity.
      1. 80 per cent of laptops could have fully mobile network and Internet connections within two months.
      2. 60 per cent of employees could be equipped with Blackberry handhelds within six months.
   B. A WAN will make it easy to take advantage of future technological developments.
      1. A WAN will work with Pocket PC's as well as desktop and laptop computers.
      2. A WAN will have the flexibility to accommodate changes to the physical structure of the building.

your ideas before they're fully developed. You'll also likely encounter situations in which you'll need to provide an easy-to-follow sketch of your ideas to colleagues, supervisors, or clients. For instance, your boss might ask for an outline of the report that's due next week. A conference committee might require an abstract (a more elaborate form of outline) of a paper you plan to present. A client might request a slide presentation indicating the work you intend to complete (a proposal in point form). Outlining is a strategy all workplace writers need to master.

Experimenting with alternatives to outlines

Outlines don't hold a monopoly on visually representing the hierarchical relationship of ideas in a document. In fact, there are several alternative, more graphic ways of organizing ideas on paper or screen. If you're someone who finds it easier to think in pictures than in words, you might find that some of these methods improve your ability to sort and express ideas. Even if you're a veteran outliner, playing with different techniques can give you fresh tools for breaking through writing resistance when you meet it in the planning phase.

1. *Idea trees*

An idea tree presents ideas in chart form. The "trunk" of the tree is your main idea, from which supporting ideas and pieces of evidence branch out. Because of its expandable structure, an idea tree lends itself to group planning sessions. Just make sure that your whiteboard or easel pad has enough space to allow your ideas to grow. Figure 4.6 shows an idea tree for a marketing plan for a new multimedia product, an encyclopedia of Canadian pop music. Can you picture how the same ideas might look presented in a conventional outline?

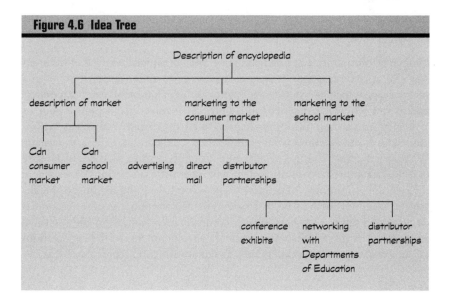

Figure 4.6 Idea Tree

2. Flowcharts

Flowcharts are especially useful for organizing writing for the web because they show the decision process readers follow when navigating through hyperlinks. They're also helpful for sketching out complex documents that require the reader to absorb and evaluate various pieces of information in order to decide on a course of action. Figure 4.7 shows a flowchart for a report investigating the possibility of creating internal project documentation using a wiki (a web-based collaborative authoring tool).

3. Storyboards

When web developers design a site, they create a mock-up screenshot of each page they need to build. They can then tack up these storyboards to build a two-dimensional chart of the various layers of pages contained in the site. For a small, brochure-style site, this map might cover a piece of Bristol board; for a medium-sized site, it might cover a small wall.

Whether you're writing for print or online media, you can build a storyboard for your piece of writing by creating a separate page for each main idea in your text. Depending on the level of complexity, you might even want to create storyboards for the main supporting ideas as well.

Working with individual storyboards allows you to experiment with various arrangements and re-arrangements of ideas, as if you're moving furniture in a room. If an idea doesn't seem to work in one place, you can move it a couple of centimetres to the left or bump it to the next level, without having to delete or cut-and-paste. This organization by trial and error can lead to some surprising insights, as you play with pairing and juxtaposing different ideas. The storyboarding method can simplify the daunting task of organizing a document with many different parts. Figure 4.8 shows a storyboard for such a document.

Organizing within a community of practice

Different communities of practice define well-organized writing in different ways. To a journalist, a well-organized news story traditionally starts with a strong lead, which is a terse, one-sentence description of what happened, where and when it happened, and who was involved. To a philosopher or a literary scholar, on the other hand, a well-organized essay starts with a graceful, elegant opening paragraph, leading gradually to a thesis statement. Whatever method you use to get your thoughts organized, then, make sure that final structure of your document will meet the expectations of readers in the relevant community of practice. Unless you have good reasons for breaking the mould, your best bet is to examine the structural features of similar documents written by others in your company or organization and use these as models. The more closely you pattern your documents to the expectations of your readers, the more likely they are to absorb and accept your ideas.

Figure 4.7 Flowchart for a Feasibility Study on Using Wiki

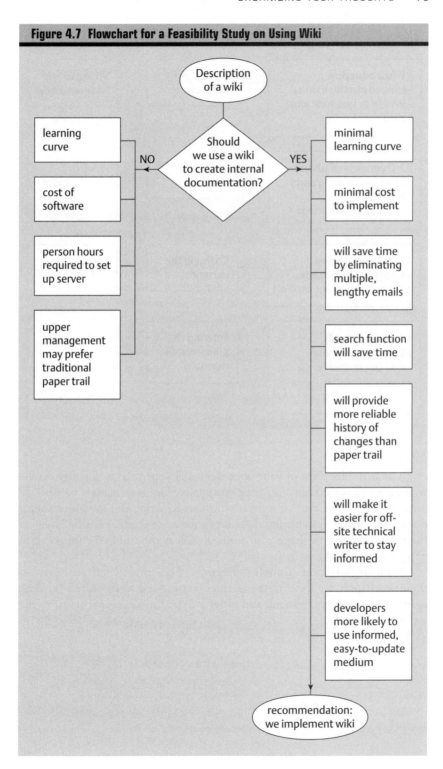

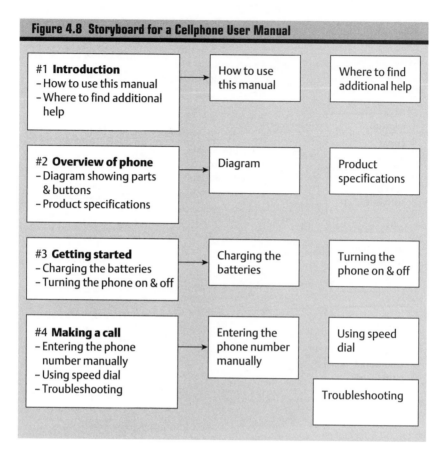

Figure 4.8 Storyboard for a Cellphone User Manual

The final blueprint of your document will depend as well partly on the writing processes dominating your workplace. The way writers collaborate on a document, the type of software they use to write, and the processes for document cycling (circulating documents for review) and revision all affect the means you use to shape your ideas as well as the finished configuration of a piece of writing.

Solid organization strongly influences a document's effectiveness. In the next chapter, we'll examine strategies you can use to measure your draft against structural requirements and other criteria for success particular to the writing task.

Exercises

1. Locate the organizational flaws in the following outline sections:

   (i)

       I. Advantages of wireless LAN

          A. No ugly cables in office

          B. Company intranet accessible from anywhere in the building

       II. Lower life-cycle costs than wired network

          A. Rapid installation

          B. Easy reconfiguration

   (ii)

       I. Response to the new interface design

          a. From paramedics

          b. From men

          c. From women

       II. Essential laptop peripherals

          a. External CD burner

          b. External zip drive

          c. Anti-theft device

          d. Headset

          e. Combination lock

          f. Notebook alarm

   (iii)

       I. Steps required to configure the printer

          a. Load the printer driver

          b. Determine compatibility of system default driver

          c. Click on Printer icon to view default driver setting

          d. Compare default driver setting with chart on p. 76

          e. Follow Install Wizard to install driver

(iv)

    I. Types of fish that can be electronically tracked

       a. Salmon and trout

       b. Tuna

       c. Shark

       d. Freshwater fish

2. Create an outline for a report on *one* of the following topics:

- ways to improve the campus cafeteria
- the feasibility of creating (more) bike lanes in your town or city
- aspects of a college or university a prospective student should consider before applying for admission
- coping with the generation gap regarding computer technology
- the desirability of legislation regarding cellphone use

3. Freecycling

   (i) Free-write for ten minutes on one of the following topics:

- my first job
- advantages of enrolling in a co-op program
- mobile computing
- disadvantages of cellphones
- how to improve Internet access
- plagiarism

   (ii) Re-read your free-writing until you find the "nugget" of an interesting idea worth exploring further. Use this idea as the basis for another ten-minute session of free-writing. Repeat the process until you have a clear theme and at least two points to develop it.

   (iii) Write a coherent paragraph (or two) elaborating on the theme you identified above.

4. Imagine that the mayor of your town or city wants to build a wireless network in the downtown core. It would be available to all for free. Use a visual organizing method (such as an idea tree, a flowchart, or a storyboard) to sketch out a letter to the editor arguing for or against this plan.

Chapter 5

Total Quality Management
for Your Draft

As an account manager for a mid-sized web development firm, Georgiana develops new business by crafting and pitching proposals. The company's owner, Rahud, is conducting Georgiana's annual performance appraisal, and one of the questions he asks himself is "How persuasive is Georgiana with clients and potential clients?"

In order to answer this question accurately and objectively, Rahud needs to refine his question to address individual behaviours Georgiana has exhibited (or failed to exhibit) since the last performance appraisal. He might consider some of the following:

- How polite is Georgiana when dealing with clients?
- How organized are Georgiana's reports and presentations?
- How well does Georgiana anticipate potential objections from clients?
- How many of Georgiana's proposals have generated new business?

To determine how well Georgiana is functioning as an employee, Rahud evaluates her performance, not her personality. Now, let's put ourselves in Georgiana's shoes. How can she evaluate her own performance as a proposal writer? Should she judge her success by the length of her documents? By their aesthetic appeal? By their conformity to the company template? By the number of passive verbs they contain?

Ultimately, the only verifiable measure Georgiana can use is the same one Rahud uses: the result. Workplace writing succeeds in terms of what it does, not what it is. Using a performance-based approach to writing assessment, Georgiana can learn to predict the strengths that will enable a document to achieve the desired outcome and the weaknesses that will stand in the way.

The best way for Georgiana to ensure that her writing meets her end goals is to conduct her performance assessment in stages. As a document develops, she should engage in a recurrent process of revision and editing. Rather than focusing on merely "polishing" her final copy, she needs to design her own Total Quality Management system for producing effective proposals. Total Quality Management (TQM) will serve as our Big Idea for this chapter, as we explore the interrelated, recurrent processes of revision and editing.

Whole-document revision as TQM

Whole-document revision grounds the TQM approach to writing. Just as it revolutionizes the way a company does business, TQM radically alters the writer's vision of the creative process. In writing, as in managing, focusing on total quality means letting the end user dictate the criteria of excellence. It also means letting go of the idea that inspecting the final product is enough; instead, quality requires a constant review of the production process.

Before TQM became a hot business trend, Quality Assurance (QA) efforts for many companies were limited to end-of-the-line inspections. However, leaving quality checks until the end of a production process wasted both time and materials. Clearly, the time to check a car's engine is before the entire chassis is built, not as the vehicle is rolling off the production line towards the dealership.

TQM shifts the focus from manufacturing to customer service so that each stage of product development promotes customer satisfaction. Ford's well-known slogan, "Quality is Job 1," reflects this new orientation. Apparently, the automaker no longer sees its primary focus as selling cars and trucks—it prefers to talk about superior standards, which have to answer to the customer's idea of excellence.

Let the same philosophy guide your writing process. Many writers omit a systematic QA procedure, or they perform a limited edit that's the equivalent of a quick glance at the paint job. When they do carefully assess the quality of their output, they often attend mostly to their own input. However, no matter what your production costs or your emotional investment in the project, it's the end user who fixes the value of your written product, not you.

Implementing TQM for your writing requires that you learn to distinguish between the three distinct phases of rewriting: revising, editing, and proofreading. In particular, it requires you to view rewriting as a global and holistic activity that doesn't so much correct writing as complete it.

The phases of rewriting

If you were in the midst of improving a draft, how would you describe your actions to a friend? Some writers might say, "I'm editing my work." Others would say, "I'm checking over my writing for errors" or "I'm proofing my document." Although they are often interpreted as being equivalent, none of these descriptions actually equates with the statement "I'm revising." Learning to differentiate the kinds of rewriting enables you to screen your whole document thoroughly without becoming overwhelmed by the number of possible changes to make.

Re-reading your work with a critical eye is like a doctor diagnosing a condition from the symptoms. Let's say, for instance, that you tell your doctor you're experiencing headaches, joint pain, mental fogginess, and occasional nausea. The physician could begin her diagnosis by sending you directly to a neurologist or ordering exploratory surgery to check for a brain tumour. If she began by ordering an immediate operation, though, my guess is you'd probably be looking for a new doctor very quickly. More likely, the doctor will start her medical "reading" of your condition by asking you some questions about your symptoms, your medical history, and your lifestyle, progressing from general to specific queries. If her questioning can't pinpoint a direct cause of your complaints, then she'll likely order blood work to eliminate certain other easily identifiable underlying conditions. Only if the blood work is inconclusive will she refer you to a neurologist or order a CAT scan herself.

The process of "diagnosing" the flaws of a written text works best when it, too, follows a system of analysis that begins with a broad perspective and gradually narrows to a microscopic view. What seems like common sense in the doctor's office doesn't, however, always seem like common sense at the writing desk or keyboard. Because they lack a reliable system for screening some of the more general weaknesses that can hamper a piece of writing, many writers begin their re-reading of a draft by going directly to the operating table. They skip revision and proceed directly to editing simply because editing flaws are the kind of "mistakes" or "errors" they know how to spot. Rather than dealing with the important overarching questions concerning a document's structure and logical development, they limit their diagnosis to matters of punctuation, grammar, and spelling.

I've stressed before that, although we can trace distinct phases of writing in which effective writers engage, I'm not trying to impose a my-way-or-the-highway writing process. You need to find your own path through the writing cycle, your own repeating rhythm that enables you to use both sides of your writing brain to produce quality thought on paper. When it comes to reworking a complete draft, however, I do recommend a definite method: work through your piece of writing in three separate passes. The first time through, focus on *revision*; the second time, focus on *editing*; and the third time, focus on *proofreading*. If you don't deal with the larger matters (structure and logic) before the smaller (grammar and punctuation), you risk losing the sense of the forest in the midst of the trees. That is, if your eye is scanning for missing periods and uncrossed t's, then it will likely miss the imbalanced arguments and weak topic sentences. You'll end up with a piece of writing that reads well sentence by sentence but creates a weak overall impression.

Revision

Novice writers tend to rely on their ear or on gut instinct to guide revision attempts. They may, for instance, read a document aloud to listen for problems with "flow," or they may rearrange paragraphs because something "just doesn't feel right." Now, I'm the first to admit that writing is a somewhat mysterious process; it's a journey of discovery every time we put pen to paper or fingers to keyboard, since we're never quite sure how our ideas will evolve or where they'll take us. As we've seen, both our conscious and our subconscious, our creative and our logical minds, play a role in crafting written thought. However, when it comes time to revise a completed draft, we need a deliberate procedure for assessing the quality of our work. Having trained ourselves to quiet the voice of Sign Mind during the drafting process so that we could get our thoughts in print as speedily as possible, it's now time to let the voice of our inner critic speak up.

We need, however, to put certain guidelines in place to control Inner Critic in order not to get so carried away with self-criticism that we lose all perspective on our work. Donald Murray is a Pulitzer Prize-winning journalist as well as a retired writing instructor, and even he confesses, "The first [post-draft] reading is a constant battle with despair. I feel I write so badly. It's so far from what I had hoped it would be. It's sloppy, a mess, worthless" (p. 219).

Such disparaging thoughts can cause writers to create second drafts that are inferior to their first efforts. They can also give rise to what I call second-stage writing resistance, which can be much harder to overcome than the first. Once we manage to step back and read our work with a critical eye, it's possible to become crippled by the imperfections of our draft. Expert writers, such as Murray, however, understand that rewriting is partly a psychological game you play with yourself. To evaluate your work thoroughly and effectively, you need to be able to consider it as dispassionately as you would a newspaper article written by a stranger.

If writer's despair is one condition that can interfere with objectivity, writer's narcissism is another. It's not by coincidence that so many authors through the ages (men as well as women) have compared writing to the act of giving birth. For many of us, delivering written language is such an ordeal that we can fall in love with the fruit of our own creativity and lose our ability to see its real strengths and weaknesses. I'll confess that I often fall into this trap. Writing is such a gruelling process for me that I tend to become unreasonably attached to the words I manage to produce. Once they're finally out there, on the page, they have an amazingly self-confident air about them, which I'm tempted to see as a mark of finality.

I've learned that the only way I can distance myself from a draft is by taking some time. Ideally, I like to put a night's sleep between me and a new draft. However, when I'm facing a tight deadline, even a couple of hours will help. Even when I'm really rushed, I take at least a fifteen-minute break in which I turn the printed draft over on my desk and grab a cup of tea or perform some distracting activity (such as flipping through a magazine, washing the dishes, or running down to the mailbox and back). Without putting deliberate mental space between me and my text, I know I'm incapable of making intelligent judgments about the strengths and weaknesses of my writing.

If we look at the root of the word, revision means, literally, "re-seeing." It requires a kind of second sight, an ability to perceive your own work through a new lens and identify any weaknesses in its construction. It also requires a precise vocabulary for describing the global structure and the internal organization of a piece of writing.

Understanding document configuration

The first step in re-visioning a piece of writing is to assess its overall contours, to recognize the shape of the organizational pattern that holds it all together. Some of the most common patterns you'll find in workplace writing include the following:

- definition
- comparison and contrast
- cause and effect
- chronological description
- physical description
- advantages versus disadvantages
- SWOT (Strengths, Weaknesses, Opportunities, Threats)
- problem and solution
- solution and justification

You might think of your document's organizational pattern as its system configuration. Once you recognize the way your ideas are configured, you can evaluate whether you've chosen the most effective arrangement. Let's imagine that you're working as a supervisor at a technical-support call centre. One of your yearly duties is to write a performance evaluation for each of the eight employees who reports to you directly. The company's perform-ance review process is fairly casual, and there is no official form for you to complete. Instead, you create an informal report (two to three paragraphs) to share with the employee and file in the company records. How should you organize your evaluation?

Your first instinct might be to create a chronological description, or narrative, of the employee's performance over the past year. Your first draft might read as follows:

> In January, Sue received three special thank-you emails for her excep-tional customer service. She improved her phone skills by attending a cus-tomer service seminar in February. Twice in March, she was slow filling out her time sheets. Sometimes, she forgets to document all the computer prob-lems she encounters. In May, she helped train two new employees, which was a great help to management. She also covered for another employee who had to take early maternity leave.

Although this paragraph provides quite a bit of information about Sue's activities on the job, the way that this information is organized does not really suit the purpose of the writing, which is to evaluate, not merely describe, her performance. Rather than listing events in their order of occurrence, the report should highlight Sue's strengths and weaknesses as an employee. A more appropriate way to arrange the ideas, then, would be to begin by dis-cussing her strong points and then mention the areas in which she needs to improve. You might even use the headings "Strengths" and "Opportunities for

Improvement" to help you sort and record your observations. This approach will better serve you, Sue, and the company. You'll be able to provide clear justification for the raise you're recommending Sue receive; Sue will know exactly what she needs to do to improve her performance; and the company will have precise documentation to protect itself from potential legal challenges over the treatment of its workers.

As this example demonstrates, it's necessary to understand the function of the whole in order to troubleshoot for problems with the parts. To determine the value of a specific section, you must first grasp the document's general purpose. Only then can you decide which information is pertinent to your document goals.

Consider the following situation as an example. Imagine you're a business analyst at a small IT consulting company. Your boss has asked you to respond to a Request for Proposal to create a user-authentication system for a local college. Your initial thought might be to concentrate on providing a detailed description of your company's credentials and the technical features you're able to create. However, since your goal is to persuade the college to choose your solution over the solutions offered by other companies, you'll improve your chances of success with a more strategic approach. Rather than using description as your method of organization, you could follow a problem-to-solution organizational pattern. That way, you'll be able to highlight the difficulties your client is facing and then demonstrate how your company can eliminate them.

Whichever way you choose to configure a piece of writing, always let the principle of emphasis guide your organization so that you accentuate the information that most serves your reader's needs. How do you know whether you've emphasized the ideas you want to stress? Try this quick check. Re-read your first and last paragraphs to verify that they contain the ideas you consider the most important and persuasive. If they don't, you may have strayed from your focus. The beginning and the ending of a document are the most effective places to underline your key points. If you don't grab your reader's attention in these spots, then you may miss the chance to emphasize the thoughts you really wanted to impress upon your audience.

Using a post-composition outline

Once you've established a general organizational framework, you might create a diagram of your document's internal architecture—in other words, an outline. Constructing an outline after you've finished your draft allows you to see at a glance the framework and development of your ideas. This enables you to focus on your thinking, without being distracted (for the moment) by mechanical glitches in expression. A post-draft outline enables you to spot two common types of structural problems: (1) imbalance and (2) confused levels of generality. The best way to explain these is to show you a few examples.

Eliminating imbalance

Here is an outline for an email report Tomas has written to recommend that the company discontinue paper forms for processing travel claims:

I. Problems caused by current paper system

    A. Interference with productivity

    B. High cost

    C. Storage issues

II. Advantages of electronic system

    A. Low cost

III. Implementation requirements for electronic system

    A. Web development

    B. Employee training

    C. Hardware for electronic backup

The diagram of Tomas's document clearly shows a structural imbalance, since the single advantage of the electronic system seems outweighed by the several implementation requirements. To address this problem, Tomas needs to show more specifically how an electronic system will eliminate each of the weaknesses of the current system. He also needs to explain how the implementation challenges will be overcome.

The situation Tomas faces is very common. Missing evidence (insufficient or inappropriate facts to support the writer's claims) is one of the most common causes of weak writing. Too often, writers seem to assume that their readers will supply the missing pieces themselves. But, unless you're writing a piece of detective fiction, where it's part of the pleasure of reading to unravel the mystery, such an assumption is wrong-headed. You wouldn't leave out lines of code in a piece of software, just trusting that the user would be able to work through the error messages and figure out how to make the program work, would you?

Here's how Tomas might flesh out his outline so that he can make his report more persuasive.

I. Problems caused by current paper system

    A. Interference with productivity

    B. High cost

    C. Large storage space

II. Advantages of electronic system

    A. Improved productivity

    B. Low cost

    C. No storage space

   III. Assessment of implementation challenges

      A. Web development will be performed in-house

      B. Employee training will be minimal

      C. Hardware investment will be a one-time cost offset by savings

As you can see, Tomas will have to do considerable rewriting, not just surface tinkering, to balance and enlarge his report. However, by examining the architecture of his document before tweaking his individual sentences, he's using his revision time effectively. To begin by correcting mechanical flaws would have been counter-productive, since he'll be completely reworking large sections of his document.

Like brainstorming, revising requires much creative wastefulness. By the time he's completed his final copy, Tomas will likely have thrown out much of his original draft. Does this mean he's a poor writer? Not by any means. Picasso once said, "I make a picture, and then proceed to destroy it" (Zervos, p. 53). Proficient writers know that a valuable idea is worth interrogating, demolishing, and rebuilding from the ground up.

Eliminating confused levels of generality

Whereas Tomas's problem was chiefly imbalance, another common structural problem results from getting confused about different degrees of generality. In the last chapter, I described an outline as functioning as a series of nesting boxes. Ideas of the same degree of generality—that is, of similar magnitude and importance—belong together in the same "box" or level of the outline. However, in the process of composing, it's easy to lose track of the sorting order of your ideas. Creating an outline after you've written your draft can help you discriminate between main sets and subsets—it can show you places in your document where you have tried to stuff too much material into one box or have put an idea in a separate box when it really belongs grouped together with other ideas. In other words, outlining visually distinguishes dominant and subordinate concepts so you can restructure to make the hierarchy of your ideas function correctly.

When creating a post-draft outline, it's important to represent accurately the disposition of your ideas. For the exercise to be helpful, you need to diagram the true shape of your document's organization, not the shape you imagined it would have when you started to compose. Chances are that you have your main points firmly established in your head. However, they won't do your reader any good there. You need to make sure that they form the main pillars of your document's structure. To verify this, make sure that you construct your outline by paying careful attention to your section headings and topic sentences (sentences that express the main idea of a paragraph.) One strategy for creating an outline is to summarize the topic sentences of every paragraph in a quick list. You can then distinguish the main ideas from the supporting ideas so that you can indent and number the lines of your list accordingly.

Here's an excerpt from an outline that Gola has created using this method. She's writing a feasibility report on the possibility of converting a workplace to a wireless network. Can you spot the flaw?

I. Advantages of wireless LAN

   A. No ugly cables in office

   B. Company intranet accessible from anywhere in the building

II. Lower life-cycle costs than wired network

   A. Rapid installation

   B. Easy reconfiguration

If we picture each of the ideas in this outline as a box, we would have two different container sizes: a large size for the general concept of advantages of a wireless LAN and a smaller size for the specific advantages of the system. Figure 5.1 graphically presents the distinction between the overarching and supporting concepts. What Gola's outline indicates, however, is that she has not appropriately sorted the ideas in her draft. Instead of nesting all the spe-

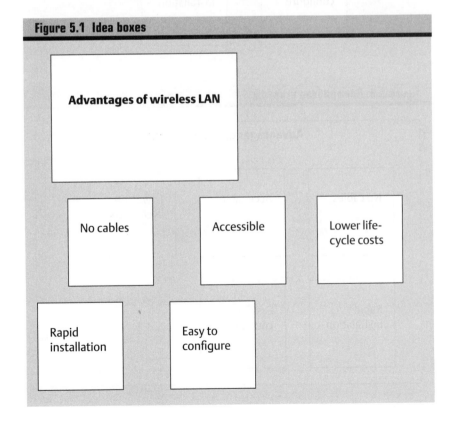

Figure 5.1 Idea boxes

Advantages of wireless LAN

No cables

Accessible

Lower life-cycle costs

Rapid installation

Easy to configure

Figure 5.2 Flawed idea grouping

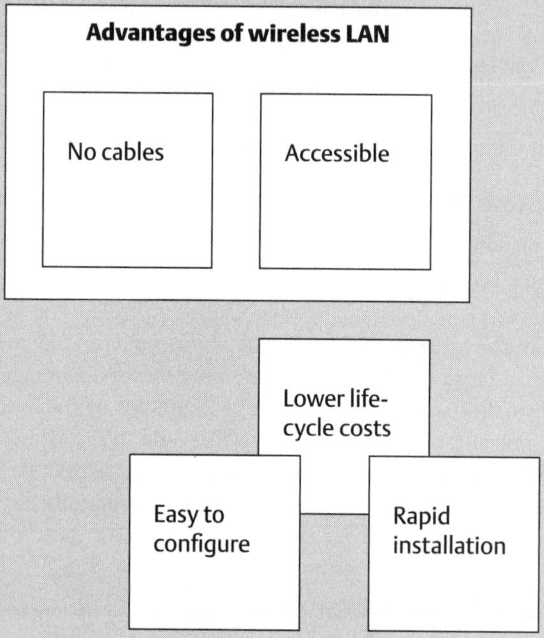

Advantages of wireless LAN

No cables

Accessible

Lower life-cycle costs

Easy to configure

Rapid installation

Two supporting ideas cannot nest inside another supporting idea at the same level of generality

Figure 5.3 Revised idea grouping

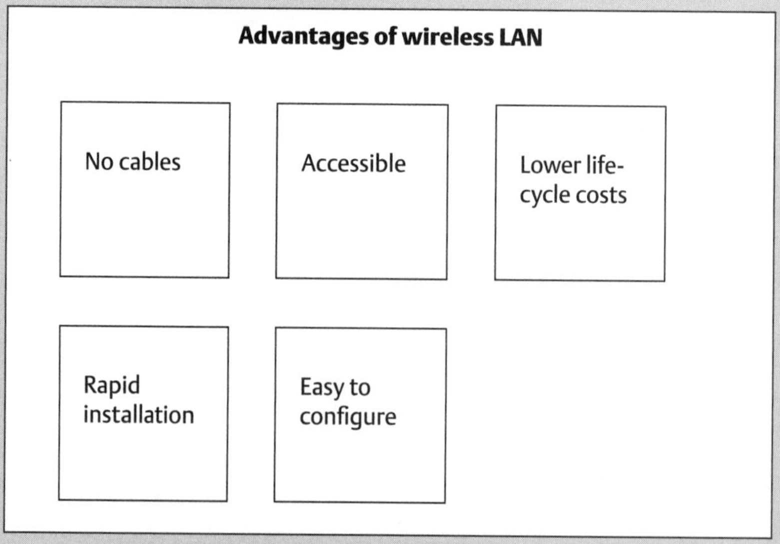

Advantages of wireless LAN

No cables

Accessible

Lower life-cycle costs

Rapid installation

Easy to configure

cific ideas (examples of benefits of a wireless system) inside the general idea (advantages of a wireless LAN), Gola has elevated one of the supporting ideas to a higher level than it deserves.

This mis-sizing of idea-boxes creates a sorting problem. The idea of lower life-cycle costs doesn't merit its own large box. (It's not a new idea able to stand on its own but rather a supporting idea of the first main point, further testimony of the advantages of a wireless LAN.) Therefore, it's not large enough to contain the other two ideas represented in the outline as being subordinate. Figure 5.2 uses idea-boxes to show the mistaken way Gola has grouped the ideas in her draft; Figure 5.3 shows the logical way her idea-boxes should fit together.

Based on this new sorting scheme, here's how Gola's revised outline of the report section looks:

I.   Advantages of wireless LAN

    A.   No ugly cables in office

    B.   Company intranet accessible from anywhere in the building

    C.   Rapid installation

    D.   Easy reconfiguration

Having established a hierarchy of ideas, Gola has a straightforward blueprint to guide her rewriting process, which will probably involve adjusting paragraphs and reworking some topic sentences.

Whereas Gola's error was to treat a specific idea as a general idea, another common structural mistake is to omit those general, categorizing ideas altogether. Consider the following example, an excerpt from an outline for a product description of a laptop computer:

I.   Essential peripherals

    A.   External CD burner

    B.   External zip drive

    C.   Anti-theft device

    D.   Headset

    E.   Combination lock

    F.   Notebook alarm

How would you re-sort items A through F? As a start, you might identify a new category at the same level as "Essential peripherals," since not all of the items listed seem to fit under this heading. We need another large-size idea-box into which we can put the non-essential objects listed in lines D through F (headset, combination lock, notebook alarm). Properly speaking, these things are not peripheral devices but non-essential extras, so we might group them under the heading of "Optional accessories." Our revised version of this section of the outline would look like this:

I. Essential peripherals

    A. External CD burner

    B. External zip drive

    C. Anti-theft device

II. Optional accessories

    D. Headset

    E. Combination lock

    F. Notebook alarm

To realign our draft to match this outline, we would likely need to create a new paragraph or section and insert a topic sentence to introduce the additional concept of accessories.

Although many people think that revision means simply making minor alterations, you can see that it more often involves major reconstruction. Just as a physician sometimes has to break a bone in order to reset it, sometimes you have to tear a draft apart in order to rebuild it. Once the most radical part of the surgery is complete, revision also requires some deft cosmetic work so that the scars from the scalpel are not visible in the final document. Fortunately, there are a couple of practices you can use to ensure that the seams in your reconstructed writing don't show.

Restructuring

Making significant changes to a document's configuration can introduce new problems, such as disjointed paragraphs or abrupt shifts in direction. The final phase of revising, therefore, entails restructuring paragraphs to ensure readability and logic.

Many writers speak of well-structured documents as having "flow." What is "flow"? Depending on whom you're talking to, it seems to imply a range of qualities, such as continuity, connectedness, and coherence. Some writers are lucky; they seem to have an innate flow-meter that enables them to recognize when flow is lacking and how to remedy the deficiency. But even the most instinctive writers should be wary of relying totally on gut feeling to guide their revision. (Can you imagine a software tester trying to perform quality assurance simply on the basis of what feels right?) Applying the principles of TQM to your writing means finding standard, reliable methods to assess and improve the quality of your written product. The more precise and objective the criteria you use, the more likely your documents are to get the results you want.

Rather than trying to gauge the "flow" of a document, then, you can examine specific features in your document for consistency, especially (1) introductions and conclusions, (2) transitional sentences, and (3) keywords.

Systematically scrutinizing these common trouble spots ensures that your reader won't stumble over gaps in logic.

Matching introductions and conclusions

As you may recall from your childhood reading, the King in *Alice in Wonderland* is a very bossy but stupid fellow. Too many writers follow his model when it comes to reading their own work. When asked how a piece of evidence should be read in court, here's how the King answers: "'Begin at the beginning,' the King said, very gravely, 'and go on till you come to the end: then stop'" (Carroll, p. 207).

The cyclical composition process, however, involves recurrent re-reading that isn't necessarily linear. One of the most effective quality tests you can perform on a document you've created is to begin at the beginning, skip to the ending, go on to the middle: then repeat.

After you've completed your first revising pass through your document, here's a simple exercise to make sure the changes you've made have resulted in writing that's logically intact:

1. Read through your introductory section and summarize it in one sentence. (If you can't do this, then there's a problem with it.)
2. Read through your concluding section and also summarize it in one sentence.
3. Compare your two summary statements. Are they similar? Have you kept the promises you made to your reader? Have you said what you said you'd say, demonstrated what you said you'd demonstrate, or proved what you said you'd prove?
4. Underline the topic sentence in each paragraph, including the introduction and conclusion. Now read your document through from beginning to end, reading only the sentences you've underlined. Do you notice any missing information, any unannounced changes in direction, or any places where the material seems disconnected from the rest of the document?

The above exercise is, you'll notice, very similar to the process of creating a post-draft outline, but it proceeds much more quickly. Once you've made further adjustments to eliminate the flaws this re-reading detects, you can do it again, perhaps mostly in your head this time. This is how revision works; it's an ongoing cycle of checks that become more and more rapid the closer you get to a finished product. Even if you have the most thorough revision checklist in the world, working through it just once is seldom enough. "Flow" may sound like a mysterious, organic quality, but it takes rigorous testing and re-testing to make it happen.

Checking for transitions

Graceful transitions are the second key feature to examine when you're checking for "flow." Transitions are the bridges you build to take the reader from one idea to another. Sometimes you need an entire sentence, or even a paragraph, to help the reader shift from one thought to the next. In other cases, you might simply need to supply a well-placed word or phrase.

When guided by appropriate transitions, your readers should feel about your writing the way computer gamers feel when caught up in the middle of play. In a well-built game, users are totally focused on the wizardry happening on the screen; they're not even aware of the lines of complex code behind the experience, unless flaws in the programming cause glitches that interrupt their fun. You need to create a similar state of obliviousness for your readers. Your aim should be to steer them straight through your argument without any awkward distractions.

Transitions come in several shapes and sizes. To understand their significance, it's useful to think of a reader as journeying through a document, whether it's in paper or electronic form. (We use this metaphor all the time when we talk of a web user "navigating" through a series of online pages.) While your topic sentences indicate the milestones in a piece of writing, transitions function as signposts along the route. They alert your reader to shifts in direction, to repeated features in the landscape, and to possible hazards on the road ahead. Figure 5.4 lists some of the most common prompts you can use to lead your reader so there's no confusion as to the course of your thinking.

To perform a TQM check for transitions, revisit the first and last sentences of each section in your document. Does each initial sentence clearly

Figure 5.4 Transitional words and phrases

To show contrast:	To indicate cause and effect:
however	as a result
in contrast	consequently
on the other hand	as an effect
rather than	
in spite of	To indicate a logical conclusion
but	therefore
	thus
To reinforce:	
moreover	To indicate chronology:
furthermore	in turn
in addition	in the beginning/end
nevertheless	first/second/third
in fact	initially
	lastly
To illustrate:	finally
for example	
for instance	
in other words	
in the same way	
similarly	
likewise	

show how the material in the upcoming section relates to the material in the previous section? In places where you're about to introduce a brand new idea, a startling point, or an especially compelling piece of evidence, have you prepared the reader for the drastic change in direction?

In documents that use frequent headings, the headings themselves may do some of the work of transitions. This strategy is, however, more appropriate in situations where the generic conventions are fairly rigid and the reader knows exactly what to expect (for example, documents in which the headings are standard from one project to another).

If you intend to rely on headings to help you lead the reader from one point to another in a long document, be careful to use phrasing that's accurate and descriptive. Let's say you work for an eLearning company, Ability Software, and are writing a proposal to create a series of online modules for EQ2, a company that specializes in interpersonal communications training. The following list of headings would not be very helpful in guiding your EQ2 readers to appreciate the fit between their need and your services:

Introduction

Background

Benefits and feasibility

Description of work

Method

Schedule

Qualifications

Required resources

Conclusions

A more descriptive set of headings could, however, play an important role in persuading your audience to hire you for the project. The following revised headings, for instance, not only speak more precisely to the audience's problem (the need to find a reliable eLearning provider) but also draw attention to the logical connections between the different sections of the proposal:

Taking interpersonal communications training into the twenty-first century

Making the transition from print to online materials

Creating an online portal for interpersonal communications

Using Ability's expertise in eLearning

Working with Ability's instructional design method

Project schedule

Return on investment

Stepping forward with Ability

When you're sure you have adequate transitions to point your reader from one section of your document to the next, you can then examine transitions within sections. Inspect the first and last sentence of each paragraph to verify that you've deliberately indicated the direction of your thinking to your readers. In addition, consider the structure of individual paragraphs to determine whether you need to include internal transitions as well. (You might want to use Coe's matrix method of analysis here.) In situations where the topic sentence does not occur at the beginning of the paragraph, it is particularly important for the transition to show how the topic is changing.

In the following example, which could be an excerpt from an article or whitepaper on methods of project management, you can see how writing that is missing transitions appears choppy, disconnected, and downright baffling:

> The "waterfall" method of project management is so-called because it takes a top-heavy approach to planning. The rest of the project supposedly flows rapidly to completion. Software developers begin a project by creating reams of documentation, including requirements, specifications, and a project schedule. The problem with producing all of this documentation at the beginning of a project is that the system leaves little room for error. Once a project goes off the rails, even slightly, the elaborate stack of documentation becomes instantly outdated.
>
> Many companies are now experimenting with innovative changes to the overall system of project management. Agile methods of software engineering may offer the solution.

Here's one example of how you could rewrite the passage to improve the logical connections between ideas. Inserted transitional words and phrases are highlighted in bold:

> The "waterfall" method of project management is so-called because it takes a top-heavy approach to planning. **Once the preliminary design work has been documented**, the rest of the project supposedly flows rapidly to completion. Software developers begin a project by creating reams of documentation, including requirements, specifications, and a project schedule. The problem with producing all of this documentation at the beginning of a project, **however**, is that the system leaves little room for error. Once a project goes off the rails, even slightly, the elaborate stack of documentation becomes instantly outdated.
>
> **Because** many companies are now experimenting with innovative changes to the overall system of project management, **a more flexible system of project documentation is clearly in order**. Agile methods of software engineering may offer the solution.

Some writers resist using transitions because they see them as extra baggage. Certainly, workplace writers should always aim to pack as much meaning into as few words as possible. However, it never makes sense to sacrifice clarity for brevity. When you're trying to reduce your word count, transitions are seldom the place to begin cutting. As a matter of fact, the more strategically you use transitions, the more focused and lean your writing can become.

Verifying keywords

A final way you can verify that a revised document preserves a sense of unity is to check that you've consistently employed keywords. A keyword might be a piece of jargon, an acronym, the name of an important hardware or software feature, or a significant metaphor.

To make sure you use consistent terms from the beginning to the end of your document, it's a good practice to keep a running list of keywords and acronyms as you compose. That way, you'll make sure that a graphic element that you refer to as a "button" in the first section of the document, for instance, does not appear as an "icon" in the final section. Your list of keywords should form part of your detailed revision checklist, an absolutely essential tool for the TQM approach.

Creating a revision checklist

Many organizations today sell themselves on their ability to meet the quality criteria established by the International Standards Organization (ISO). In some fields, such as electrical engineering, companies need ISO certification in order to bid on large contracts. Companies that produce technical documentation must also follow strict quality-management processes in order to become ISO-certified.

You can create ISO-level standards for your writing by establishing regular checkpoints and checklists. Having learned to separate your revising process from your editing process, you're more than halfway to becoming an unofficially ISO-qualified writer. The next step is to create an adaptable set of criteria that you can use to evaluate the effectiveness of a piece of writing in terms of its structure, logic, accuracy, and cohesiveness.

Exactly when in the revision process you choose to use this checklist is up to you. Some writers use it after they've already done some restructuring. Other writers like to turn to a checklist at the beginning of their revising so they have guidelines to lead them through the iterations of the rewriting cycle. However and whenever you choose to use your checklist, the important thing is to make it as specific as possible. It should address the features and challenges of the particular kind of writing you're doing, and it should force you to focus on the peculiar writing flaws you are prone to producing.

Plan to modify your checklist to meet the demands of different writing tasks. Figure 5.5 gives you a list of questions from which you can build your own revising guide.

Figure 5.5 Sample revision checklist

Organization

___ Does your document follow a layout that will be intuitive for your reader?

___ Have you arranged your material so that your reader can go directly to priority information?

___ Is your pattern of organization easy to perceive?

___ Have you used headings to help your reader see your pattern of organization?

___ Does your introductory material (including front matter) provide any necessary context and indicate what the reader should expect from the document?

___ Have you clearly explained how the figures and tables support your ideas?

___ Have you explicitly indicated what you want your reader to do as a result of reading your document?

Accuracy

___ Have you provided your readers with all the information they need to do what you want them to do? (For example, you might want them to absorb the information, adjust their perspective, make a decision, or act directly on your ideas.)

___ Have you used authoritative, up-to-date information sources?

___ Have you explained your method of analysis, your key assumptions, and your criteria for evaluating data?

___ Where conflicting data exists, have you acknowledged and dealt with it objectively?

Logic

(Note: You might want to consult your post-draft outline or flowchart to check the following items.)

___ Have you concisely expressed the main idea of your document within the first couple paragraphs? Have you made clear the document's purpose or goal?

___ Does all of the information in your document support the main idea? (Get rid of any digressions, or rewrite them to show their relevance.)

___ Are there places where you're missing the evidence to support your claims?

___ Are there imbalances in your argument or discussion?

___ Have you grouped your ideas in a clear hierarchy?

___ Thinking of your particular readers, is there information in your document that your audience could interpret as compromising or challenging your main idea? (You don't necessarily have to eliminate such information, but your interpretation of it needs to be watertight.)

Coherence

___ Can you easily find a topic sentence for each paragraph?

___ By examining topic sentences of your sections and paragraphs, can you clearly trace the development of your ideas from one paragraph to the next?

___ Have you alerted your readers to ideas that are particularly important?

___ Considering your audience's background, have you expressed any ideas that are new, unexpected, or controversial? If so, have you used transitional words or phrases to introduce these ideas? Have you couched them in positive, persuasive language?

___ Have you included signposts (transitional words or phrases) to indicate changes in the direction of your argument or discussion?

___ Does your concluding section fulfill the promises you make to the reader in your introductory section?

___ Do your recommendations follow directly from your conclusions? (They should not introduce new material or opinions that you haven't explained in the rest of your document.)

___ Have you used keywords consistently throughout your document?

Clarity

___ Have you written for specific readers?

___ Have you introduced unfamiliar information by referencing the familiar?

___ If your audience is non-technical, have you used analogy (comparison) to simplify abstract or difficult concepts?

___ Have you used definitions to help describe a particularly complex product or process?

___ Have you used specific examples to illustrate key concepts?

___ Have you used graphic aids (charts, maps, graphs, tables, diagrams) to supplement your text?

Persuasiveness

___ Have you emphasized the information that's most important to your readers (not necessarily to you)?

___ Have you used a pattern of organization that's familiar to your readers?

___ Have you referenced evidence and sources of information that your readers particularly trust?

___ Have you explicitly stated what it is you want your reader to do as a result of reading your document?

Finally...

___ Does your document fulfill the following basic directive?

Say what you're going to say.
Say it.
Say what it is you've said.

Editing

Once you're satisfied that your document (or section of your document) exhibits sound structure and logic, you're ready to proceed to the editing phase of TQM. At this stage, your focus shifts from the macro to the micro level, as you concentrate on such matters as grammar, punctuation, spelling, mechanics, usage (word choice), and citation.

Standard Edited Written English: the common rules of the road

No matter what part of the world you're driving in, you're likely to encounter octagonal stop signs and, at least on busy highways, lines of paint that separate one side of the road from the other. Although the conventions of traffic signals are not universal, there is much commonality. That's why it's possible for a visitor from North America to rent a car in the United Kingdom, even though vehicles there drive on the opposite side of the road. Likewise, despite regional variations in spelling, word usage, and even punctuation, there are certain conventions of Standard Edited Written English (SEWE) that apply across the board.

SEWE should be readable to anyone who speaks English. It avoids slang and dialect terms because, although these are often colourful and meaningful for certain groups, they can be confusing for a wider audience. In informal conversation in Newfoundland, for instance, it's perfectly acceptable to say, "I loves to play 3D Ultra Pinball." In other parts of the English-speaking world, this would be considered grammatically incorrect. Newfoundland grammar is not "wrong," of course—in its context, it makes sense. However, when communicating with people elsewhere in Canada and beyond, writers in Newfoundland adhere to a particular set of conventions recognized around the world.

Do the "correct" conventions of grammar and punctuation expected in SEWE really matter in today's largely informal workplaces? Yes, they really, really do. But don't just take my word for it. Listen to the evidence from the business world. In 2000, two American professors, Jeanette Gilsdorf and Don Leonard, conducted a survey that measured the response of senior executives to typical breaches of SEWE. The survey presented the executives with sentences exhibiting a range of errors and asked respondents to indicate the degree to which they were bothered by each sentence. The sixty-four executives from large U.S. corporations clearly agreed that correctness still counts. Asked to rate the level of "botheration" on a scale of 1 to 5, they gave the following seven errors a rating of at least a 3.5: sentence fragment, run-on sentence, missing comma, misused apostrophe, faulty parallel structure, and comma splice.

Unlike some writing instructors, business executives are not preoccupied with maintaining the purity of the English language and preserving conventions for history's sake. Their interest is entirely practical. They know that incorrect writing slows readers down, frustrates them, makes them doubt the writer, and obstructs the business of the moment. To avoid such perils, train yourself to assess your writing rigorously in terms of its correctness, clarity, and conciseness.

Editing for correctness

Scrutinizing a document for errors in expression (grammar, punctuation, spelling, mechanics, and word choice) doesn't have to be as tedious as combing for needles in the proverbial haystack. Just as you can make the overall task of rewriting more manageable by breaking it into the sub-tasks of revising and editing, you can also divide your editing process into stages. One of the secrets of effective editors is that they train themselves to look for one type of flaw at a time. On the first pass through a document, for instance, a professional editor might look just for punctuation problems. After that, she might look just for usage problems or subject-verb agreement problems. In the final pass, she might look to correct inconsistencies in headings, page numbering, and citation.

The first step toward becoming an effective editor of your own work is to track the kinds of errors you commit most often. If you're not aware of your main problem areas, you might consider starting an editing journal. Each time you notice a fault in your writing, record it in your journal, along with the date and the title of the document. Before long, you'll have a picture of the kinds of writing problems you need to remedy. Figure 5.6 shows a typical page from one writer's editing journal.

Developing the ability to debug your writing may involve learning (or re-learning) the necessary vocabulary. It's not within the scope of this book to define all the possible technical errors and how to redress them. To do that, you'll need to obtain a thorough reference manual, such as *The Canadian Writer's Handbook, Fourth Edition*. For a list of recommended books (some with a humorous approach to the subject), please turn to the Suggested Further Readings at the end of this book.

Figure 5.6 Tracking Errors

Date	Document	Error	Sentence	Correction
Aug 1	weekly progress report	sentence frag.	Given that we have only one more test left to run.	We should finish early, given that we have only one more test to run.
Aug 5	email to Don Reid	misspelling	We seem to be working in a vaccum.	vacuum
Aug 10	proposal for CherryBrooke	dangling mod.	After meeting with you last week, the program has been altered.	After meeting with you last week, we altered the program.

Editing for clarity

Although we sometimes treat clarity and conciseness as if they're luxury qualities in writing, a growing international movement recognizes them as absolute essentials. The Plain Language movement, which grew into a force to be reckoned with during the 1980s, lobbies for simple, transparent language, especially in public documents. Plain Language advocates believe that when public documents (such as laws) are so difficult to read that they're inaccessible to much of the population, they violate the principles of democracy.

Today, most of Canada's provincial governments have implemented official Plain Language policies to govern their publications. Most of these consist of basic, common-sense guidelines. "Plain Language" means using the ordinary language of the target readership. It doesn't involve dumbing down the content of complex documents, but rather choosing language and sentence structures that are clear, direct, and easy for the intended readers to understand. Plain Language uses brief sentences and paragraphs, short words, and intelligent design practices to enable straightforward reading.

The principles of Plain Language challenge most writers, but you can fulfill them if you master the editing strategies described in this chapter. *Plain Language Clear and Simple*, a publication by the Canadian government (Human Resources Development Canada, 1996), emphasizes the following techniques:

- put the information most valuable to your reader up front
- explain in the introduction how the document structure works
- use a conversational tone and everyday words
- write directly to the reader, using "you," "we," and "I"
- address only one main idea per paragraph
- keep sentences short (average length of 15–25 words)
- use active verbs
- provide obvious connections between ideas
- avoid jargon
- use verb forms rather than noun forms ("participate" rather than "engage in participation")
- design pages to allow plenty of white space
- create short, descriptive headings

As you strive for clarity, watch for two grammatical problems that often interfere with plain language: ambiguous pronouns and dangling or misplaced modifiers. (Your reference guide will help you identify and correct these.) Also watch for usage errors, which occur when a writer misappropriates the meaning of a word or confuses the meaning of two words that have similar pronunciation. Whenever you're editing, keep a dictionary at your fingertips.

Editing for conciseness

Writers sometimes fall into wordy habits because they perceive Standard Edited Written English as "formal English" or "academic English." Professional written communication should not, however, be either stiff or highbrow. In North America, elaborately formal, verbose business correspondence went out with top hats and tails. Today, the appropriate tone for most business and technical communication is one that is friendly and conversational.

You can avoid wordiness by paying attention to the following habits in your writing:

1. Passive verbs

When a verb appears in the active voice, the subject performs the action in the sentence: *The cat chased the dog.* When a verb is in the passive voice, the subject of the sentence has the action performed upon it: *The dog was chased by the cat.* Passive constructions are naturally more wordy, since they require a form of "to be" as a helping verb.

Passive verbs weaken much technical writing because writers often equate them with an impersonal style, which is sometimes required. In trying to avoid using "I" or "you," writers slip automatically into the passive voice, as in the following pair of sentences:

Sentence using personal style

For the system to work effectively, you must enter your forecasting data by month's end.

Sentence using impersonal style

For the system to work effectively, forecasting data must be entered by month's end.

Just because stylistic conventions prevent you from using "I," however, there's no need to avoid active verbs too. A passive verb may be the first alternative that comes to mind, but both the ear and the eye prefer active verbs, action-oriented words that grab our attention and communicate information concisely and precisely.

To prevent awkward passive phrasing, you can create sentences with anonymous or impersonal agents. For instance, we could rewrite our example sentence as follows:

Anonymous agent

For the system to work effectively, managers must enter forecasting data by month's end.

Impersonal agent

The system will work effectively if it receives all forecasting data by month's end.

Passive verbs take so much abuse (almost every writing manual maligns them) that you might wonder why we even have them. There are times when passive verbs serve appropriate functions, however. When you're trying to avoid assigning blame, for instance, a passive verb can come in handy. Imagine that you need to explain an accounting error in a report to a colleague in another division, but the person who made the error is your immediate supervisor. Which of the following sentences would you choose to use?

Yelena balanced the spreadsheet incorrectly.

The spreadsheet was balanced incorrectly.

2. Redundancies

If time really is money, then you waste your readers' resources as well as their patience every time you use empty repetition. Here are some common redundant expressions to eliminate from your writing.

Redundancy	Alternative
twelve o'clock noon	12 p.m.
the colour red	red
mutual consensus	consensus
totally unanimous	unanimous
each and every	each
future prospects	prospects
PIN number	PIN (Personal Identification Number)
end result	result
final decision	decision
free give-away	give-away
co-operative team player	team player
over and above	over
brand-new innovation	innovation
recur again	recur

3. Padded expressions

Padded expressions, like redundancies, add excess words to your sentences, making them cumbersome. Whereas redundancies say the same thing twice, padded expressions say nothing at all. They function as unnecessary "filler."

Novice writers often fall into the trap of adding padded expressions in the belief that it will make their writing somehow weightier. Beware, however: padded expressions bear negative weight. Rather than making your writing more solid and substantial, they fill it with meaningless fluff that detracts from the substance of your ideas. To streamline and clarify your writing, avoid such say-nothing phrases as the following.

Padded expression	Alternative
at the present time, at the moment	now, currently
in order to	to
as a matter of fact	in fact
whether or not	whether
for the purpose of	for
in the event that	if
owing to the fact that	because
in the process of [+ verb]	[verb]
by means of	by
in the case that	when
all of a sudden	suddenly
in a quiet manner	quietly

Two more common phrases can also contribute to wordiness: "there is" and "it is." When these occur at the beginning of a sentence, you can probably cut them without changing your meaning. Here's an example to demonstrate:

Wordy sentence: There is a tool, called Quickform, that generates a spreadsheet template.

Revised sentence: The Quickform tool generates a spreadsheet template.

4. Nominalizations

A nominalization is the noun form of a verb. ("Participation" is the nominalization of "to participate," for instance.) You can often detect a nominalization by its –*tion* ending.

Nominalizations weaken sentences by forcing nouns, not verbs, to bear the meaning. In most situations, verbs should function as the workhorses of a statement. Consider, for instance, how simply changing the verb renders the meaning increasingly clear in the following series of sentences:

He entered through the door.

He walked through the door.

He strode through the door.

Now, consider how many additional words it would take to create the meaning of the last sentence if you were restricted to using the verb "walked." You would be stuck saying something like this: *He walked confidently with long strides through the door.*

It's easy to fall into the habit of overloading your writing with nouns if you struggle with a limited verb vocabulary. If you have command over only simple, commonly used verbs—such as "to walk," "to put," "to place," "to have," "to be"—then your writing will tend to rely on wordier constructions based on strings of adjectives and nouns. Using the following examples as a beginning, you may find it useful to keep a personal list of the nominalizations that burden your writing most frequently.

- performance
- functionality
- utilization
- operation
- maintenance
- communication
- integration
- adaptation
- innovation

By tracking your errors and wordy tendencies over time, you'll be able to assemble a personal checklist that will enable you to apply TQM to the editing stage. Here's a detailed editing checklist to get you started:

Editing checklist

Matters of correctness

Comma faults

___ commas with a series of items

___ comma before a coordinating conjunction (for, and, nor, but, or, yet, so)

___ comma after introductory phrase or clause

___ comma to separate non-essential elements

___ comma before a quotation

Subject-verb agreement

___ collective nouns

___ indefinite pronouns

___ sentence fragments

___ run-ons

___ comma splices

___ misplaced apostrophes

___ improper use of colon

___ improper use of semicolon

Matters of clarity

___ pronoun-antecedent problems

___ dangling modifiers

___ usage

___ faulty parallel structure

Matters of conciseness

___ passive verbs

___ redundancies

___ padded expressions

___ nominalizations

Proofreading

Proofreading is the final stage of the editing process. Some people seem to be born with an innate attention to detail that gives them a proofreader's eye, but, for the rest of us mere mortals, here are a few helpful hints for detecting errors.

1. Read your writing aloud.
2. Read your writing, sentence by sentence, from the end of the document to the beginning.
3. Keep a running log of words you misspell, especially those your computer's spell-checker can't identify, and memorize the correct spellings.
4. If you use a computer to compose, print out your draft to edit and proofread it.
5. Print out your drafts in a larger-than-usual font.
6. Ask a second reader to proofread important documents.
7. Proofread formulas, spreadsheets, and diagrams separately from text.
8. Mark errors with a coloured pen or pencil and check them off one-by-one as you correct them.

As with revising and editing, creating a list of items to check when proofreading is a personal matter. However, the following checklist provides a starting point:

Proofreading checklist

___ correct spelling (especially of proper names)

___ no missing page numbers

___ page numbers in the same place on the page throughout

___ accurate Table of Contents and Table of Figures (where appropriate)

___ in-text references and figure titles match

___ consistent margins

___ consistent font size and indentation for headings, subheadings, and figure titles

___ signature (if required)

___ consistent spacing after end punctuation

__ consistent placement of punctuation relative to quotation marks (normally inside the quotation marks)

__ conventional treatment of numerals (normally spell out for numbers under 10)

__ accurate equations, formulas, and numerical data

__ complete documentation of secondary sources

Final thoughts on TQM

TQM as a team process

No revising or editing process is complete without input from a second reader, preferably someone who is part of, or at least close to, your target audience. Writers need testers just as much as software developers do, since it's impossible to detect all the bugs in your own work, even with the most comprehensive revision checklist as your guide.

In many work situations, writing is a team sport. Collaboration may follow formal procedures if the organization has an established draft-review process. More often, though, collaboration happens informally, as employees help one another with aspects of revision. The director of business development asks someone from the product development team to write a technical description, which he then revises to include in the company business plan; the president reviews a press release drafted by the marketing manager; a colleague asks you to give your opinion on an email message he's about to send a disgruntled client.

Collaborative workplace writing complicates the idea of authorship. Most of the writing you create on the job doesn't belong to you at all, since the documents you create are company property. Moreover, in many cases, before you sign your name to a document, you'll have received substantial input from one or more of your colleagues or supervisors. On the other hand, you're still ultimately accountable for the document's final form. If a customer calls to complain about spelling errors in a piece of documentation you produced, for instance, the explanation that Garth helped you edit is not likely satisfy your boss.

When giving or receiving advice on a piece of writing, be prepared to use your patience and negotiating skills. Because few writing teams experience such mental synchronicity that they're able to compose in a group, keep your mind open to experimenting with various models of collaboration.

Some teams work best by delegating phases of the writing process to different members. Suzie might conduct background research; Karl might draft an outline; Anwar might do the editing. Team members might divide the document into sections, with each writer composing a section, and with revisions either happening in a group session or assigned individually.

Other teams work best by following a less linear process. They might, for instance, take turns producing whole drafts. Suzie might start the ball rolling by creating a free-flowing initial version for the group to critique. Based on this feedback, Karl might then rework the entire document. After another group review, Anwar might create a third version, which, after a little more group tinkering, serves as the final copy.

Writing teams can collaborate effectively via email or in face-to-face meetings. In either situation, though, they work most productively when they put clear ground rules in place. Here are some examples of such rules:

- Comments on drafts should be submitted within two days of a document circulating.
- Criticism should be phrased positively and address the writing rather than the writer.
- If a team member will be unable to meet a deadline, he or she should tell the team leader at least three days in advance.

Depending on the context, each writing team in which you participate will evolve its own operating principles and procedures.

Whenever you collaborate with other readers and writers, the most effective way to elicit useful comments (and not just spelling corrections) is to provide a list of questions, similar to a testing protocol. Keep things simple by focusing your reader on no more than two or three questions at a time. You might, for instance, ask a reader to point out sections of the text that she finds confusing or unclear. Or you might ask her to concentrate on detecting flaws in your logic or weaknesses in your evidence. ("Do you think I have enough support for my ideas?") Another strategy is to direct your reader's attention to a couple of critical areas of your document where you've had particular trouble making your thoughts clear. If you already know where the weak spots are, you can make the most of your reader's limited time and energy by drawing immediate attention to these areas.

Besides telling your reader how to direct feedback, it's often useful to mention matters on which you don't want comments. Since few people recognize the difference between editing and revising, it's a good idea to clarify that you're not, at the revision stage, interested in fixing up errors in grammar, punctuation, or syntax (sentence structure). It's also a good idea to follow up with your readers by giving them feedback on their feedback. Let them know what you found most helpful in their suggestions and how their commentary has helped you strengthen your document. Such a response doesn't just fulfill common courtesy; it acts as positive reinforcement, too, training them to give you even more constructive input next time.

I have one final word of advice about writing collaboratively: when working with others, document the writing process as carefully as you'd document the coding of a piece of software. Keep copies of your own notes and drafts as well as commentary from others. That way you can make sure the writing process stays on track, even when many contributors play a part.

TQM and intellectual honesty

Sometimes contributors to your writing team are people whom you've never met or even contacted. Especially when you're creating a whitepaper (a detailed description of a technical solution, often used for marketing purposes) or a proposal, you may need to conduct background research. When you incorporate the ideas or words of other writers, you need to credit them appropriately. In fact, you need to credit them twice.

First, you must introduce the idea or quotation by indicating that it came from someone else. You might say, for instance, "According to James Smith, professor of metallurgical science at the University of British Columbia. . ." or "Dr. James Smith maintains that. . ." When acknowledging a source, make sure to inform readers of his or her credentials. What makes his opinion trustworthy? In what sense is she an expert on the topic?

Besides alerting your reader to the fact that you've relied on writing produced by others, you must also recognize the contributions by using formal documentation. The documentation style to use will depend on the writing context. Different organizations consult different style guides as their authority, but most adopt some version of an author-date citation method. (Rather than appearing as footnotes, in-text references list the author and date of the publication in parentheses.) The American Psychological Association (APA) style is a common author-date method and the one I've chosen for this book. The Association for Computing Machinery (ACM) also has its own variation of an author-date system, and you'll likely encounter still others on the job. The only sure way to determine which documentation style to follow is to consult previous documents produced by writers within the organization.

Although some students view plagiarism as an issue that matters only to university and college instructors, IT companies worry about intellectual property issues even more than professors do. They jealously guard confidential product information and research data because they know that, without it, the company would lose its competitive edge and even its reason to exist. One IT professional I know had to work through the night one Christmas Eve to guard against hackers breaking into files concerning the spice recipe for Colonel Sanders' Kentucky Fried Chicken.

To protect both yourself and your organization from charges of "stealing" the intellectual property of other writers, train yourself to take careful research notes. The best way to document sources accurately is to do so from the beginning.

Now that we've discussed how to produce writing that's clear and correct, we will explore ways to make your writing even more appealing. Turning from the micro level back to the macro perspective, we'll examine overall strategies for enabling your writing to act persuasively on your target audience.

Exercises

1. Create a post-composition outline for a piece of writing you have already prepared for this course. Does your outline point out any structural problems you need to address?

2. Insert transitions to improve the readability of the following paragraph:

    > Wireless home networks have become extremely popular. They're inexpensive, easy to install, and available at most retail computer stores. They have their problems. Many consumers are unaware of the security risks they pose. It's much easier for a criminal to hack into a wireless network than a wired network. A hacker positioned outside your house could access all of the personal information you store on your home computers, download your banking information, and access that confidential report you've been writing for a client. He could read the love notes you emailed to your girlfriend last week. There are many attractive reasons for setting up a wireless home network. Do these positives outweigh the negative risks?

3. Below is an outline for a report describing testing outcomes for a new piece of software. How many different ways can you imagine to organize the topics? Generate one or two alternative outlines for the report.

    I.   Testing procedures
        a. speed test
        b. security test
        c. usability test

    II. Test results
        a. speed test
        b. security test
        c. usability test

    III. Conclusions

4. Rewrite the following email progress report, eliminating its chronological structure and reducing wordiness.

Micheline,

On April 12th, we first approached the client, Murphy Homes. We asked Stella Marino, who is the Vice-President, whether the company was completely satisfied with its network. She said no, and we said we'd do up a quote at the earliest opportunity we could manage.

The first problem was that the usual router supplier, who, as you know, has been encountering some significant financial difficulties as of late, had gone out of business. This made it very difficult for us; it took us half a day for us to find an alternative supplier, since we were looking for someone who would be able to provide technical support in French as well as English. (Many of the people who work at Murphy Homes have French as their first language.)

Once we found a new supplier, we were able to proceed. The new supplier was Vincent Technologies of Vancouver. However, progress was held up by the fact that Cheryl Wilson was ill for two days. As the finance officer for the division, Cheryl is responsible for drawing up project budgets. Cheryl returned to work on April 16th, then we hit the weekend, so we were held up again.

Now that it's Monday, we're back on track with the detailed quoting process. I've set up an appointment to meet with Stella in person tomorrow, when I'll get answers to a few of the remaining questions we need answered before we can provide a quote. Then, I'll ask Macky to make a few recommendations regarding cable choices, and I'll ask Jaxon for information pertaining to the costs for labour and installation. After all this information has been collected, I will prepare the quote and deliver it to Stella. Given the time constraints we're under, I'll do this by fax. (Given the confidential nature of the information, Stella has requested that we refrain from using email communication at this time.) With any luck, I should be able to copy you the quote by Wednesday—Thursday at the latest.

Regards,

Ivona

5. Edit the following passage to make it more precise.

> To put together a loaf of bread, start by taking a pinch of yeast and placing it in a bowl, along with some warm water. Add a taste of sweetener. Once the yeast has started to bubble, place it a medium-sized bowl with three well-rounded cups of flour. (For best results, use a combination of whole wheat and white flours.) Stir and let rise.
>
> When the dough has risen, punch it down, and let it rise a bit longer.
>
> When the dough has completely risen again, put it on the counter and press it with the heel of your hand, turn it gently, fold it over, and press again. Repeat until it's ready to bake.

6. Choose a page-long piece of writing from daily life—perhaps a government document, a passage from a textbook, or a piece of your own writing—and rewrite it in Plain Language.

Chapter 6

Making Your Writing Persuasive

Desmond squirms in his seat just thinking about it—"it" being the slide presentation the boss has assigned to him. His task is to describe the firm's various services to a potential client, with the aim of soliciting new business.

It's that word "solicit" that's making Desmond wriggle. It reminds him of signs he's seen outside apartment buildings saying, "No soliciting allowed." He always thought people posted those to keep out aggressive, sleazy salespeople. Now, much to his discomfort, he feels he's being asked to join their ranks. "I'm no pushy peddler," he grumbles into his coffee mug. "I just can't force myself to come on strong. I'm not a used-car salesman, just a developer who's probably too honest for his own good."

I'd hate to be the one to break it to Desmond, but the truth is that most workplace writers function as salespeople most of the time. Sure, your official job title may be Network Administrator, Business Analyst, or Software Developer, but your core job duties will no doubt involve selling—whether you're trying to get people to "buy" a product, a process, or an idea.

As Robert Louis Stevenson has said, "Everyone lives by selling something." The Ancient Greeks grasped this concept. Each year, they held sacrificial rituals in honour of Peitho, the goddess of persuasion. However, like we moderns, they had a limited, rather tainted notion of the act of persuasion. Like us, they associated it with cunning and trickery. They imagined Peitho as a handmaiden to Aphrodite, the goddess of love. Thus, she represented the wily craft of seduction, the ability to lure the unwary into compromising circumstances.

Because popular culture portrays persuaders as con artists, it's no wonder that so many of us loathe the idea of selling. Persuasion isn't just for hucksters, however, and it's not just for a few sales-oriented kinds of documents. Persuasiveness plays an essential role in most workplace writing, formal and informal. This chapter looks at strategies for persuading readers, focusing on three different modes of persuasion, called *logos*, *ethos*, and *pathos*. It also provides help with assessing your audience's needs and adapting proven methods to influence behaviour.

Managing impressions

More than forty years ago, a pioneering social anthropologist named Erving Goffman (1959) verified through his research Shakespeare's poetic claim that "All the world's a stage, / And all the men and women merely players." Goffman determined that on-the-job interaction involves a kind of "performance" in which both actors and audience play a role. Each of us manages the impressions other people develop of us by creating a kind of stage character or "persona" to suit the demands of the particular scene we find ourselves playing at the moment. The various choices we make in presenting ourselves—from the clothers we wear, to the pitch of our voice, to the model of our car—constitute the "front" we construct to create a certain image of ourselves in the minds of our spectators.

Readers recognize that you're projecting an image of yourself as you select and arrange your words. The "front" you create through written language emerges by means of a variety of components, including sentence structure, word choice, arrangement of ideas, even document design and typeface. When writers don't think enough about the persona they create on the page or screen, they can baffle their readers. Exhibit A for this point comes from my husband, who pumps out a steady stream of email each day in his role as business developer for a software company. Sometimes I'll send him personal reminders at work, such as this one:

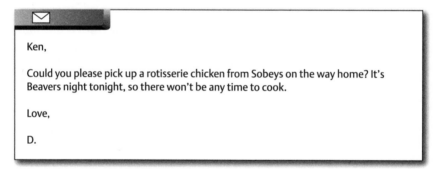

Ken,

Could you please pick up a rotisserie chicken from Sobeys on the way home? It's Beavers night tonight, so there won't be any time to cook.

Love,

D.

Most times, I'll receive an answer in the very familiar tone you would expect from someone who has lived with me for fifteen years. But occasionally, if he's replying in haste between messages to clients, Ken accidentally writes to me in his formal workplace voice:

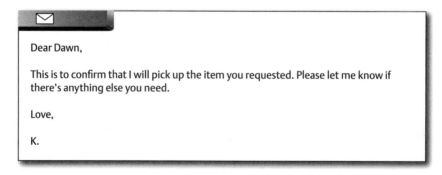

Dear Dawn,

This is to confirm that I will pick up the item you requested. Please let me know if there's anything else you need.

Love,

K.

As his wife, I can chuckle at the variations between the different personas Ken projects over email. If I were a new girlfriend, though, or a colleague at work, or a long-time customer, would I feel the same way? Or would I be trying to figure out what I'd done to deserve the sudden cold shoulder?

As you sharpen your writing abilities, you'll learn to develop numerous different "fronts" to suit different circumstances. When you address a memo to the CEO, you'll adopt a more formal, respectful persona than you'd use in an email to your friend who works in the next cubicle. Even when you're not conscious of creating a front, you still project one. Be aware that readers will automatically construct a character from your words. Do you really want to leave the impression you create solely up to the imagination of your skeptical audience? In written communication even more than in person-to-person communication, none of us can afford to avoid what Goffman and his successors have termed "impression management."

The Olympic sport of rhetoric

The traditional name for managing audiences through skill with words is "rhetoric." Today, the word often carries negative associations, as in: "The company says we're all family, but that's just meaningless rhetoric." The term, however, has a venerable history, going back to the ancient world.

The Greeks and Romans considered rhetorical ability an essential skill for public life. When we examine Aristotle's definition of rhetoric, we can see why: rhetoric, he says, is "an ability, in each [particular] case, to see the available means of persuasion" (1991, p. 36). In other words, rather than distorting information, practising rhetoric enables us to make fair-minded judgments concerning what we speak and hear, write and read.

In Ancient Greece, young men spent years rigorously training their rhetorical muscles so they could win glory for themselves in the law courts, the government assembly, or even the Olympics. By following in their footsteps, you can master the rhetorical skills you need to succeed in modern workplaces. The first step in "becoming a rhetor" (Mackinnon, 1993) is to make three little Greek words your mantra: *logos, ethos, pathos*. These are the three classical modes of persuasion.

Logos = logical argument

You persuade someone through *logos* when you use linear reasoning. The proof you provide to support your position appeals to your audience's rational side. It might include, for instance, factual evidence, scientific research, or survey results.

When you persuade by using *logos*, the structure of your writing should be well-defined. You might reason from cause to effect, or from problem to solution. Alternatively, you might state your opinion on a topic and then back it up by providing a wealth of credible examples to support your point of view. Typically, persuasion based in *logos* relies heavily on words that emphasize logical connection, such as "because" and "therefore."

Ethos = authority

You persuade someone through *ethos* when you emphasize your authority. The success of this technique depends largely on how qualified and reliable your reader judges you to be.

How you assert your authority will vary depending on your audience. With a co-worker, you might casually mention successful projects to which you've contributed. With a client whom you've never met, you might state your credentials more directly, referring to publications you've read or offering testimonials from other clients. Another tactic might be to acknowledge opposite points of view to show that you're well-informed and fair-minded.

Pathos = emotion

You persuade through *pathos* when you appeal to your reader's feelings. As advertisers and copywriters know, there are as many ways to create emotional colour as there are pixels on a high-resolution monitor. You can play to your readers' positive feelings (excitement, happiness, pleasure) about a topic, or you can elicit their negative feelings (fear, distrust, pain). Either way, it should be your audience's orientation to your subject—not yours—that determines the strategy you follow.

Techniques to arouse emotion in your reader might include descriptive language, repetition of resonant phrases, reminders about past commitments, direct questions or challenges, imaginative scenarios, and stories. When you attempt to persuade through *pathos*, you need to think like a screenwriter. Aim to engage your readers dramatically so that they react to your words and ideas at a primal, intuitive level.

Logos + *ethos* + *pathos* = complete persuasion package

Think of the last time you made a major purchase. What mode of persuasion influenced your buying decision? It likely took more than one kind of convincing to compel you to part with your money. Effective writers, therefore, make it a habit to cover all three modes by weaving aspects of *logos*, *ethos* and *pathos* into their documents. Let's say, for instance, you're trying to convince the boss to let you move from programming into web development. You could try a straightforward *logos* strategy by pointing out that you're more than ready for the job: you've completed all the necessary training and you have a strong track record of adapting to new projects quickly. To develop this argument, you might build your *ethos* by displaying your familiarity with some of the latest ideas or information learned during your training. You might also add some *pathos* to the mix by demonstrating your enthusiasm for web development, by appealing to the boss's desire to be regarded as a progressive employer, or perhaps even by evoking mild fear of losing you as an employee.

Choosing the most appropriate mode of persuasion

When you're considering which mode of persuasion to emphasize in a document, you need to ask yourself two key questions: (1) which kind of persuasion appeals most strongly to my audience? and (2) which kind of persuasion appeals most to me?

The first question reminds us how important it is to put your audience's needs first. Suppose you've just finished developing a piece of software that allows cellphone users to activate home appliances remotely. You've been asked to create a set of slides for the company's sales force to use with two different audiences. The first audience consists of the research and development team at Mega Wireless; this group is considering working out a deal to include your software as an option on all new service packages. The second audience consists of consumers, most of them women, attending the country's largest home show. How would your two sets of slides differ? What might they have in common?

Even though you're presenting the identical product, the contrasting profiles of your audiences should result in two very different rhetorical strategies. Let's assume that your audience profile tells you that most of the members of the Mega Wireless group are male engineers, between thirty-five and fifty years old. This group, if we can believe common wisdom, trusts numbers, scientific evidence, and well-organized, rational thinking. *Logos* will likely matter more to them than *pathos*. Since your audience is a well-educated group that sees itself as elite, you'll also need to persuade through *ethos* by establishing the credibility of your company and your product.

For the consumer audience, on the other hand, you can let *pathos* be your primary guide. Since the information you select to present will likely not be highly technical, the structure of your presentation may be more free-flowing than the show you create for the engineers. You might use slogans, rather than bulleted lists, and the lists you do use will likely use language that arouses an emotional response. You might also invest more time in thinking about how the visual display evokes feelings in your audience. As with the engineers, you'll need to think carefully about *ethos*. In this case, though, you'll probably focus on bringing out the personal likeability of the presenters rather than their professional credentials.

When it comes to choosing a rhetorical emphasis, it's important to understand your own susceptibility to the different modes of persuasion as well as you do your audience's. Otherwise, it's very easy to overestimate the effectiveness of a particular strategy. If, for instance, you are a person who tends to be convinced by so-called "hard facts," you might make the mistake in the above scenario of assuming that most female consumers of household products are, too. You might create a beautifully crafted set of presentation slides illustrating the impressive technical features of your software only to find it falling completely flat with the target audience.

We're not always convinced by the mode of persuasion we think has the strongest pull on us. Sometimes we are unaware of what's really affecting our attitudes or behaviour. Moreover, the most powerful mode of persuasion can differ depending on the situation. When I'm reading an article in an academic journal, I'm persuaded primarily by *logos*. On the other hand, when I'm choosing a consumer good in a store, I'm much more likely to be swayed by my emotional reactions—to colour, design, and the personality of the salesperson.

Skilfull writers, then, win over their audiences by using a combination of strategies that appeal to the reader's intellect, emotions, and sense of trust, although not necessarily in that order. Since we tend to favour the persuasive techniques we find attractive, it's a wise idea to double-check that you've covered all three bases.

Needs analysis

Let's imagine you want to recommend that the system administrators at your college or university erect a more elaborate firewall around the school's main servers. You plan to write two letters: the first will go to the Head of Campus Computing Services; the second will go to the Dean of Applied Sciences. In each case, how can you anticipate the person's needs in order to make your case persuasive?

We might view the Head of Campus Computing Services, Gerald Greene, as being strongly motivated by the need for safety. Part of Gerald's job is to make sure that student records and other private academic information are protected from hackers and viruses. Your message to him might emphasize the risks to students if their information can be accessed by hackers and also point out the benefits of investing in stronger security.

Would the same approach work with the Dean of Applied Sciences? The dean is Geraldine Grenadier, a civil engineer by training. You suspect she can't tell a trojan from a worm. Although Geraldine is likely concerned about computer safety in a general way, her main concerns probably relate to the faculty and its reputation. You might, therefore, emphasize how improvements to network security will make more people want to take the Faculty of Applied Science's online courses. You might also mention that the technology you're recommending is state-of-the-art, subtly encouraging Geraldine to see herself (and imagine others perceiving her) as a leader who is at the forefront in tackling current problems faced by the university.

When examining audience needs, it's useful to consider various categories of wants and desires. There are basic physical and physiological needs, for instance, such as the need for food, clothing, and shelter. There are also needs related to security, stability, belonging, and recognition. In addition, there are needs for personal growth (intellectual, emotional, and spiritual).

Modern psychologists have invested much energy in trying to explain and predict how different kinds of needs evolve. For workplace writers, the most significant insight from the psychological research is that human needs often overlap, sometimes without us being aware. Considering the underlying needs of readers—not just their expressed concerns—allows us to influence the forces that really motivate them.

Six practical tools of persuasion

For three years, social psychologist Robert Cialdini went undercover to infiltrate a variety of companies and find out their secrets for eliciting and directing consumer needs. His findings reinforce that most of us are swayed not by hard logic alone but by a combination of reasons, needs, and emotions. He identified six "weapons of influence" (I prefer to think of them as more neutral "tools") used to provoke a reflex-like reaction that he calls a "click-whirr" response. *Click*, the persuasion switch goes on; and *whirr*, we go into action without thinking.

One very simple way to encourage a positive "click-whirr" response to a request is to provide a reason for it. To prove this point, Cialdini cites research conducted by Harvard psychologist Ellen Langer (1978). Langer conducted her experiment in the photocopy room of a busy university library. Her method was to test the effectiveness of different ways of phrasing a request to skip ahead in the line-up for the photocopier. When she gave a reason ("Excuse me, I have five pages. May I use the Xerox machine because I'm in a rush?"), 94 per cent of people let her skip ahead. When she didn't give a reason ("Excuse me, I have five pages. May I use the Xerox machine?"), however, only 60 per cent of people let her skip. Now, here's the startling part: even when the reason was not very strong, the word "because" seemed to work as a magic charm. Only 7 per cent of the research subjects refused to let Langer go ahead of them when she gave this rather nonsensical explanation: "Excuse me, I have five pages. May I use the Xerox machine because I have to make some copies?"

If Aristotle were to comment on Langer's study, perhaps he'd suggest that even the mere appearance of *logos* is a highly compelling method of persuasion. Cialdini's six tools exert a similar influence on the thoughts, feelings, and actions of the recipient, and they can be very handy when writing a persuasive document:

1. Consistency

A strong motivation for human action is the belief that we're acting in accordance with our beliefs and past behaviour. We like to preserve our self-esteem by appearing consistent. Cialdini describes a "nearly obsessive desire to be (and to appear) consistent with what we have already done" (p. 57). For instance, in a study of people who placed bets on horses at a racetrack, the subjects expressed a much higher level of confidence in the horse's ability to win after they'd placed their bet than before (Knox & Inkster, cited in Cialdini, p. 57).

You can make the desire for consistency work for you by showing your readers how the choice you'd like them to make aligns with their past decisions. For example, let's say you're trying to convince a group of venture capitalists to invest in a new high-tech company. You might remind the investors of their track record as far-seeing leaders who have profited in the past from their ability to see the potential of cutting-edge technologies.

2. Reciprocity

"You scratch my back, I'll scratch yours," said one caveperson to the other, and thus human economies began to evolve. Anthropologists tell us that the principle of reciprocation—the idea that we should do something kind for someone who's just done something kind for us—is the glue that holds human cultures together. It's so ingrained in our "biogrammar" of acceptable behaviour that it takes a great deal of effort to resist an automatic response.

For instance, Cialdini describes how, one Christmas, a researcher mailed greeting cards to complete strangers. The reciprocal response to this action was, in Cialdini's words, "amazing." The researcher's mailbox overflowed with holiday cards from people who had never even heard of him, let alone met him (Cialdini, p. 17).

A secondary aspect of the reciprocity principle is that we feel we should give up something when someone has given up something for us. For instance, let's say you and I are negotiating a contract. If you abandon one of your demands, I'll automatically feel pressure to concede you a point in return. The bottom line is that, whatever the favour, cultural forces work very strongly to compel us to return it.

You can make the urge to reciprocate work to your advantage by treating each persuasive message you write as a kind of negotiation. Offering a concession or making a friendly gesture can go a long way toward converting your readers to your point of view.

3. Social proof

When my sister and I were teenagers, my parents tried to combat the forces of peer pressure by raising the clichéd question: "If so-and-so jumped off a bridge, would you jump off, too?" When you put the forces of conformity into that ridiculous statement, it's easy to answer, "Of course not!" But it's far less easy to resist similar questions that advertisers ask us all the time, such as "If your good-looking neighbours just bought this electric grill, shouldn't you?" or "If your children's soccer coach drives a minivan, shouldn't you?" It's even harder to deny appeals that involve celebrities or well-known authorities. ("If your doctor takes this medication, shouldn't you?" or "If Michael Jordan wears these sneakers, shouldn't you?") Because we're social creatures, we determine what is correct by watching what others around us do, and we adapt our own behaviour accordingly.

You can evoke the power of this "social proof" most successfully if you understand the community to which your readers belong. When you're selling an inventory-management program to a company that produces natural supplements, for instance, it might not work to use as social proof the fact that the country's major pharmaceutical manufacturer has adopted the product. However, if you can show that others whom your readers respect—perhaps a leading producer of naturopathic remedies—use the program, you'll tap into a very convincing means of persuasion. Direct testimonials would make your appeal even more convincing.

4. Authority

A number of experiments have confirmed that one of the most effective ways to persuade is to create a sense of authority. When communicating in person, you might do this by paying attention to the way you dress and to the physical objects with which you associate yourself, such as your jewellery, your car, or even your pen. (Some executives will pay upwards of $200 USD to sport a fashionable ballpoint.) When you're communicating in print, you can also convey authority visually through the document design choices you make.

Even so seemingly small a matter as the choice of typeface can affect the overall persuasiveness of your message. Imagine, for instance, that you're seated in front of a lawyer's desk, about to sign an important agreement. Here's what the text looks like:

> *The undersigned parties, Tracy Carruthers and John Doolittle, hereby agree to the following terms of service...*

Goodness knows that legal language is difficult enough to decipher in its own right; it certainly doesn't need any graphical interference from an unorthodox font choice. But notice that the font doesn't just interfere with readability; it also interferes with the lawyer's credibility. Most of the legal and professional documents we see appear in something standard, like Times New Roman. Anything bizarre-looking is unlikely to gain our complete confidence. I'm not a lawyer myself, but my instinct warns me away from any legally binding document that looks like a child's birthday party invitation.

Most of us place a high value not only on "professional" appearance but also on certain professions. To make this attitude work for you, dress your writing with theories, data, and opinions from such "experts" as doctors, scientists, engineers, professors, and business leaders. If you can get a quotable quote from an expert, you'll appear even more knowledgeable and reliable.

5. Liking

Building a friendly rapport with your reader is another effective way to create *ethos*. Sometimes, in fact, likeability can outweigh authority when it comes to establishing trust with your audience. So how can you get your readers to like you, especially when you may not have the happiest news to deliver? Here are some pointers:

(a) Attractiveness encourages liking

While maintaining their authoritative look, make your documents (whether electronic or paper) as eye-pleasing as possible. Allow lots of white space; use a font size that's easy to read (minimum of 10-point on paper, 12-point on screen); break long documents into sections with descriptive headings; use different fonts for main text and headings; and follow any prescribed formatting requirements to the tee. Research shows that such attention to aesthetics really work. For instance, one study (Berleant, 2000) found that computing proposals that used headings in a sans serif font (such as Arial) were more likely to succeed than proposals that used headings in a serif font (such as Times New Roman).

(b) Similarity encourages liking

Communication experts have long known that one of the best ways to increase persuasiveness is to mirror the communication style of your audience. Imagine that you walk into a room for an interview with a major software developer. When you meet your prospective employer, he is wearing cut-off jeans, sandals, and a faded T-shirt that reads "Rock On In Righteousness." He introduces himself as Jon, in a friendly, easygoing tone. In response to this, you would not be wise to insist on calling him Jonathan—or, even worse, "Mr. Hathaway"—and you certainly wouldn't adopt your most serious, over-enunciated, newscaster voice.

Such minor adaptations to another's style are perfectly natural for us to do when we're communicating in person. In writing, you can achieve such flexibility by matching your audience's writing in terms of such elements as vocabulary level, use of jargon, sentence length, and sentence structure.

(c) Positive associations encourage liking

In the 1930s, psychologist Gregory Razran noted the impact of the "luncheon technique" on the perceived persuasiveness of a message (cited in Cialdini, p. 193–94). Organizations host so-called "free" meals because it's been scientifically proven that people are more receptive to what they hear if they're eating while they hear it (assuming that the meal is a pleasant experience).

There are a couple of ways you can make the "luncheon effect" work for you as a writer:

- serve cookies and coffee with every memo you deliver, or
- establish clear links between what you're selling (your ideas, product, or service) and other things that have positive associations for your reader.

(I'd suggest that the second application is by far the easier to implement!)

Imagine that you are the head of Research & Development in a mid-sized company that manufactures networking equipment. You receive the following email messages from two innovative employees:

(Email 1)

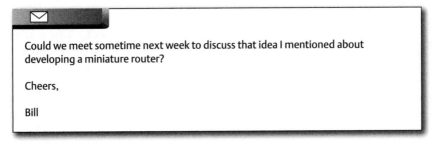

Could we meet sometime next week to discuss that idea I mentioned about developing a miniature router?

Cheers,

Bill

(Email 2)

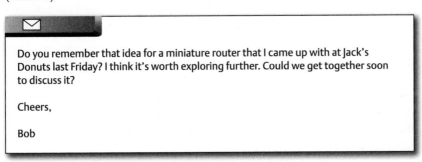

Do you remember that idea for a miniature router that I came up with at Jack's Donuts last Friday? I think it's worth exploring further. Could we get together soon to discuss it?

Cheers,

Bob

Most of us, so the theory goes, would respond better to the second email, due to its luncheon effect. This example happens to involve food and drink, but you could create a similarly positive impact by associating the subject of your message with anything pleasant—perhaps a hobby, a favourite location, a happy event, or a prosperous venture.

6. Scarcity

The fear that a possibility may soon evaporate can create a compelling reason for your reader to act. I don't suggest that you end your email messages with the intense emotional pleading found in direct-mail advertisements (*Order now to get your limited-edition Ray Charles sunglasses. We're down to only 500. Don't miss this opportunity of a lifetime!*). I do recommend, though, that you take advantage of the persuasive concept of scarcity by making your messages time-sensitive. Make it a point to do two things in every persuasive message you write:

- State exactly what it is you want you readers to do once they've absorbed your message.
- Specify a time frame for completing the desired action.

As a junior employee, you may find this difficult because it feels disrespectful to tell your superiors what to do. To make the scarcity principle work, however, you don't need to bark out commands like a general giving orders to the troops. It's possible to maintain a polite, respectful tone while clearly laying out the next steps for your reader to take.

Here's a typical scenario you might encounter on the job. Let's say you're responsible for arranging a training event for some developers. You've spoken with a representative from the training provider, and she's available to deliver a workshop in two weeks. The boss has okayed your budget, but, before you can confirm the arrangements, you need to verify that the date does not conflict with any meetings. Here are some possible ways you might end your email requesting your supervisor's final approval for the training session:

(a) Could you please get back to me on this by Monday so I can make sure we don't lose our spot on the trainer's schedule?

(b) As long as we book by Monday, we should be able to hang on to our reservation with the trainer.

(c) The trainer says she's already booking for next month, so it would be good to firm up the details no later than Monday.

Each of the above endings expresses a sense of urgency by pointing out the scarcity of the desired product (the training). At the same time, each of them also maintains an appropriately courteous attitude toward the socially superior reader.

Using the scarcity principle with proper respect won't make you seem impudent, but it will make you appear well organized and proactive. Tactfully used, the notion of scarcity, like Cialdini's other persuasion tactics, can create the image of a confident, trustworthy writer behind the words.

Putting it all together

Although many enterprising consultants make a living by advocating sales methods that are "guaranteed" to work, there really is no single, fail-safe model for creating documents that sell. A writer or speaker persuades an audience through the combined influence of various strategies and effects. If speakers in ancient Greece needed to think shrewdly about how to cover all their bases—reasoning, emotions, and credibility—we need to so all the more today, now that sales messages bombard us 24-7.

If you're afraid that selling means badgering an audience into submission, you can take heart in knowing that research discredits the "hard sell." A more effective method is simply to practise ethical rhetoric. This means considering how your words contribute to the persona you're creating on the page, and how that persona encourages reader confidence and agreement. In the next chapter, we'll see how crucial this kind of strategizing becomes in the realm of email.

Exercises

1. The following sentences attempt to persuade the reader primarily through *logos*. Revise them to appeal to the reader through *ethos* or *pathos* (or both). Use your imagination to fill in any necessary details.

    Example:

    logos — The sedan uses fuel more efficiently than 85% of the other compact cars on the market.

    ethos and *pathos* — The sedan is one of the most environmentally friendly cars on the market. Its super-clean engine was designed by a team of research scientists committed to combatting climate change.

    (i)   The ergonomic structure of the WristEasy mouse pad reduces the symptoms of carpal tunnel syndrome by enabling the user to keep the wrist flat.

    (ii)   According to a recent efficiency survey, XYZ Corporation could increase productivity by outsourcing the e-mail its customer service centre receives.

    (iii) The most effective way for a team to produce a piece of collaborative writing is to divide the document into pieces and ask each team member to draft a section. This method has worked well for our division for several years.

    (iv)   Although we're operating on a tight budget, our market research indicates we should increase the resources we allocate to usability testing of our manuals.

2. Locate a recent speech by a politician on a controversial topic. How many strategies of persuasion can you identify? Would you recommend any different or additional strategies to make the speech more persuasive?

3. Pick one of Cialdini's six "weapons of influence" and write an advice column telling readers how to recognize it and defend themselves against it.

4. Locate a brief technical description of a piece of software or technology you know very well. Rewrite the description as a promotional piece by (1) picking a target audience, (2) identifying your audience's needs, and (3) using at least one of the "six persuasive strategies" discussed in this chapter.

Part 2

Creating Effective Electronic Text

Chapter 7

Mastering the Art of Email

Loic and Dallas spend their workdays three cubicles apart in a government department of thirty-two employees. Both are short-term contractors involved in building a database to track information related to a large project just launched by a federal grant. They've known each other only a few weeks.

Loic has made it clear that he tolerates few interruptions while he's coding. Whenever Dallas has a question, therefore, he sends Loic an email, and awaits the reply. Today, Dallas is chafing to hear back from Loic, because his own work is stalled until he gets a response. As he waits impatiently, he hopes Loic's message will not be as cryptic as the last one, which seemed to sidestep the question completely. "I just don't like that guy," Dallas thinks.

The friction between Loic and Dallas exemplifies what one exasperated IT executive told me: "Email is the biggest problem in business today."

A universal threat to workplace communication

As senior managers know from experience, and as communication researchers have documented through numerous studies, email constitutes both a more limited and a more complex communication channel than many of us realize. That's why Karen Spaulding, CEO of a software company called Metaworks, encourages her developers to get up from their cubicles and talk to one another rather than rely on email. She suggests that email tends to create the misleading impression that the communicator's job ends once he or she hits *Send*. As Spaulding reminds her staff, however: "The only way you're going to know if the other guy got your message is to get them to feed it back to you."

Mignona Cote, senior manager of information security for Nortel, echoes Spaulding's concerns, stressing that an email sent is not necessarily an email read. Cote's biggest complaint is with "over-communicating"—many of the roughly three hundred messages she receives each day are unnecessary. The habit of sending out messages that are irrelevant to many of the recipients seriously interferes with productivity at Nortel, Cote believes.

Skilfully used, email can be a very effective communication channel. When used thoughtlessly, however, it can generate ambiguity, confusion, and hurt feelings.

Best practices of email communicators

When we're composing an email message, we may feel as if we're pouring our thoughts directly into our reader's ears. Ironically, though, the more natural email seems, the more difficult it can be to use. The first, clunky email clients made the mediated aspect of computer-mediated communication painfully obvious. Nowadays, however, sophisticated user interfaces cause us to forget that technological barriers still exist between the sender and the receiver.

We confront those barriers when we run up against "e-tone." Communications consultant Nancy Friedman says that e-tone happens "when I write my email with a particular tone of voice in mind and you read it with a totally different tone" (Stauffer, 199, p. 4). The discrepancy occurs partly because email strips away many of the social cues we normally use to feel our way through a conversation. It also occurs because the faceless realm of cyberspace encourages "hyperpersonal" (Walther, 1996) communication. Emotions tend to run high online, where people view writing style as expressing emotion and character.

Crafting an email message is a bit like participating in an MUD. From the recipient's point of view, each textual choice we make—such as our greeting, word choices, and sentence structure—casts us in certain role. In the following sections, you'll find seven best practices that will enable you to project an online persona that's as likeable, professional, and persuasive as you are in real life.

1. Pay attention to the entire email package

According to Canadian image consultant Sharon Skaling, "First impressions are formed within eleven seconds of meeting someone, giving you barely enough time to speak." Online encounters are no different. The impression you create with an email begins with various aspects of the message's packaging, including the sender's address, the subject line, and the greeting.

Sender's address

Many of us have several email accounts. You might, for instance, have one through your workplace that's for work-related messages only, a personal one through a web-based mail service such as Google or Yahoo, and perhaps another that you use just for online shopping. Think carefully about which accounts you use for which sorts of messages. An email address of *cyberbunny@yahoo.com* may be a cute moniker to use when sending online notes to your friends, but it would not create the best impression with a potential employer. Consider your email address as part of your online personality, and apply appropriate discretion.

Subject line

It's a message-beats-message world out there in today's cluttered in-boxes. No matter how important your message is in your eyes, there's a good chance your reader doesn't really want to read it. When it comes to processing email subject lines, many people want to scan through their in-boxes and detect as quickly as possible the messages they can delete. The most effective subject lines avoid the purge by meeting four essential criteria: they're (a) singular, (b) descriptive, (c) concise, and (d) as positive as is ethically possible.

(a) Singular—Although it may seem contradictory, you actually save the reader time by dealing with just one subject per email. By keeping to a single topic, you make it easy for your readers to sort and prioritize messages. They can tell at a glance whether they need to open an email immediately or move it to the "Read later" file. Here's an example of a subject line that fails the singularity test: *Routine requests from head office and an important announcement.* If the "important announcement" really is important, the writer should deal with it in a separate email so that it won't be missed.

(b) Descriptive—Avoid generic labels, such as "News," "FYI," or "Important Reminder." Not only will these fail to catch your reader's eye, but they may also fall prey to a spam filter. Keep in mind, too, that your reader may pass your message on to other readers. Creating a descriptive subject line that's easy to interpret will prevent the confusion that can happen when messages become removed from their original context. Instead of the vague "Urgent request," favour the more specific "Requirements for launch of product X."

(c) Concise—Now that so many people are reading email on the tiny screens of handheld devices, it's risky to assume that a subject line is short enough just because your desktop monitor can accommodate it. To tighten up your subject lines, eliminate articles and pronouns, such as "the," "an," "your," and "my" ("Proposal revisions" rather than "My revisions to the proposal," for example). You can also use jargon and abbreviations where appropriate (that is, when you're absolutely sure that your various audiences understand the terms). Here are some examples of wordy versus concise subject lines. Can you think of alternative ways of improving the originals?

Wordy	Concise
Recently-approved amendments to the constitution	New constitutional amendments
Objections to the new building plan from Fred, Ted, Blyth, Yentl, and Stan	Group 3's comments on blueprints
Revisions to manuscript of the user documentation for RoboFix 7	User doc revisions—RF7

(d) As positive as is ethically possible—Because the conditions of cyberspace encourage emotional reactions, a negative subject line can easily trigger the alarm bell. Even when you have to write an email that contains bad news, avoid blatantly pessimistic, shocking words that automatically increase the reader's heart rate, such as "problem," "impossible," and "disaster." Avoid red-flagging a message, unless you're dealing with a genuinely urgent matter.

It can be challenging to seize your reader's attention without inviting panic. Something like "Problem with the budget" or "Budget overrun" will certainly get your boss's attention, but so would "Budget concerns" or "Budget update," which are more neutral choices. It's your responsibility to portray the situation accurately, but you don't have to use doomsday language to do so.

Greeting

Before you shake hands with someone you're meeting for the first time, that person has already constructed judgments of you based on your facial expression, the colour of your hair, the cut of your suit, and perhaps the quality of your shoes. The firmness or limpness of your handshake can seal those impressions. In a similar way, the greeting with which you open the body of your email functions as your virtual handshake. Current netiquette (email etiquette) permits you to skip the greeting altogether if you're addressing a group of readers, but when you want to establish rapport, the right greeting is an important element in your message. Here are some guidelines:

a. *Double-check titles and spellings.* If you're aiming for a formal tone and the person to whom you're writing has a professional title, such as Dr. or Rev., use it. Unless you have evidence to the contrary, assume that a woman prefers to be addressed as "Ms.," not "Miss" or "Mrs." Always double-check spellings of both first and last names. (Messages addressed to "Mrs. Harwood" or "Dear Donna" have a very short shelf life in my inbox.)

b. *Take the cultural context into account.* If you're writing to a person from a culture outside of North America, it's safest to assume that a formal greeting (such as "Dear Herr Vogelbacher") is most appropriate. If English is not your reader's first language, it's best to avoid slang expressions anyway, so "Howdy" and "How's it hangin'?" are definitely out of the running.

c. *Avoid time-sensitive greetings.* You have no control over when your reader will open your message, so don't say "Good morning"—your audience might be reading the email at midnight.

2. "Ground" your message

When someone opens a meeting by saying, "Let's first make sure we're all on the same page on this," that person is establishing something that the psycholinguists call "communicative grounding" (Clark and Brennan, 1991). A grounded conversation proceeds effectively because the participants share a set of premises; they at least agree on what the topic is, even if they approach it from different points of view. A good grounding matters all the more in emails, as confusion can easily arise.

Imagine that Tara sends the following message at 10:05 a.m., immediately after a brief hallway conversation with Les, regarding some sudden changes in a software project:

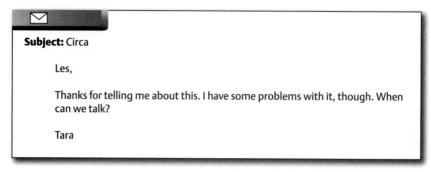

Subject: Circa

Les,

Thanks for telling me about this. I have some problems with it, though. When can we talk?

Tara

If Les receives the message just moments after Tara sends it, he'll have no trouble understanding her gist. But let's say that he's in a meeting that drags on until 3 p.m., then reads Tara's message along with the other thirty-five emails that have accumulated in his inbox since the morning. By then, he may have no idea what she's talking about.

Even when replying to emails with the original topic or thread quoted beneath your message, it is worth taking the trouble to make your references explicit. Tara, for instance, could make her message much easier for Les to understand by altering it as follows:

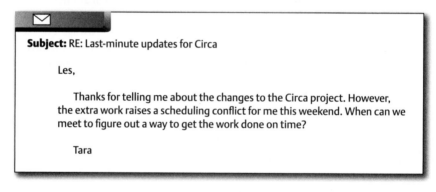

Subject: RE: Last-minute updates for Circa

Les,

Thanks for telling me about the changes to the Circa project. However, the extra work raises a scheduling conflict for me this weekend. When can we meet to figure out a way to get the work done on time?

Tara

3. Arrange your ideas for maximum persuasive impact

Just as journalists who write for TV must learn to tell the news in sound bites, people who communicate by email must master the art of the e-bite. As screens on mobile devices continue to shrink, it becomes more and more crucial for email writers to arrange information in small, carefully prioritized chunks.

Although, in theory, your readers can scroll down as far as you want them to go, in actuality, readers are—well, there's no kind way to put it—lazy. You can never assume that someone will make an effort to read your entire email. Assume instead that you must "hook" your reader with a compelling opening statement.

Therefore, put your most important information in the opening paragraph, if not the opening line. In longer messages, repeat your key ideas, and also the action you expect your reader to take, in the last line of your message. That way, you'll accommodate the reading practices of most workplace readers, who tend to skim rather than thoroughly read on-screen text.

This kind of structuring requires that you carefully review your email before sending it. We return to the paradox of email: the form of business writing that seems quickest and easiest actually demands the most scrupulous attention. Far from being an activity reserved for paper-based documents, revision constitutes an essential phase in the email-writing process.

4. Compensate for linguistic hypersensitivity

Someone who becomes visually impaired tends to develop extraordinary capabilities of sight, hearing, and touch to compensate for the lost sense. Similarly, in the text-only world of computer-mediated communication, email readers become extra responsive to tone, word choice, and even sentence structure.

A few simple practices can help build stable relationships in this environment. You can buffer any potentially jarring information, put your reader's interests before your own, and use positive language wherever ethically possible.

Buffer any potentially jarring information

To minimize the fallout from negative news, try cushioning the blow. Used sparingly, an effective "buffer" gives readers time to prepare mentally for bad news so that they're able to process it rationally and calmly, rather than respond in a fit of emotion. Communications expert Kitty Locker mentions the following buffers (2005, p. 206):

a. A statement of an accepted fact or truism
b. A description of a positive aspect of the situation
c. A recap of events
d. A reference to an enclosure or attachment
e. A thank-you to the reader for performing a specific action

Because cyberspace is such a high-risk environment, buffers are needed much more often in emails than in paper correspondence. If you think your reader could find your message disturbing in any way, I'd recommend putting a shock absorber in place. Returning to that imaginary email regarding your overdrawn budget, for instance, here are some of the cushioning statements you could use:

Reference to a positive aspect of the situation

> Thanks to the new software, the Ardgate project is nearly complete, and we're running two full weeks ahead of schedule. This efficiency has, however, come at a premium...

Reference to an attachment

> As the attached spreadsheet indicates, we now expect the Argentia project to come in 20 per cent over budget...

Recap of events

> Because we purchased new software, it looks as if the Argentia project will exceed its current budget by 20 per cent...

Reference to an accepted fact

> Looking back through the records, it seems that each major project we've undertaken in the past two years has exceeded its projected budget by fifteen to twenty-five percent. It looks as if the Argentia project will be no exception: we're now forecasting a budget overrun of 20 per cent.

Thank-you to reader for performing a specific action

> Thank you for approving the purchase of the new software. I'm writing to let you know that, as a result of this unexpected cost, we now expect the Argentia project to run 20 per cent over budget.

Put your reader's interests before your own

Ours is not a planet of altruists. As the research on impression management loudly demonstrates, we Earthlings normally expect that other Earthlings will act with the primary motive of protecting their own ideas, finances, and social position. To overcome habitual suspicion and to earn your reader's trust, craft your words to project empathy. Make a sincere effort to see the situation from the reader's perspective.

I'm not talking about paying lip service to someone's patience or glibly glossing over someone else's difficulties. Fake feelings—like fake art—will always be detected. Here's what I'd consider an example of a writer trying, unsuccessfully, to feign empathy:

> I understand how busy you must be as an admin clerk, but my timesheets are very important to me, and I need them processed no later than noon today.

Notice that this sentence contains no fewer than four first-person pro-nouns (two *I*'s and two *my*'s). Clearly, although the individual professes to "understand" the clerk's position, the writer's focus is very me-focused.

Writing radiates genuine empathy when you take the trouble to examine the various aspects of your correspondent's situation, and engage in genuine problem-solving. Here's a revised version of the above statement that shows legitimate, credible fellow-feeling:

> I know you're very busy with the month-end paperwork today, so I've submitted my timesheets pre-signed. I'd appreciate your putting them through by noon so we can avoid having to re-bill my hours next week.

As you can see, one of the most valuable habits email users can learn is to arrange ideas so that the reader's worries and wishes, rather than the writer's, drive the document.

Keep your tone pleasant

When required to take a firm stand, writers sometimes adopt a brusque and uncompromising style. Students who use such a tone in my course assignments often tell me that they want to come across as unambiguous and decided. The problem is that if you compose an email using harsh language, you could alienate your readers to the point that they fail to absorb your point.

Bearing in mind the emotional reactivity that computer-mediated com-munication encourages, I'm struck by how well Aesop's ancient fable about the north wind and the sun applies here. The story tells of a competition between the two forces of nature, the object of which is to see who can be the first to force a man to remove his cloak. As the wind whips up a mighty gale, the man draws his cloak closer to protect himself from the cold. As soon as the sun begins to shine gently, however, the man grows warm and takes off the garment. The moral of the story is "Persuasion is better than force" (Aesop, 1880, p. 233). Translation for email writers: Genuine empathy beats browbeating every time.

Choose pronouns carefully

Pronouns—such as "you" and "me," or "us" and "them"—may be some of the shortest words in the English language, but they can also be the most powerful because they position us in relation to others.

Politicians and business leaders know the power of a well-placed "we." Consider as a prime example the motivational words that Winston Churchill delivered in the British House of Commons in 1940, following the evacua-tion of British forces from Dunkirk in the Second World War. His famous speech concludes: "We shall fight on the beaches, we shall fight on the landing grounds, we shall fight in the fields and in the streets, we shall fight in the hills; we shall never surrender" (Churchill, 1945, p. 223).

Now, those members of the Allied nations who tuned in from around the world to hear Churchill's words must have realized that the British Prime Minister himself had no intention of strapping on galoshes and a knapsack and hiking off to the trenches. Nevertheless, Churchill's use of the inclusive "we" rather than "you" harmonized his leadership efforts with those of the common soldier.

When, like Churchill, you're trying to motivate a reader to join your campaign or second your cause, it's often an effective rallying strategy to use the inclusive "we." ("By giving this trade show *our* best combined effort, *we'll* get a serious leg up on the competition.") If you're trying to avoid pointing the finger of blame at someone, you may also find it useful to use the first-person plural. ("Since *our* sales quotas are down this month, *we'll* all have to aim to target five additional phone customers a day.") You should be careful, though, not to assume blame for a fault that is not yours; remember that email creates a permanent record that can be used for performance evaluation or legal purposes.

When, on the other hand, your goal is to convince your readers that you're operating with their interests at heart, then you may find it most useful to emphasize "you" and "yours." Consider the difference in effect that derives from altering the point of view in this very simple sentence:

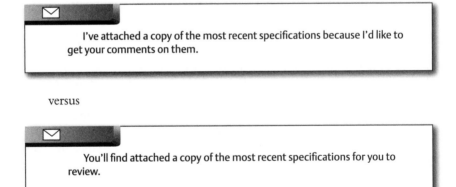

I've attached a copy of the most recent specifications because I'd like to get your comments on them.

versus

You'll find attached a copy of the most recent specifications for you to review.

Although the changes appear very slight, they dramatically influence the timbre of the e-voice. I'd describe the voice in the first sentence as self-centred because the emphasis falls on what "I" need rather than on what "you" can do. Although equally results-oriented, the voice in the second sentence comes across as more courteous. Rather than making a demand, it extends an invitation, placing the importance on the reader's efforts and judgment.

Avoid dictating feelings

Few of us like to be told what to think or feel. But that's exactly what well-meaning writers do when they make such comments as "You'll be glad to hear that Sally El-Diri has just received the award for Salesperson of the Year," or "I know you're probably disappointed about the scheduling for this project, but we had little choice in the matter this time."

Given the emotional volatility of computer-mediated communication, it's best to avoid such presumptive references to another person's emotional state. Pretending to read someone else's feelings can easily trigger a hostile reaction. Imagine, for instance, that Pat, a fierce rival of Sally, receives the official company email announcing Sally's promotion. Far from feeling "glad," Pat may be thinking such seething thoughts as "How dare she assume I'm happy about Sally's promotion? Hasn't she heard how that witch stole my biggest client from under my nose?"

As for your own feelings, even when you're feeling delighted or anguished, I'd think twice before bringing your emotions into the spotlight. Putting your feelings on display will not encourage rapport unless your reader shares them. By venting, you're gambling with your reader's trust.

Taking these warnings into account by no means excludes *pathos* from email communication. To truly connect with your readers via email, you need to generate an online personality that's amiable as well as competent. The more human qualities you portray through your textual presence, the less "mediated" the computer-mediated communication seems. But instructing your audience to feel certain emotions, or merely describing your own, seldom works. (That's why emoticons do little to rescue a serious email blooper.)

Think positive

The so-called "sandwich method" of creating positive emphasis works well in email messages, at both the paragraph and sentence level. When you must introduce a negative word or idea, you can deflect attention from it by positioning it between two positive elements. For example, let's say that Aaron needs to tell his supervisor, Liam, that the prototype he's building won't be ready until Wednesday, a day late. As a first draft, Aaron composes the following email message:

Liam,

I'm sorry, but I've been working so hard on getting all the bugs out that I won't be able to deliver the prototype to you until Wednesday. I know that this is a whole day past the deadline, and I apologize for taking so long with this.

Aaron

After re-reading his message, Aaron revises it to make it more positive:

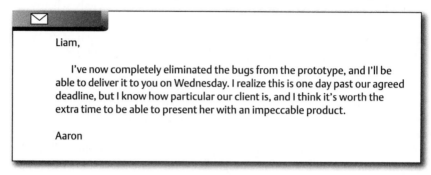

Liam,

I've now completely eliminated the bugs from the prototype, and I'll be able to deliver it to you on Wednesday. I realize this is one day past our agreed deadline, but I know how particular our client is, and I think it's worth the extra time to be able to present her with an impeccable product.

Aaron

Notice that one of the first things that Aaron eliminates is his repeated apology. Rather than saying he's sorry for doing too thorough a job (not a very logical position, when you think about it), Aaron has now decided to highlight the care he's taken with the prototype. He clearly states his bad news so that there's no ambiguity, but sandwiches this between the positive introduction and a confident conclusion justifying the delay.

Whereas Aaron's e-voice in the first message suggests a timid, perhaps incompetent employee, the second message creates the image of someone who's confident, responsible, and customer-centred. It's important to note that Aaron has not distorted or exaggerated the information in his revised message in any way. He has committed no ethical infractions, but simply given attention to how his words create his online personality.

Besides arranging your sentence to create the most positive impression, you can maintain an upbeat tone by eliminating doom-and-gloom words, particularly those beginning with *dis-*, *mis-*, *in-*, *im-*, and *un-*. I recommend you also steer clear of words with negative emotional associations, such as *anxiety*, *nervous*, *afraid*, and *sorry* (a word that Canadians, especially women, tend to mistake as a standard expression of courtesy). In addition, to keep your e-voice self-assured, avoid words that make actions appear difficult to accomplish. Using the word "difficulty" or "problem" to describe a situation, for instance, can make it seem harder to perform a task than the word "challenge." Finally, when dealing with clients, beware of hot-button words that undercut your credibility, such as *delay*, *unfortunately*, *damage*, *downturn*, and *loss*.

Screen your drafts as well for more subtle expressions of self-doubt. As a first step, eliminate the words *hope*, *hopeful*, or *hopefully* from your workplace dictionary. As reknowned sales trainer Rick Page has said, "Hope is not a strategy." Expressing intent rather than ability implies a lack of confidence. Consider the following:

This working arrangement is designed to maximize our output to aim for a delivery date of April 2007.

This sentence does not include obviously negative words, but it creates a tentative impression. The proposal's author could instantly beef up the confidence quotient by using more direct, affirmative verbs:

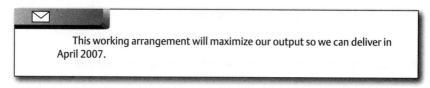

This working arrangement will maximize our output so we can deliver in April 2007.

5. Proofread, proofread, proofread.

In one sense, the facelessness of email levels the playing field for communication. In an interpersonal encounter, the person with the flattest abdominal muscles or the classiest watch will likely appear most persuasive; in an online conversation, however, all participants have the same physical appearance.

That's one theory, anyway, but surely it's a naïve one. If anything, the ongoing power contests that characterize face-to-face conversation become more intense online, where the options for self-presentation are reduced to rhetorical choices alone. To be persuasive, an email writer can't rely on good looks or fancy clothes but instead must exhibit good grooming through correct grammar, controlled syntax, and a precise vocabulary.

In her study of the cyber-protest against the release of Lotus MarketPlace (a CD-ROM containing information on millions of individual American consumers), Laura Gurak (1997) shows that, among strangers online, ethos emerges almost purely through textual representation. This finding radically changes our existing notions of what it means to demonstrate a "good character." Although reputation still plays a significant role in electronic communication, credibility often develops directly from writing skill. As another researcher, Jan Fernback, has concluded, "the commodities of power in cyberspace may be wit, and tenacity, and intelligence rather than brawn, money, or political clout" (1999, p. 213). Suddenly, the mechanics of writing no longer seem issues for schoolmarms alone.

Rightly or wrongly, our society interprets the ability to follow conventions of grammar, spelling, and punctuation as a reliable index of intelligence. Online communication, we know, dramatically increases the importance we ascribe to this. So I'm not kidding when I say that proofreading your email messages could make the difference between receiving a promotion and not.

Garth Smedley is in charge of product development for Coemergence, a company that creates software to support competitive intelligence. He sums up the significance of good email grooming this way: "Poor spelling can seriously affect someone's career." Smedley stresses that Coemergence, like many companies, includes a "Communication" category in the annual performance evaluation, which means that poor spelling and grammar reduce an employee's overall score.

To score high points with your online correspondence, I suggest you print out important email messages to proofread them in hard copy. (Your eye is more likely to catch errors on paper than on the screen.) For very important messages, you might also consider sending a preview copy to yourself so that you can see exactly how your message appears on screen (allowing for browser differences, of course) before releasing it.

6. Offer opportunities to follow up through supplementary channels

You've crafted and re-crafted your email message. You've composed a dynamite subject line, put your key ideas up front, used positive language, and even checked for spelling errors. You're confident you've reduced the risk of having a poor e-tone to approximately 0.01 per cent. Even so, the job is not yet done.

To ward off possible misunderstandings, it's always wise to make it easy for your reader to raise questions through another communication channel. Your professional signature should take care of most of the details, such as your work phone number and fax number. However, you may also want to raise the possibility of an in-person meeting or include an additional phone number. The easier you make it for your reader to reach you, the more you increase the likeability and credibility of your e-voice.

7. Routinely pause before hitting *Send*

The way that email appears to reduce non-verbal cues can seem a significant advantage. The feeling of anonymity that one gets facing a blank screen can cause us to believe it's easier to deliver an unpleasant message via the cyber route rather than in person or over the phone. Because I'm the kind of person who would rather walk across a bed of nails in bare feet than deal with interpersonal conflict, I know this temptation only too well. Therefore, before I send a message dealing with a sticky situation, I stop to ask myself this question: "Are you being an email wimp, or is this really the best communication channel to use in this situation?" Many a time, routinely pausing before I press *Send* has forced me to choose another channel and thus saved me from escalating conflict.

Because of the low security of email, I recommend that you pause before sending any message, not just those that you deem emotionally charged. As Bill Gates, Enron's accountants, and countless other less famous individuals have learned to their great cost, anything you send via email constitutes a permanent written record. The well-worn advice to avoid putting in an email message anything you wouldn't want to see on the front page of the *Globe and Mail* still makes good sense, even though firewalls and encryption programs become more sophisticated every day. In fact, the continuing growth of companies that develop software to guarantee email security points to the ongoing risk.

There's one more compelling reason for taking a brief time-out before you hit *Send*—the over-communication pandemic. Before you copy in your supervisors or colleagues, stop to ask yourself whether those people really need the message. Do they have an actual use for the information? Do they need it to make a decision, to justify an action, or to adjust their own actions? Have they specifically requested it? If the answers to all these questions are negative, then you would probably make a more positive impression by withholding your message than by cluttering up their inboxes.

Putting it all together

Rather ironically, my advice on how to create pointed, successful emails has been lengthy. The challenges of online correspondence are so complex that it can sometimes be difficult to keep track of all of them, let alone overcome them. To help you apply the writing strategies we've explored, I've created a chart summary of email best practices (Figure 7.1). It's not necessary to use each strategy I've listed with each email you write. Some emails bear more weight than others and require the deluxe rhetorical treatment, while other messages you can safely produce with far less attention to detail. Conducting a thorough audience analysis will enable you to recognize which category of email writing task you're facing. In addition, consciously following the best practices of successful email communicators as often as you can will enable you to internalize the principles so that the guidelines eventually become second nature.

Figure 7.1 — Summary of email best practices

1. Pay attention to the entire email package
   - sender's address
   - subject line (singular, descriptive, concise, positive)
   - greeting

2. Ground your message

3. Arrange your ideas for maximum persuasive impact

4. Compensate for linguistic hypersensitivity
   - buffer any potentially jarring information
   - put your reader's interests before your own
   - keep your tone pleasant
   - choose pronouns carefully
   - avoid dictating feelings
   - think positive

5. Proofread, proofread, proofread

6. Offer opportunities to follow up through supplementary channels.

7. Routinely pause before hitting *Send*

I'll let Karen Spaulding, who has more than twenty years experience communicating from within both large and small organizations, have the last word on email. She says: "Things do not have to be communicated to the nth degree, and they do not have to be perfect. They have to be understood."

As we'll see, making yourself understood on web pages and presentation slides involves implementing many of the same strategies that create effective email messages. Although each medium has its particular challenges, we're still in the realm of digital rhetoric, where choices of form and expression shape the persona the world sees.

Exercises

1. Create an effective buffering statement for each of the following situations:
   (a) Your boss asks you to head up the United Way campaign again this year. You must decline.
   (b) Your project is two weeks behind schedule because your son had chickenpox and your computer had a virus.
   (c) Because you underestimated costs, you need to request approval to increase your project budget by 10 per cent.

2. Revise the following sentences to emphasize the positive.
   (a) Users who choose the default installation do not have many font choices, since most specialty fonts are reserved for the custom installation.
   (b) Although I have no direct experience with professional speechwriting, I have been an active participant of Toastmasters for three years.
   (c) You failed to sign your travel claim, so, unfortunately, I can't process it.
   (d) When you create your PowerPoint slides, do not underestimate the importance of using parallel structure.
   (e) I hope the enclosed proposal will provide all the information you need to make a decision.

3. Test your online diplomacy skills by revising the following comments to make them suitable to send via email to your supervisor.
   (a) I really need a week off; I'm just whacked after all that overtime last week.
   (b) Why can't those idiots in Finance get something right for a change? This is the third week in a row they've screwed up my paycheque.
   (c) I'm dying to get onto that project team!!!

4. Following is the body of a collection letter written in 1915 (Gardner, p. 190). Revise it to make it suitable to send to a modern-day customer. Remember to give your message an appropriate subject line, greeting, and closing.

Your account, as appearing on our books, shows an unpaid balance of the amount indicated above. We have previously sent a detailed statement, but as yet we have received no reply.

This may be through some oversight, or possibly your remittance is already on its way, in which case we will promptly credit it upon its receipt. If by any chance there is some reason why you are withholding payment, may we ask that you kindly inform us of it.

You will readily understand that the very nature of this business calls for a rigid adherence to the doctrine of prompt pay, both as applied to ourselves and to our customers; and our best customers are those most willing to pardon us for insisting that they live up to our terms.

We shall be greatly obliged for your prompt attention to this matter.

Chapter 8

Creating High-Performance Web Pages

It's quite possible, thought Sean, that Joyline is insane. Or at least mildly mentally incapacitated. She's asked me to create a product description for the new website, but she's only allowed me 300 words. How on earth am I going to encapsulate the amazing functionality of this product in that miniature space? After all, we're talking about a product so revolutionary that it's soon going to make the Blackberry look as antiquated as a rotary telephone.

Sean could take a lesson from David Letterman's Top Ten lists. Now that we live in the age of the electronic text, we also live in the age of writing-by-list. Traditional paragraphs like this one are becoming obsolete in electronic media. To overcome his dilemma, Sean will need to adjust his assumptions about the structure his product description will take, the writing style he'll use, and the amount of detail he'll include.

Although many web developers distinguish between the copy (the text for the site) and the design (the graphical elements, general layout, and structure of the site), the really good developers know that it's all of a piece. On the web, to separate writing from design is like trying to view a painting apart from the canvas.

Drawing on the rhetorical principles we've examined, the following sections deliver a set of practical tips for creating compelling online content.

Tip #1—Write for users, not readers

No one actually "reads" online—at least not the way you'd curl up in a comfortable armchair and read a novel or magazine. Instead, we use web pages the way we'd use an encyclopedia. "Surfing" only partially describes how move from page to page and site to site. "Hunting" and "foraging" are more apt terms. That's why the age of Googling has spawned a new industry dealing specifically with how to make sites show up more often in search-engine results.

People use writing on the web the same way they use a computer program. If you want to attract and retain their attention, then, you'll need to write for users, not readers. One way to achieve this is to pepper your text with keywords that people are likely to use when searching for information on your topic. On a more general level, however, writing for users means thinking of your pages not as *content*-driven but rather as *function*-driven.

Think of users as wealthy big-game hunters on a guided expedition. They want to be taken to the lion as directly as possible so they can get a clear shot, bag their prize, and be back to the camp in time for cocktails. They tend to be so impatient that they'll allow a web page mere seconds to satisfy their needs. Effective pages, then, need to deliver the goods in great haste. As Irene Hammerich and Claire Harrison, authors of *Developing Online Content,* note: "The key to a seductive website is immediate gratification" (2002, p. 38).

Communications consultant Ginny Redish (2004) suggests you provide such gratification by considering the user's goal in visiting the site. (Remember the first principles of the TACT method: to think about the *type* of document your *audience* requires to achieve particular goals within a particular *context.*) Following are some of Redish's recommendations for producing four distinct varieties of web pages:

Home pages should orient the reader to the site. They should clearly identify its purpose and structure, without a lot of busy chitchat to distract the reader. Because people want to figure out where they need to go and then move along as quickly as possible, it's more accurate to think of your home page as a doorway than as a lobby. Avoid, therefore, the temptation to welcome the reader, indulge in self-promotion, or philosophize about your organization's "mission." As usability consultant Steve Krug quips, "Happy talk must die" (2000, p. 46). Instead of wasting time in idle chitchat, sum up the essence of the organization in a catchy, pithy phrase, or "tag line." Here are some effective tag lines of real companies to ponder as examples:

- IronSentry: Simplifying Email Management
- Premiere Van Lines: The Art of Moving
- LimeLight Communications Group: Delivering Inspiring Speakers
- Rapid Relay: Ground Transportation Connections

Navigation pages should concentrate on presenting clear, straightforward menus, with as little additional content as possible. Readers in this phase of the information hunt aren't yet ready to digest large passages. At this stage, says Redish, users want simply to skim and choose, so extra details will only encumber them.

The main principle is to focus on one function at a time. Just because we live in the era of multi-tasking doesn't mean people enjoy having to split their focus between multiple activities. Base your page design and content on the knowledge that web users are happiest when they're single-tasking.

Content pages should, like navigation pages, allow users to skim and choose, but for a different purpose. Once information-hunters reach a content page, they're ready to read the material you have to present, but they're still seeking the ideas or data that interest them. They hop from keyword to keyword, heading to heading, pausing only to grab the minimal information they need to meet their objective (to find their answer, solve their problem, or make their purchase).

As we'll see, it requires thoughtful structuring to create so-called "sticky" pages that attract and retain users' attention and help them obtain the information they need. Although it's often tempting to "repurpose" a paper document simply by loading it into an HTML editor or a content-repurposing software program, making the transition from page to screen requires not cosmetic adjustments but profound changes.

Forms pages should make it easy for users to input information. Here, the typical user situation is reversed; rather than trying to convince users to accept your content, you need to persuade them to give you the content you want. The realm of form design lies outside the parameters of this book, but a few basic principles are worth mentioning here:

- A forms page is not a navigation page or a content page.
- The more clearly you spell out your purpose in requesting the information, the more likely your user is to supply it.
- Conciseness and consistency make forms easy to fill out.
- The "personality" of your website comes across through the forms you design just as surely as it does through the other types of content you create.

Tip #2—Create a web persona, not a web page

Just as your email messages engender an online personality, so do your web pages, especially the written content in them. Even though design and text work together, "content is king in the user's mind," according to usability researchers Jakob Nielsen and John Morkes. Drawing on laboratory research, they explain: "When asked for feedback on a web page, users will comment on the quality and relevance of the content to a much greater extent than they will comment on navigational issues or the page elements that we consider to be 'user interface'" (Morkes & Nielsen, 1997).

Like people, websites can appear friendly or standoffish, warm or cool, genuine or phony. One way to evaluate the perceived emotional sincerity of your web persona is to read your writing aloud. Does it feel natural and easy? Would you feel comfortable delivering it as a phone script or saying it to someone in conversation? You'll know your web persona sounds real if you're able to answer "yes" to such questions.

Assessing tone is a good first step, but creating a persona that users will like and trust requires that you do more. *Ethos* is everything. Simply indicating the source of the site's content can help greatly in this regard. Remember also that the "About Us" section of any website is the most obvious spot for users to go to scrutinize your credibility. On this page, and throughout the site, you can create rapport by referring to your company or organization as "we" rather than, let's say, "Smith & Smith Solutions." Employee photos and profiles also help users perceive your company or organization as a "you" rather than an "it." Even as small a detail as including the name and contact information of your webmaster can humanize your website.

How do you know what kind of personality characteristics, besides sincerity and trustworthiness, your site should convey? Before you start profiling your persona, pay a trip back to the drawing board to revisit your audience analysis. The clearer picture you have of your users, the easier you'll find it to construct a character to meet them.

When you're thinking about the characteristics you'd like users to ascribe to your site, you may find it useful to consider the following question: if your site were a restaurant, what kind of *maitre d'* would you want to greet your guests? If your users come from a laid-back, easygoing group, then maybe you want a bright-eyed, energetic host who approaches customers with a wide smile and a "Hi there? How you doin' today?" If, on the other hand, your users tend to be sophisticated and reserved (perhaps even skeptical), then you're probably looking for somebody quite different. Instead of bubbly, you want self-assured and polite, someone who's friendly but respectful.

Here's a pair of examples to demonstrate how two sites can embody dramatically different personas in the way they approach their users.

Example #1

University Copy Centre

> Our computers run 24/7 so you don't have to run all over town trying to print that essay that's due tomorrow morning. You'll find us at the top of the escalator in the Student Centre. Just follow your nose to Joe's Java Hut—we're right next door.

Example #2

Bridgeway Business Centre

> Clients have access to computers with Internet 24 hours a day. The centre is located at 602 Canal Street, across from the Bridgeway-Rushton Mall.

As you can see, the examples communicate the same essential message—that the copy shop in question has computers that are available any time of day or night. However, does one sound friendlier to you than the other? Based on the tone of the text, what assumptions do you make about the author of the copy? If you were surfing from site to site looking for somewhere you could print an essay, which of the two copy centres would you be more likely to visit?

Notice the way that the above examples create a definite persona for the implied user as well as for the site itself. For a web text to succeed, it must imply a user role that's "playable" (Coney & Steehouder, 2000). The text for the University Copy Centre site, for instance, assumes that people visiting the site are students who need to print essays. What if, however, the user is not an essay-writer at all? What if she's a Physics major who needs to do some late-night Internet research to help her understand an upcoming lab? Would she be able to picture herself using the services of the University Copy Centre, which include Internet access? If not, she may keep surfing until she finds another business that seems more ready to meet her needs, even though the campus option would actually be more convenient for her.

Tip #3—Follow the journalist, not the essay writer

Since web users peruse pages at a frantic pace, and since even the most diligent among them tend to be reluctant scrollers, smart writers organize material as they would for an email: they put the most important idea up front.

Writing instructors are fond of referring to this arrangement as an element of traditional "journalistic style." Pick up today's newspaper and you'll see this style in any news article (but not an opinion column or a feature article). The most important facts come directly under the headline, in an opening sentence known as the "lead."

As journalists know, however, simply drawing in readers at the beginning of a story doesn't guarantee they'll linger to hear the end. You have to keep hooking and re-hooking them as the story progresses. William Horton (1997), author of *Secrets of User-Seductive Documents*, maintains that electronic documents such as web pages must offer sequential incentives to users so that they'll persist in reading. You need to figure out how to lure users on from line to line.

Horton emphasizes transitions and structure, arguing that a clear sense of the direction of your thought will help readers eagerly anticipate what's coming next. He recommends linking an idea at the end of one paragraph to the first idea of the next, setting up a consistent enticement-reward system for readers.

Tip #4—Structure your content in chunks, not paragraphs

Laboratory studies have shown that it takes readers 25 per cent more time to process text on a screen than it does text on a page (Nielsen 1997). Researchers once blamed poor screen resolution, prompting a wave of new, supposedly easy-to-read fonts designed especially for the screen. (Georgia and Verdana were two of the most popular.) However, subsequent studies have shown that these new fonts have not improved onscreen reading speeds (Boyarski et al. 1998).

We can compensate for slower reading in several ways. The first strategy is to present your information in "chunks" of easy-to-locate, easy-to-digest units. That way, users can select the pieces of information that interest them and read those pieces in whichever sequence they choose.

You can visually cue web surfers to recognize chunks of information. To separate one chunk from another, you can use bulleted lists, extra white space, horizontal rules, or differing fonts. Some of these cues are subtle, but they have an impact on the way a visitor navigates your material.

It's important that you don't miscue your reader by visually signalling that information belongs to a chunk when it really doesn't. For instance, consider the following example from a (fictitious) site promoting a telecommunications company:

Last year, more than 200 new clients took advantage of our Prime Partner services. These include the following:

- Unlimited long distance calls

- 10% discount on high-speed Internet

- Free text messaging with any Silver or Gold wireless plan

- $50 gift certificate to use at any of our retail outlets

- Don't forget that we've waived the enrollment fee for the month of August. To take advantage of this offer now, click here to access the online registration form.

If the aim here is to persuade potential clients to become Prime Partners, then the person who wrote the copy may be disappointed. By lumping the enrollment instructions together with the list of specific services, the writer risks confusing—and therefore losing—the user.

Imagine this scenario. Let's say you've already researched the Prime Partner plan, and you've come to the website looking specifically for an online enrollment form. (In other words, like most users, you're out to perform a mission, not just wandering for recreation.) Based on visual cues, you might assume that all of the bulleted items describe services and skip the entire list.

On the other hand, someone who doesn't know anything about the Prime Partner deal might be momentarily thrown off balance by the abrupt shift in the final point. From the point of view of the web writer, this is hazardous because a confused user does not tend to be a trusting user. By appearing disorganized, the writer undermines the site's credibility.

Tip #5—Pay careful attention to headings

Once you've grouped your ideas into manageable chunks, you need to provide clear labels for those units, normally in the form of headings.

It never fails to amaze me just how few writers use headings effectively. Many authors seem to view them as purely ornamental, as if it's nice to have one or two just for appearance's sake. Headings, however, serve more than one important function. For readers coping with information overload (that's most of us), headings provide convenient footholds for navigating rapidly through a text. By setting up expectations as to what's coming, they also enable users to read selectively. Employing headings effectively is one of the simplest ways I know to earn an audience's respect and gratitude.

On the web, headings perform as vital a role as headlines do in newspapers. Marketers tell us that we live in an "attention economy," in which the main resource in demand is time—the time readers and listeners have to attend to the continual avalanche of information. To persuade users to invest precious attention in web copy, create headings that are descriptive, concise, and parallel.

Descriptive headings let the user know exactly what's next on the agenda. They enable busy "readers" to fulfill their goal, which is to avoid reading whenever possible. Like descriptive subject lines for email messages, descriptive headings use precise, concrete language, as in the following examples:

Nondescript heading	Descriptive heading
The current situation	Current contract with AMP Cable
History	Past attempts to reduce development time
Qualifications	Springwater's experience designing POS systems
Background	Why we need another Level II secretary

Whenever the genre and format allow it, I'd recommend you capture your reader's attention with headings that indicate exactly the content to follow. If you're having trouble converting a conventional, bland heading to something more accurate and captivating, you might find it helpful to express your headings initially as questions rather than phrases.

Let's take a brief detour to the land of report-writing to see how this tactic works. Imagine that Lina, leader of the Product Development team, is writing a report for her boss, Stephan, on how to improve communication between freelance technical writers and software developers. The preliminary headings she conceives for her report might look like this:

- History of the problem
- Analysis
- Recommendations

Lina quickly realizes, however, that these headings don't give Stephan a clue about the content of her report. As a first step toward making her headings more descriptive, she tries posing them as a series of questions:

- Why do we need to improve communication between technical writers and developers?
- What has been done about the communication problem in the past?
- What are some new solutions we could try?
- What are the pros and cons of each solution?
- Which is the best solution?
- How can we implement the solution?

Now Lina has delineated a much clearer structure for her report. She's shown Stephan an obvious path from problem to solution so that he's not left wondering, "So what? Why should I care about any of this? Why do I need to read this?" Her next step is to turn her questions into succinct phrases. She revises her headings along with the other aspects of her report, and produces these results:

Causes of communication barriers

Past attempts to overcome communication barriers

Possible ways to improve communication
   – hire writers earlier
   – recruit writers with technical backgrounds
   – require writers to work on-site
   – encourage writers and developers to socialize

Changing our recruitment strategy to improve communication

As you can see from Lina's case, headings evolve along with a document. As your ideas change and develop, your headings should too. You've probably also noticed that, as Lina's thinking about her topic became clearer, she developed subheadings. Even when circumstances indicate that you should use conventional, pre-fabricated headings (as some organizational templates require), you can usually take the liberty of breaking down those familiar labels into more descriptive subheadings. By so doing, you'll respect your audience's established reading habits but avoid sacrificing clarity.

Fortunately, when you're writing for the web, your audience expects you to be innovative. Web users tend to be rather jaded. They're looking for original, attractive headings to grab their attention. Crawford Kilian (1999) says that web writers need to deliver users the "high joltage" information that delivers "the simple jolt of being readily understandable in one quick glance" (p. xviii). Strategically placed, carefully worded headings can go far toward creating that desired effect.

Concise headings capture the user's attention with the minimum number of words. Even first-level headings (the largest headings on a page) should contain themselves to a single line. If you make them longer, they'll start to look like body text, not heads, and they'll lose their effectiveness.

To compress your headings, apply the same principles you use to create brief subject lines for your email messages. Avoid articles (*a, an, the*), use concrete language, choose words with few syllables, and make the verbs carry the freight. In many situations, you'll also find you can instantly trim a heading by addressing the reader directly as "you" or by using a personal pronoun instead of the corporate name. As we've seen, using personal pronouns can produce the added benefit of creating a welcoming site persona.

Here are a few examples of wordy headings reduced to more concise forms:

Wordy
The reasons consumers should purchase an extra memory card

Concise
Why you need a memory card

Wordy
Applebaum Computer's Commitment to Quality Customer Service
Concise
We pick up and deliver

Wordy
Inexpensive web hosting solutions for small to medium-sized enterprises
Concise
Low-cost web hosting for small business

Besides being descriptive and concise, headings should also be parallel so that you create a balanced "look and feel," as designers say, and help those jaded users better retain the information.

Parallel headings follow the identical syntax (pattern of word arrangement) throughout a document or web page. For instance, if your first heading begins with a verb that is followed by a noun, then subsequent headings should do the same. In the following examples, you'll see that each of the three headings follow a pattern—noun, preposition, product name:

- Features of the DWX-500 Digital Camera
- User instructions for the DWX-500 Digital Camera
- FAQ about the DWX-500 Digital Camera

By preserving the same syntax in every heading, you make it easier for users to skim and speed-read their way through your website. In this situation, repetition doesn't bore the user. On the contrary, establishing a clear pattern and sticking with it will earn you the user's gratitude. Parallel headings provide users with easy-to-grip toeholds in the text, so they can jump from one section to another. In long texts, they also help unify the writing, something that can be difficult to do online, where you have little control over the order in which your reader processes your sentences.

You may feel that my sample parallel headings above are rather lengthy because they repeat the full name of the product. The repetition is deliberate. Since you can't predict just where in your text a user will jump in or jump out, you must provide clear orientation signals to accommodate different entry and exit points. In the world of hypertext, you can't assume that a reader who enters a piece of writing at the level of a subheading will view the main heading as well.

Tip #6—Build captivating lists

The crucial matter of parallelism applies to bulleted lists as well. It's not just a question of making your page look pretty, although symmetry and balance are indeed important design principles. Research hints that parallelism can increase persuasiveness. Drawing on insights from cognitive science, University of Maryland professor Jeanne Fahnestock (2003) explains as follows: "When several parallel items are perceived in a series, the second or third items follow a path of construal prepared by the first. They satisfy an immediate expectation. Our minds are constructed to be receptive to repeated verbal or visual forms in any of their possible dimensions" (p.148).

This suggests that simply giving our bulleted lists a parallel structure helps us captivate online readers. Here's an example of a bulleted list that lacks parallel structure. How many different ways can you think of to address this weakness?

Automated banking machines have caused several improvements:

1. faster service
2. more accurate transactions
3. there are no statements to mail

The imbalance occurs in the third point. Whereas the first two points are phrases, the last one is a complete sentence. As is common, the lack of grammatical parallelism indicates a larger, conceptual problem. The focus of the argument the list presents is actually divided. Whereas the first two items take the point of view of the customer (who is able to take advantage of faster, more accurate service), the last item abruptly shifts the point of view to the bank (to whose advantage it is to reduce mailing costs). Here are a couple of possible rewrites that overcome the problem. (You have likely thought of other possibilities, too.)

Revision 1

Automated banking machines have caused several improvements:

1. faster service
2. more accurate transactions
3. cost-effective electronic statements

Revision 2

Automated banking machines have caused several improvements:

1. customers obtain faster service
2. customers receive more accurate transactions
3. customers get up-to-date electronic statements

These two revisions resolve the perspective problem in two different ways. Revision 1 creates unity by viewing the advantages from a global perspective, whereas Revision 2 adopts the customer's perspective throughout. While Revision 2 exhibits a sharper focus, I'm sure you've noticed that it's also rather wordy. Here's how an additional revision to Revision 2 might appear:

Revision 2A

Automated banking machines deliver customers the following advantages:

1. faster service
2. more accurate transactions
3. up-to-date electronic statements

One final word about creating effective bulleted lists. To link a bulleted list to the text that precedes it, you need a colon, which performs a trumpeter role, announcing forthcoming information that will illustrate or support the point. To sound the fanfare properly, the colon must appear at the end of a complete thought, expressed as either a heading or a complete sentence, but not as a sentence fragment.

It's not always easy to recognize this distinction. In fact, in creating Revision 2A, I fell into the very trap I'm cautioning you to avoid. Here's what my first attempt looked like:

Automated banking machines have improved customer service by providing:

1. faster service
2. more accurate transactions
3. up-to-date electronic statements

What's the matter here? To spot the irregular punctuation usage, substitute a period for the colon at the end of the introductory statement. It's obvious now that the thought is incomplete. The final revision rectifies this breach of Standard Edited Written English.

Tip #7—Follow through on information design

Because we predict future behaviour based on past behaviour, we tend to be most comfortable with people who act predictably. Thus, we need to make sure that we enact a given web persona consistently by monitoring a wide range of factors that come under the umbrella of "information design." Individual elements include headings, fonts, list formats, word choice, paragraph length, and sentence structure.

Information design principles grow out of the premise that the physical appearance of a text never functions as a mere façade to dress up language. Rather, it embodies written thought, and thus is inseparable from it. The German word for "typeface," *schriftbild*, aptly encapsulates this true nature of writing as a mode of both graphical and linguistic representation (Stöckl 2005, p. 206). Literally translated, *schriftbild* means "writing picture."

To derive the benefits of effective information design, you'll need to begin by considering textual content as contributing to a site's graphical effect. Then, you'll need to expand your notion of that content to cover more than just "copy." Think of "web writing" as referring to any text you see on the screen. That includes text that traditionally falls into the designer's, (rather than the writer's) jurisdiction, such as the words on navigation buttons, menus, and forms.

Have you ever witnessed someone undermine a professional appearance with one poorly chosen accessory or piece of clothing? Imagine, for instance, that you're a supervisor interviewing a potential employee, and a young woman walks in dressed in a tailored pant suit—and wearing a pair of beat-up basketball shoes on her feet. How seriously do you take her claim that she's "worked closely with executives in a high-profile office for several years"? Like the job candidate's unfortunate smelly sneakers, inconsistent writing—wherever it appears on a web page—can irreparably injure a website's visual impact.

Let's say that you're creating copy for a corporate site, and you refer to the company throughout with the pronouns "we" and "our." Your amiable tone could be seriously compromised if the site designer plugs in ready-made copy for the "About Us" page that refers to "Simplex Solutions Limited," "the company," and "it." Damage to your tone could occur if you refer to the "Customer Care Department" in your text but the contact form refers to the "Customer Service Team." Any inconsistency poses a potential threat because it could distract, confuse, and irritate your impatient users.

If God is indeed in the details, as a famous architect once remarked, then style sheets can help you keep track of divinely important information. Long before Cascading Style Sheets (CSS) for HTML, copy editors started the practice of using paper style sheets to monitor the various design elements, such as heading size, typeface, colour, leading (line spacing), and indentation. In its most basic form, a style sheet simply provides a record of each design decision a writer makes. Most word-processing programs now include a feature that makes it easy to generate a customized style guide as you compose.

Tip #8—Use hyperlinks sparingly, not for special effect

To link or not to link, that is the question—probably the most perplexing one you'll face as a web writer. On one side of the debate, there are those who argue that writers should take advantage of hypertext whenever they can, since hotlinking is what makes online reading differ dramatically from paper-based reading. On the other side of the question, there are those who argue that hyperlinks distract highly distractible users and make online reading more laborious.

A reasonable approach is to choose the middle road. Hyperlinks are valuable because they enable writers to break up text into multi-screen chunks, thus reducing the need for scrolling. Used judiciously, they enrich the multimedia experience. Wouldn't creating web pages without hyperlinks be like purchasing a sports car with all the latest bells and whistles but never leaving your driveway?

To pursue this sports car analogy a bit further, when you're trying to draw the fine line between enough hypertext and too much, consider who your drivers are and where they're driving. If you're writing text for learners (perhaps part of an online tutorial or in-context Help), then your drivers may want to see plenty of road signs, and they may also require the freedom to take their time and explore back roads. In such a situation, it might be advisable to employ hypertext frequently so that users can access definitions of unfamiliar material, get help putting that material in context, and choose a path that suits their individual learning style. If, on the other hand, you're writing text for experienced, high-speed drivers who are in a hurry to get where they're going, then you might want to limit your use of hypertext to avoid slowing them down.

However much you use hypertext, you'll need to reflect on what Hammerich and Harrison term "the rhetoric of departure and arrival" (p. 181). The way you handle hyperlinks conveys an attitude, encouraging users to impute characteristics to your web persona. When you think about it, clicking on a hyperlink requires a leap of faith on the user's part. They have to trust that you won't take them somewhere inappropriate or abandon them by failing to show them the way back. To sustain a reliable persona, it's essential to preserve that trust. You can achieve this, Hammerich and Harrison suggest, by creating courteous departures and "safe landings" (pp. 181–84).

A courteous departure tells users where the hyperlink leads so they know exactly what to expect. Here's a scenario that violates this principle:

Click here to learn more.

Although this link is appropriately brief, it's the online equivalent of a highway exit sign that says, "That-a-way." Could it lead to a more detailed textual description of the product or service? Perhaps. It could also lead to a visual description (photos or diagrams), to client testimonials, or to a contact form. Because "more" is so ambiguous, the signpost sets some of your users up for frustration.

To avoid such confusion, establish clear expectations in the user's mind. If the link leads to a contact form, say so: "Use our convenient contact form to reach us." If it leads to a detailed technical description, then say that: "The technical description provides further details." In either case, avoid keeping the reader in suspense. Spine-tingling mystery is the stuff of detective fiction, not web pages.

Once you've indicated where the link will take users, you need to ensure that those users arrive safely there. That means checking and double-checking for broken or dead links, especially if you're linking to an external site. It also means linking as closely as you can to the specific text or image so that your user doesn't have to plow through layers of material to find the desired piece of information. (Be careful here, though, because "deep linking" to a page below the first level of an external site can raise copyright issues.) In some cases, you may have to include travel tips ("Scroll down to the bottom of the home page to access the contact list.").

Some of the decisions concerning hyperlinks commonly fall to the so-called web "designer," rather than the writer. However, carrying out effective information design sometimes requires team members to rethink assigned roles—be prepared to work around fences and across gaps in your organization so that the writing and design work in tandem.

Tip #9—Be brief, ~~not wordy~~

Think of conciseness as increasing the value of each word you write, and condense, condense, condense.

We've seen how the process of "writing" involves far more than producing letters on a page or screen. In fact, the leaner the text, the more "writing" is required before and after composing takes place. When you're crafting an electronic text, be prepared to invest extra time in revising—and revising, and revising—your words.

Jakob Nielsen recommends that web writing be twice as concise as writing for paper formats. To achieve this, take advantage of all the design elements that HTML facilitates, particularly bulleted lists and tables. Use the techniques presented in Chapter 5 to eliminate chatter, lengthy jargon, and filler phrases.

If you're really struggling to cram your meaning into the extreme space limitations of a web page, then maybe the shoe—that is, the medium—doesn't quite fit. Rather than maiming a longer piece of writing in order to publish it on the web, consider presenting it in PDF format for people to print.

Bonus tip—Apply tips for web writing to ordinary writing

Although you may not believe that web writing lies in your future, thinking like a web writer will help you to succeed in a variety of other writing tasks. Contemporary business communication is adopting many of the techniques of digital rhetoric (such as short sentences, frequent bulleted lists, and leading topic sentences). Nowadays, we're moving toward what we might call an IText style.

Writing theorists have recently coined the label "IText" to describe "the blend of IT and texts" (Gerber et al. 2001, p. 270) that constitutes digital writing, online and offline. ITexts function in unique ways because they occur at the point where written language and the means of producing it merge. Form fuses with communication medium to challenge the traditional ways we define what "writing" means.

In the next chapter, we'll examine more closely the relationships between form, medium, and function, as we explore some writing genres common to the IT workplace.

Exercises

1. Applying the writing tips discussed in this chapter, adapt the following passage to make it appropriate for publication on the web. (Your final draft should be half the length of the original.)

    > Today, many businesses, both large and small, fall into the error of assuming that a piece of text originally prepared for print-based publication will translate automatically into effective online text. Nothing, however, could be farther from the truth. To begin with, writing on paper tends to be far more expansive than is appropriate on the web, so most texts need to be significantly reduced—normally by about half—in order to make the transition from page to screen. In addition, most paper-based texts follow imaginatively impoverished layouts, whereas web writing needs to make maximum use of simple, but effective design to gain the writer's attention. Finally, there are a number of specific behaviours web writers need to avoid. These include using slang or regional expressions, requiring horizontal scrolling, and adopting a line length longer than 60 characters.

2. Improve the following lists by aligning the points using parallel structure, and correcting any improper usage of the colon.

    a. Recruiters say that young Canadians can make themselves attractive job candidates by:

    -   Developing strong interpersonal skills
    -   Learning to solve problems independently
    -   Experience in working with people from diverse cultures
    -   Building on a strong core of technical ability

    b. Reading on the web is slower than reading from paper for the following reasons:

    -   Scrolling frequently interrupts the user
    -   Eye strain
    -   Poor text resolution on computer monitors
    -   Unnecessary graphics distract users

    c. Web developers and web content providers need to collaborate closely because:

    -   Consistency is key to a website's success.
    -   Opportunity for savings in time and money
    -   A collaborative environment encourages ongoing revision, especially when it's a question of a longer project.

3. Rewrite the following passage to suggest a more friendly, energetic persona.

   Company Background

   Liminal Productions has been operating as a full-time, full-service production company since 1985. During that time, it has initiated many well-known projects, including the HarbourSafe video series.

   Liminal Productions was started by Mr. Bruce Joggins, who graduated from Sheridan College with a diploma in computer animation in 1983. Mr. Joggins had always felt a keen desire to pursue a career in the field of animation, and a grant from the Youth Entrepreneurship Forum allowed him to realize this dream.

   Gradually, Mr. Joggins has built up his client list over the years by providing premium customer service to each and every customer. His People First award to the employee with the best monthly record in customer service has helped a great deal in this regard. Today, Liminal Productions runs the premier animation studio in western Canada.

4. Make the following headings more concise.

   a. The key differences between the former product and the new version
   b. The advantages of our product over the competition's product
   c. Instructions on how to assemble the router
   d. Registration procedure for this year's corporate retreat

Part 3

Adapting to Professional Forms

Chapter 9

Genre Guidelines for Some Common IT Documents

You may not be able to tell just by looking at the page, but there's something very different about the chapter you're now reading: I wrote almost the entire book on a PC, but I composed this final chapter on a Macintosh computer. At first, this wasn't easy. Even though the Mac interface is more intuitive and user-friendly, I had to overcome several ingrained assumptions about how a computer should work before I became comfortable with it.

As an on-the-job writer, you'll need to revisit frequently your own assumptions about how writing works. Thanks largely to the predominance of ITexts, conventions are rapidly evolving. It's no longer adequate to be able to follow set formats for reports, proposals, and other common classes of workplace documents. As Mignona Cote, a senior manager at Nortel, told me, "We're moving too quickly to use traditional communication models."

At Nortel, for example, formal reports hardly exist any more. Rather than producing lengthy paper documents, employees write two-to-three-paragraph email messages or create PowerPoint presentations. Cote encourages staff to think beyond habitual ways of delivering written information. She promotes what she calls "scoreboard reporting," which enables employees to quickly rank recommendations, or "dashboard reporting," which uses coloured traffic signals to indicate whether a writer approves or rejects an idea. "Quick and flashy," she says, is the way to go.

Cote's comments remind us that genre is best understood as a matter of function as well as form. Carolyn Miller (1984) established this when she challenged writing instructors to define genre primarily as "social action." In the midst of ever-shifting technologies and formats, focusing on a document's intended social action (use and purpose) can clarify appropriate choices concerning such rhetorical elements as structure, tone, style, and design.

Those are choices you'll have to make for yourself as you undertake various writing tasks. I could easily provide you with a fistful of useful templates for such common writing tasks as The Report, The Proposal, or The Press Release. I'm afraid, though, that in the end you wouldn't find such standardized solutions very useful. Instead, I offer in this chapter some flexible guidelines for five common genres you're likely to produce in the workplace: slide presentations, progress reports, proposals, design documents, and instructions. As you read through these, please remember that you can apply them successfully only if you supplement them with careful audience analysis. The guidelines in themselves will not substitute for a full rhetorical strategy, but they should help you develop one to suit your particular situation.

Slide presentations

Since slides are a medium of communication rather than a genre, your slide presentation could fall into any number of categories—such as the proposal, the report, the informative presentation, or the sales pitch. The medium does influence the characteristics of each genre, however, which is why I want to deal with it separately here. It's important to recognize its strengths and also its limitations.

The most commonly used software for putting together slide presentations is Microsoft's PowerPoint. Derek Anderson, a manager with a large audio/video production company, AVW-TELAV Audio Visual Solutions, witnesses thousands of PowerPoint conference presentations each year. He warns that most of them fall prey to the temptation of letting technology eclipse content. "People fall in love with technology," he observes, "but if they put as much thought into the content of the slides as the design they'd be better off." When a presenter overuses the features in the software, Anderson questions the person's competence: "I don't know whether it's PowerPoint controlling the show, or the individual." Anderson recommends keeping slides simple, short, and uncluttered so that the audience can focus on the speaker.

Anderson isn't alone in his opinion that PowerPoint should be used sparingly, if at all. Yale professor Edward Tufte has delivered notorious attacks against software-supported presentations. His pamphlet, *The Cognitive Style of PowerPoint*, goes so far as to blame PowerPoint for dumbing down discussions not just in the corporate world but also in schools, churches, and scientific contexts. In fact, in one of his most controversial claims, he argues that the use of PowerPoint slides helped cause the crash of the space shuttle Columbia (Tufte 2003, pp. 7–11).

In an article for *Wired* magazine, Tufte sums up his numerous complaints against slide presentations this way: "The standard PowerPoint presentation elevates format over content, betraying an attitude of commercialism that turns everything into a sales pitch" (2003, Sept.). Tufte's criticisms of the technology may be harsh, but he's reacting against an enthusiasm for PowerPoint that is also extreme. In many situations, presenters assume that PowerPoint will help them make their points, without stopping to think whether the software will actually enhance clear communication or hinder it.

Part of Tufte's outrage seems to stem from the common practice of using slides as stand-alone documents. There's a vast difference between creating slides to accompany a presentation (the task for which PowerPoint is designed) and creating them to substitute for a written report. In reality, though, communication is often so rushed that people use PowerPoint as a kind of shortcut, and slides end up circulating on their own.

Whenever you're required to prepare a slide presentation, then, it's wise to ask how the slides will be used. Will they be posted online, for instance, or copied to the client in lieu of a proper summary? If possible, try to persuade your supervisor to use a more appropriate format for publishing a record of the presentation's ideas. If you don't win that argument, you might need to create two sets of slides: one to use with your presentation and one to circulate independently. Yes, this will require double the work, but the benefit is in avoiding a communication fiasco to mimic the shuttle disaster.

Assuming you're using PowerPoint to create slides for a live presentation, here are some general guidelines to help you avoid becoming a slave to the software:

1. *Recognize what PowerPoint can and can't do.*
   Stick with using the software for what it's designed to do—deliver skeletal, low-grade visual support for oral presentations. Realize that PowerPoint offers you limited screen size, with poor resolution. If you have a number of complex points to get across or a complicated visual (such as a detailed graph or table), then you probably need a handout rather than a slide. (Or you might use a handout to supplement your slide.) PowerPoint should not completely replace other kinds of visual aids any more than it should substitute for weak speaking skills.

2. *Avoid templates and wizards.*
   Unfortunately, ready-made templates and wizards lure speakers into the false belief that presentation software has made rhetoric passé. As with other forms of computer-mediated communication, however, the technology actually demands more work from us, not less.

   Before the advent of PowerPoint, presenters already had a full roster of details to manage, including their gestures, the pitch and volume of their voice, the rate of their speech, the structure of their ideas, and the timing of the presentation. Nowadays, speakers must still pay attention to all these, plus they have to design, integrate, and operate computerized visual support for their message. No template can enable a presenter to handle all these demands adroitly; only a responsive, customized rhetorical strategy can hold the whole show together. Nine times out of ten, you simply can't bake an effective PowerPoint presentation from a mix, so don't even try.

3. *Distinguish your main points from your subordinate points.*
   Rather than trying to cram every idea you have into your presentation slides, choose carefully. Which are the key phrases or concepts you really need your audience to retain? If you could summarize your presentation in a single paragraph, which ideas would you include?

   If you find it difficult to pick out your main ideas, you might want to try writing an abstract for your presentation. Such an exercise forces you to distill your presentation down to a handful of key ideas. You might also find it useful to review the material in Chapter 4 on organizing ideas into a hierarchy. If you're finding it hard to discern your principal points, your confusion may actually be a warning signal that the structure of your ideas is too flat.

When designing your slides, keep in mind that oral presentations require more "signposts" than do written documents. Because live audiences don't have the luxury of re-reading your material, you need to review the material for them clearly. Strong presentations clearly position new material in the context of information that has come before. They also use obvious transition words to alert the audience to upcoming changes, such as the introduction of a new point, the reinforcement of a previous point, or a shift in the direction of the argument.

4. *Think visually.*

When you're mounting your main ideas on your PowerPoint slides, keep in mind that the text on your slides should complement, but not necessarily duplicate, the wording of your presentation. Many speakers seem to miss the main point of PowerPoint—that it serves as a visual aid for an oral message, not a mere carbon copy.

Recently, this point came to my attention when I accidentally brought home a "described" version of a movie, produced for the visually impaired. At first, I was rather startled by the narrative voice, which explained, moment by moment, exactly what I could already see the characters doing. Very quickly, though, my eyes and ears adjusted, and I was able to tune out the narration and focus simply on watching the screen. In this situation, the shift in my attention was deliberate, but how many viewers of PowerPoint shut down unconsciously on either the audio or video track?

It's difficult for us to process information from two separate channels simultaneously. To escape cognitive overload, we tend to ignore on one channel, especially if the information coming through seems to repeat the information we're already receiving via another channel. To get the most out of PowerPoint, then, think primarily in pictures and aim to produce a visual story to support, not supplant, your spoken words. Graphs, charts, and simple images can strengthen the impact of your presentation by dramatizing key elements, such as statistical achievements, growth patterns, and changes in relationships.

5. *Consider the ethics of visual rhetoric.*

Although charts, tables, and graphs may seem to convey information more impartially than language, in fact they use a visual language that produces its own biases. As Robin Kinross, among others, has pointed out, there's no such thing as neutral design; all visual representations, like textual ones, involve an element of persuasion, whether or not the designer is conscious of it. Gui Bonsiepe was one of the first thinkers to point out that the art of design inevitably intertwines with the art of persuasion to produce a visual rhetoric. His logic worked as follows:

> Information without rhetoric is a pipe-dream which ends up in the break-down of communication and total silence. "Pure" information exists for the designer only in arid abstraction. As soon as he begins to give it concrete shape, to bring it within the range of experience, the process of rhetorical infiltration begins. (Bonsiepe, "Visual/verbal rhetoric," p. 30)

Even a simple choice, such as whether to use a pie chart or a bar graph, can significantly influence an audience's interpretation. A pie chart, for instance, will tend to emphasize the big picture because it embodies data in terms of its relationship to the whole. A bar graph, on the other hand, draws attention to groups of data as discrete, competing categories. And, once you've decided on the overall form of your graph, you've only just begun to negotiate your way through a labyrinth of design decisions. Where and how should you label the visual? Should you title it? Which font(s) should you use? What about colours, shading, and line widths? How should you size the visual? How should you orient it on the page? Each of the selections you make reflects your point of view concerning the material, and the options you choose will affect the meaning your audience derives from the figure.

Because PowerPoint is really designed to accommodate only simple images, users of the software need to be acutely aware of the rhetorical value of their design choices. If you find yourself trying to squeeze too complex a visual onto a slide, then you may need to use a paper handout instead or perhaps break the data into two or more screens. When you do present graphs, tables, or charts in PowerPoint, make sure that you include accurate, legible titles and labels, even if you mention these orally.

6. *Respect the conventional principles of good design.*
Although slide design should evolve from rhetorical purpose, most experts agree on some basic design principles that are worth bearing in mind:

- Use no more than three to five colours. (Here's where the built-in templates can actually help, as they provide attractive, easy-to-view colour schemes.)
- Tailor your colour scheme to the room in which you'll be presenting: light text on dark background for a bright room; dark text on light background for a dim room.
- Use the same colour for the same type of information throughout your presentation. For example, if you use royal blue for the first top-level headings, reserve royal blue for top-level headings throughout the slide show.

- Exercise cultural sensitivity when choosing a colour scheme. The meanings we associate with colours are not universal. For instance, while the colour of mourning is black in the West, in China, it's white.

- If you're using a company logo, position it in the same place on every screen. Consistency is a fundamental principle of all good design.

- Provide a heading or title for every screen. These serve as orientation signals for people whose attention drifts.

- Consider the PowerPoint screen as a grid and balance the distribution of text and images across it. (Avoid using only the left side of the screen, for instance.)

- Ensure that images and symbols obviously support your message. Miscellaneous, unrelated images do nothing to "jazz up" a presentation. Instead, they distract and confuse your audience. (Your listeners will spend more time trying to figure out how the bright green leprechaun relates to the fourth-quarter sales figures than they will reflecting on the sales numbers themselves.) Such "chartjunk" (Tufte, "Powerpoint") is just waste of pixels.

- Verify that images will appear clearly. PowerPoint is a far cry from Photoshop. You will likely need to play with both the format and resolution to make your image visible for your audience.

- Steer clear of animated graphics; they make it very difficult for your audience to focus on either the words on your slide or the words coming out of your mouth. For the same reason, it's best to avoid background sound effects.

- Use a sans serif font (such as Arial) in at least a 22-point typeface. Stick to standard fonts, especially if you'll be delivering your presentation using a computer other than your own.

- Restrict text to no more than seven lines per screen. If you preserve your 22-point font, you'll find you can't fit in more than this anyway.

- Use parallel structure for bulleted points. (Review Chapter 8 for help with this.) Check, double-check, and triple-check spelling and punctuation. There's something about a glowing screen that makes technical errors even more glaring than when they appear on paper.

7. *Give credit where credit's due.*
   Without the convention of footnotes, it can become a tricky matter to indicate in an oral presentation the sources of your information. If you use the ideas or data of others, however, you need to let your audience know. Some of the ways you can fulfill this ethical responsibility include the following:

   - Indicate the source orally.

- Offer to provide full information about sources to interested audience members after the presentation.
- Create a concluding slide that lists references.
- Distribute a handout listing references.

Depending on your situation, you may want to use more than one of the above suggestions. As always, let your knowledge of the specific audience and context determine the appropriate presentation of your information. The way you refer to your sources can play an important role in establishing your credibility and thus your persuasiveness as a presenter.

8. *Use your body as your primary presentation aid.*
Chris Little is an actor-turned-sales-representative for MathResources, a company that produces educational software. His advice for producing truly powerful PowerPoint presentations is, like Derek Anderson's, remarkably simple: never forget that your presentation is about you and your ideas, not your software and slides. Like an actor, you need to prepare and rehearse as much as you can and then, when you're speaking, let go and enjoy the moment.

As with the design-related suggestions above, we can only touch briefly on presentation techniques in this book. It's worth noting the following tips from Little, however:

- **Find your feet.** Plant them firmly on the floor, shoulder-width apart, and keep them there unless you have a reason to move them. Some movement can keep a presentation alive, but aimless fidgeting creates visual static between you and your audience.
- **Look them in the eye.** In Western culture, direct eye contact encourages a feeling of trust. If your presentation is short and your audience is large, it's better to make eye contact with a few people in different parts of the room than to try to flit rapidly from one person to another. Glancing quickly around the room is not the same as connecting with people one-on-one.
- **Get to know your voice.** In his theatre workshops, Little directs participants to yell, hoot, and howl so loudly that they feel their voices bouncing off the wall back to them. "Many people have trouble speaking," he explains, "because they're actually afraid of the sound of their own voice." Try recording yourself so that you can experience hearing your voice as others hear it.
- **Be natural.** Many people run into trouble when they adopt an artificial public-speaking voice. Little comments: "I have heard many people who are charming and well spoken one-on-one but choose to throw this away when they speak in public. You have a lot more practice being you than you do being a newscaster or talk-show host. Use that experience to your advantage." On the other hand, Little does suggest

paying attention to your vocal dynamics (pitch, tone, rate, and volume), and warns that "monotony kills."

- **Plan for the unplanned.** Presenters should focus on responding to what is happening during the presentation so they can improvise as necessary. Becoming an effective presenter means knowing how to recover when the presentation breaks down, whether due to human or computer error. Little recommends "trainwrecking" (rehearsing without stopping to correct mistakes) as a way to build confidence and adaptability.

Progress reports

Progress reports are shape-shifters, changing their form according to the demands of a variety of factors, including the following:

- the organization's accounting procedures
- the organizational model of project management
- the project or process being described
- the reporting period
- the medium
- the shelf life of the report
- the writer's relationship to the target reader(s)

In some organizations, employees file progress reports at regular intervals (daily, weekly, or monthly); in other organizations, employees produce reports only when requested or when they decide it's time to update the boss on the status of a project. In either of these situations, submitting a progress report can mean simply filling in the blanks of a standard paper or electronic form, using a prescribed template, or creating your own design. Each of these instances, however, requires that the writer attend to the rhetorical challenges of the situation, which are often complex.

"There she goes complicating things, again," you might be sighing at this point. "How can creating a straightforward record of the work I've done result in a rhetorically 'complex' writing task?" Ahhh... many an employee has learned the answer to this question the hard way. You see, the label "progress report" is really something of a misnomer. I actually think of progress reports as "CYB docs," as in Cover Your Behind.

Progress reports can make or break your career. Within the genre restrictions (which can become painfully cramped in a standardized form), you have a chance to exhibit your work ethic, your way of relating to other employees, your problem-solving ability, and other intangible aspects of your character. Since readers will inevitably judge your personality and your promotability by the "progress" you've made, it's crucial to take the time to consider the subtle impressions your report will create.

To be minimally effective, a progress report should address three essential points:

- the work planned
- the work achieved
- the work remaining

Astute writers know, however, that progress reports often need to fulfill an additional number of tangential goals that fall into the categories of "personal" or "political." Such objectives might include the following:

- to convince a supervisor you deserve recognition for exceptional effort
- to avoid blame for a project that's floundering
- to reassure a nervous supervisor that the project will succeed
- to clarify points of confusion
- to provide information for a client update
- to negotiate adjusted terms for a project (such as a larger budget or a longer schedule)
- to create a record of your performance for a formal employee review process
- to remind the boss that you exist

As you can guess, many of these unstated goals help serve a "legacy" function, meaning that they create an enduring written record of your behaviour on the job. Down the road, your supervisor or an outside auditor might retrieve a humble progress report for any number of reasons: to assess your eligibility for a pay increase, to initiate a review of the work process, to track contributions of another employee, to sort out the historical development of a project gone awry, or to re-calculate the hours or expenses billed to a project. When you consider their possible long-term effects, you can see why those routine messages in fact merit especially careful handling.

The humble progress report provides an excellent opportunity for you to corroborate your character as a hard-working, organized, responsible, considerate employee. Here are a few tips to help you exploit the full potential of progress reports, while avoiding the typical pitfalls:

1. *Consider alternatives to chronological organization*
   For brief, straightforward reports, you may find it easiest to organize information in a simple timeline. (First we did this, then this. Next we'll do this.) However, in many cases, the chronological pattern makes it difficult for readers to extract quickly the information they need. The burning questions on a supervisor's mind normally relate to timelines and the bottom line (financial considerations). A typical supervisor is less interested in a blow-by-blow description of the work in progress, and more concerned with the overall picture. Is the project on track? Will it stay within the allotted budget? Are all the team members pulling their weight? Has the crisis that cropped up last week been overcome?

If you have the freedom to arrange information according to your preference, you might find it effective to group your information under three main headings:

- Work Planned
- Work Achieved
- Work Remaining

Alternatively, if you know your reader has particular concerns about the project, you might want to address those up front. For instance, if the project has been running over budget, you might want to deal with financial matters first under the heading "Budget Update" and then proceed to list your recent accomplishments and the work left to do.

2. Avoid over-narrativizing

One of the trickiest aspects of writing a progress report is determining how much information is enough. In general, it's wise to provide the minimal information your supervisor needs to assess the development of the work.

Avoid merely describing your project as a story. Your reader is not likely very keen on knowing the intricate details of the plot. Rather, he or she wants to know final outcomes and your plan for completing the task on time. In a bi-weekly report, for example, you don't need to inform your boss of your every action over the past two weeks, as the following rambling narrative does:

> On October 28th, I received the first lines of code from Fred. Then I began work on the testing. Then I ran the program through our standard testing procedure three times, as usual. The program tested fine, with only two minor bugs, which Janine fixed. I gave the program to her on October 30th. On November 2nd, she returned the program to me. I re-tested three times again and approved the program for release.

In this case, the writer could reduce the amount of tedious storytelling by compressing key information and dates into a paragraph as brief as this:

> Program testing began on October 28th. After Janine made minor revisions, I re-tested and approved the program on November 2nd.

3. Pay careful attention to tone

An effective progress report adopts a tone that is assertive but also polite. It's not always easy to balance the two qualities. Novice writers often slip into sounding either arrogant or apologetic.

You can make your voice confident without seeming to boss the boss. You can also truthfully recognize negative aspects of a situation without grovelling in penitence. (Here's where your ability to use impersonal subjects and the occasional passive voice will come in handy.)

To achieve the right tonal equilibrium, keep in mind the following tips:

- Use a neutral vocabulary; avoid words that portray emotion (such as *hope, afraid, feel, disappointing*).
- Address your supervisor as he or she prefers to be addressed. Be aware that addressing "Bob" as "Mr. Jones" is just as much a faux pas as addressing "Mr. Jones" as "Bob." The first mistake makes you appear unsure of yourself; the second makes you seem plain rude.
- If your report takes the form of a memo or email message, pay particular attention to the closing. Avoid weak, clichéd endings that imply doubt in your own competence, such as "Trusting this is satisfactory," "I hope this is agreeable," or "I hope this meets with your approval." Also stay away from closing comments that seem to condescend to your superior, especially "Thank you for your cooperation."
- Reserve the phrases "I'm sorry" and "I apologize" for only those situations for which you're willing to take full, legal responsibility. If you aren't culpable of the crime, don't shoulder the blame.

Refer to other employees diplomatically. Avoid criticizing a colleague in print because a written remark can have a long lifespan and travel far. The language choices you make can affect personal relationships, your reputation, and even performance evaluations.

4. Keep it positive—and honest
As discussed earlier, these two goals should not be mutually exclusive. If you've goofed, don't try to hide your blunder. If the project is two weeks behind schedule, it won't do anyone any good to pretend it's not. However, there's no need to make bad news even bleaker by emphasizing the negative.

Consider this negative message:

> Unfortunately, Meccanix Imports will be unable to process our order in time, so we'll have to make do with the product that Green Street Suppliers can provide.

You could express the same news more positively like this:

> Since the Meccanix parts will be on back order until July 2nd, I've ordered the remaining equipment from Green Street Suppliers so we can deliver to the client on time.

In many situations, whether the messenger gets shot is largely up to the messenger.

5. Address problems honestly and creatively
Sometimes, for both ethical and practical reasons, you just can't soft-pedal a problem as an "issue" or a "challenge"; you must face the dragon in your

path and deal with it head-on. Most supervisors appreciate an employee who recognizes a snag early on and reacts quickly to eliminate it. The key to keeping your supervisor in good humour is to recommend a way out of the problem you identify. Even if it's not your job to deal with staffing dilemmas, recalculate budgets, or manage client relations, you can help mitigate a crisis by offering—with due respect—creative solutions for your supervisor to consider.

Perhaps, for example, there's simply no way around the following situation: three team members have caught the flu, and it has become impossible for you to complete both of the projects that are due next Tuesday. This is indeed an urgent piece of information, and you'll need to deliver it directly so that your supervisor clearly understands the gravity of the situation. You don't, however, have to create a doomsday message.

Take advantage of the opportunity to show what a proactive, innovative, take-charge kind of worker you are. Maybe, you might suggest, Johanna from Team B could step in to lend a hand, or you could use some of the slack in the budget to hire that freelancer who was so great on the last project, or the company could offer one of the clients a discount for agreeing to shift the delivery date. Even if your supervisor doesn't implement any of your ideas, you'll have planted one idea firmly—that your problem-solving abilities make you a valuable contributor to the organization.

6. Demonstrate your awareness of organizational priorities

Mark Pettigrew is vice-president of VR Interactive, a company that produces hardware and software for 360-degree imaging. He says it's vital that writers keep the ultimate goal in view. He compares this point to the way car manufacturing works—three thousand employees may work on a single car, and each needs to understand how his or her individual tasks help construct the final product. Pettigrew complains that many IT professionals appear to see no further than the particular wheel or shaft on which they're working. You can show a broader vision by framing your progress report in terms of the overall objectives of the project and the organization.

7. Be precise, especially about financial information and timelines

A supervisor reading a progress report is likely looking for answers to the questions journalists use when they're trying to get to the crux of a situation as quickly as possible: *Who? What? Where? When? Why?* and *How?* For this reason, be specific about dates, measurements, and especially financial data. Rather than promising another update for "the middle of next week," for example, say that you'll send another report "on December 12th." Rather than guessing at upcoming costs, do your homework and provide an exact quote.

Provide your supervisor with all the information needed to evaluate the progress of the work and make related decisions. A precision-crafted progress report enables the reader to determine a course of action, if such action is required, without having to request additional information.

Investing time to make your report as specific as possible (in all the right places) will save your boss both time and money. It will also save you the headache of having to create additional mini-reports before you can proceed with your project.

8. Use headings, bulleted lists, charts, and tables

Use your graphical imagination to make it easy for your reader to get to the key information. Whenever possible, use headings and bulleted lists to sort information. If conventions allow, experiment with using charts and tables to provide quick access to important names, dates, and figures. Remember, too, that slight changes in font type or size and simple graphics, such as a horizontal rule, can do much to streamline a document, thereby increasing your document's efficiency.

Proposals

Proposals keep the world of business turning. Although they can take a variety of shapes—from telephone conversations to long, detailed forms—they share a common function: to deliver persuasive offers to solve problems.

A proposal can be either internal or external, solicited or unsolicited. If it's solicited, as in a formal Request for Proposals (RFP), then you may have the advantage of explicit guidelines to follow. This is the case with government research and development grants; for example, the NSERC (National Sciences and Engineering Research Council) provides detailed instructions and a tipsheet on its website.

Some of NSERC's tips address nitpicky formatting issues, such as required font and margin sizes, while others address matters relating to the criteria and the evaluation process. Among the most valuable words of wisdom, however, is the following recommendation: "Proofread your application carefully—typographical, spelling, and grammatical errors can have a negative impact. Take the time to make a good impression—this could be your only chance to compete for these funds!" (NSERC).

Unsolicited proposals also demand such extreme care, but there are normally fewer stated guidelines (although you may find filing cabinets full of precedents to use as models). Whatever form they take, unsolicited proposals frequently pose two peculiar challenges:

- you must make the audience aware there actually is a problem;
- you must establish that you're offering a uniquely effective solution to the problem.

From beginning to conclusion, your proposal should emphasize that you —and *only* you—possess the qualifications, resources, and character to eliminate the problem. *Ethos* thus plays a central role, whether you're pitching your idea, service, or product to a venture capitalist, a government grant program, or a business. You can have the greatest idea or product in the world, but if you can't convince your audience that you have the wherewithal to deliver it, then your proposal will fall flat.

Two veteran judges of proposals, Wayne Bussey and Ron McLeod, vehemently reinforce this point. Between them, Bussey and McLeod have evaluated more than a hundred funding applications to the Telecom Applications Research Alliance (TARA). Bussey sums up TARA's assessment criteria by saying, "We invest first and foremost in people . . . Every success and every failure relates back to people." McLeod concurs: "I'll take intelligence and courage over experience any day."

It's a myth that formal proposals should be de-personalized documents. Even when conventions require an impersonal style (no "I"), you still project a persona. When creating the various parts of a proposal, consider how each component conveys your most winning attributes.

Common elements of a proposal

One of the challenges of creating proposals, which can be hundreds of pages long, is the need to reach multiple audiences, with a variety of information needs, not to mention reading habits. The key is to include plenty of headings and other signposts (graphic and textual) to allow readers to navigate easily through the document. Think of proposal-writing as an exercise in facilitating speed-reading. Enable your readers to locate quickly the information that matters most to them and skip the rest. (Here's where experience constructing web pages will serve you well.)

Although some informal proposals may take the form of a brief email or letter of intent, even these should divide into at least two sections: a clear statement of the problem and a detailed description of the solution. More formal proposals usually include the following sections, although not necessarily in the order listed.

Introduction

This is where you introduce yourself, shaking hands, so to speak, with the reader. Since first impressions are so vital, the introduction alone can make or break a proposal.

Besides providing a brief overview of the proposal as a whole, the introduction should whet the audience's appetite. I think of the "Introduction" as the "Motivation to Read." Because it's so important, you might want to delay drafting it until you've completed the rest of the proposal and can state precisely the compelling reasons for readers to consider your solution.

Background

This section names and describes the problem. (You might even title it "The problem.") In some cases, as in a business plan, it may need to establish the very existence of the problem. Let's say, for example, you're pitching to a venture capitalist a proposal to produce inexpensive electronic paper (a paper-thin screen users could inscribe with a stylus). Your audience may not perceive that there are concerns regarding the status quo—paper produced from wood pulp. To make your proposal convincing, then, you'll need to establish that the status quo is, in fact, problematic. You might point out, for instance, the expense of disposable paper, the environmental problems caused by clearcutting, and the pollution created by the process of recycling old paper.

By the time they've finished reading your "Background," your readers should be feeling mighty uncomfortable and therefore ready to consider the solution you propose. If you can't locate a real problem, you may not have a legitimate proposal. The Canadian Patents Database is full of bizarre ideas that sounded great to the inventors but failed to serve a genuine need in the market.

Benefits

When writing this section, keep one distinction clearly in mind: *benefits* differ from *features*. Your product may have 293 individually impressive components, but perhaps only a handful of those improve life for your readers. Concentrate on defining and selling those.

As you catalogue the benefits your proposal will create, make sure to stress the uniqueness of the particular solution you're suggesting. Otherwise, in a corporate situation, you could effectively generate business for the competition.

Speaking of the competition, it's usually wise to acknowledge it's out there. Graciously deal with the pros and cons of your offering in comparison so that your readers perceive you as reasonable, fair, and well-informed. Recognizing the opposite side of the question and anticipating audience objections can actually serve as useful rhetorical strategies for further establishing your credibility.

Description of work

Business jargon refers to the items you enumerate here as "the deliverables." In this section, you list the results you'll accomplish. Describe these in precise, quantitative terms. Where possible, incorporate graphics in your description by including outlines, blueprints, or schematic diagrams.

Method

Depending on the context, this section could involve substantial theoretical or technical background. Here, you define such project elements as your software engineering system, your manufacturing process, your testing procedures, and your approach to collaborating with a client or partner. Include the minimum information needed to provide an overview of your plan for accomplishing your project. It's normally wise to use plain language, since proposals commonly circulate to decision-makers who are non-experts, such as financial officers or high-ranking executives.

Schedule

In most cases, charts or tables will best present the information in this section. Your schedule should include a final completion date as well as a timeline indicating key deadlines along the way. Make sure you also provide dates for progress reports, if you'll be delivering these.

Qualifications

If you've been doing your job well, you've been emphasizing your credibility throughout the proposal. You've already, for instance, mentioned your stellar qualifications in your "Introduction." You've also demonstrated your expertise by supporting any claims you make about the project's benefits with valid research, and lucidly describing your methods in language a lay reader can understand. Finally, you've revised, edited, and proofread your proposal so that the image you present on paper is orderly, efficient, and courteous. Your qualifications should simply confirm the positive impression you've already created indirectly.

Probably the biggest mistake proposal-writers make in this section is being too timid. While it's rude to brag, it's not crass to state objectively what you know and what you've done. If you completed the last project three weeks early, that's worth mentioning. If your organization has received an industry award, or if one of your team members has an impressive (and relevant) educational background, say that too. Offer to provide references or client testimonials, if you have these. Never, however, offer to provide a reference without first verifying that the person is willing to speak glowingly of your work.

Required resources

Decision-makers will be keenly interested in this section, which outlines the specific costs you'll incur as well as staffing and system requirements. Although you'll want to be competitive, it doesn't pay to underestimate here. To protect your reputation as a reliable professional, make your predictions as accurate as you can. Where you can't provide a precise figure, you may be able to indicate a numerical range.

This section commonly incorporates charts or tables to communicate financial details. If you have a long spreadsheet, consider including it as an appendix to the document so that it doesn't interfere with readability.

Conclusions

Some of your readers will skim your document by flipping quickly from the first to the last pages. To accommodate these readers, and to refresh the memory of others, reiterate here the most compelling reasons why your particular solution is the ideal answer to the problem at hand. Refrain from simply summarizing the individual sections of the proposal, unless you're working within a prescribed format that requires such repetition. Writing an effective conclusion requires careful selectivity. You should highlight the advantages of your plan, especially for the long term, and your one-of-a-kind qualifications for implementing it.

By the end of this section, readers should understand that what you're proposing is not only necessary but also easy to implement and highly beneficial over time. They should see that they can't afford to refuse your request for action. Moreover, they should view you, the proposal writer, as an effective, congenial partner whom they can trust. Just as your introductory section functions as your opening handshake with the reader, your concluding section serves as your farewell handshake. Cement the positive relationship you've already established by striving for a tone that's friendly, polite, and optimistic. To encourage further interaction, you may want to restate contact information so that readers will follow up with you for further details.

Further tips for creating persuasive proposals

Successful proposals move the reader from grasping the problem to desiring the solution. It's not enough, however, merely to intrigue your audience. You must empower readers to take action—perhaps immediately. Provide readers with all the information they need to make a well-reasoned decision. This is not the time to build suspense by leaving your readers hanging with questions such as "I wonder how much that will cost?" or "What methods will they use to conduct the research?" By the time they've finished reviewing your proposal, readers should feel fully confident to endorse your project.

Here are a few final reminders of ways you can cultivate your reader's confidence throughout your proposal:

- Conduct a thorough audience analysis for each group of readers that will receive the proposal.
- Adopt organizational strategies you'd use for online writing to enable different audiences to access quickly the information they need.
- Emphasize in more than one place the unique advantages your proposal will create.
- Use plain language. Only in very rare circumstances does a proposal circulate exclusively to technical experts.
- Avoid clichés and overused superlatives, such as "cutting-edge," "innovative," and "ground-breaking." Instead, make your language more precise. A so-called "innovative" eLearning platform, for instance, could manifest any number of remarkable qualities. It could be "responsive," "student-centred," "fluid," "motivation-driven," or "instructor-friendly." Find the adjectives that best represent the technology's benefits.
- Pare down wordy prose. Eliminate such common causes of wordiness as passive constructions, nominalizations, and redundant expressions. (You may want to review the material in Chapter 5 for help with this.)
- Enlist graphics to work for you. Further cut down your word count by presenting schedules and financial data in charts or tables. Enhance verbal descriptions by including diagrams of a planned product.

- Mind your formatting. If you're responding to a formal RFP, even the slightest breach of prescribed conventions, such as margins that are too narrow or a font that's too small, could send your proposal to the waste bin. Even informal proposals can be highjacked by errors in expression (grammar, punctuation, spelling, and mechanics). If possible, find a second reader who can cast a fresh eye over your work and help you edit it.

Design documents

Although some organizations use the term "design document" to signify a specific type of document—perhaps one that writers create by template—I use the term to refer to a diverse range of writing relating to project management, including software requirements, design briefs, outlines, implementation plans, and software specifications.

Depending on the context, the genre expectations for design documents may be either hard or soft. Some organizations, for instance, rigidly adhere to the *IEEE Recommended Practice for Software Requirements Specifications* published by the Institute of Electrical and Electronics Engineers. In complete contrast, other organizations treat design documentation very loosely. Development happens so rapidly in some workplaces that it's impossible to write down all the changes as they occur. In other work environments, the development staff is so small that much communication about design issues happens in face-to-face conversations or casual email messages, so only a faint paper trail ever exists.

The shape of a design document depends on the project management paradigm followed by the organization. The "waterfall" approach to software development, for example, tends to lead to rigidly structured documents, and lots of them. Because the waterfall method assigns different stages of development work to different teams, employees must scrupulously record each of their intentions, efforts, and results for others to read.

On the other hand, the so-called "Agile method" of software development generates more fluid design documents. Patrick Welsh, a founding partner of Adaption Software, describes the Agile "movement" as "part of a larger, humanizing movement in software development." Agile programming involves close interaction not just among programmers but also between programmers and users, between programmers and graphic designers, and between programmers and managers. Because the development process is highly collaborative, design documents often become design conversations, conducted either live or via informal written messages. Moreover, because the Agile method emphasizes responsiveness to end-user feedback, design documents tend to evolve *ad hoc*, frequently in bits and pieces, rather than as elaborate blueprints conforming to established regulations.

In the most controversial brand of the Agile method, extreme programming (XP), developers all but eliminate the need for design documentation as they code side-by-side at the same keyboard. The demanding duet of XP requires such intense concentration, however, that programmers can only sustain it for brief periods. Until telepathy among co-workers becomes the norm, then, the need for some sort of design documentation will persist, no matter the model of project management.

Whether you're creating a design document "to spec" or making your own choices about organization and format, you are engaged in crafting a technical description. Your task is to describe either what your product will do, how it will do it, or perhaps both.

Although we often associate descriptive writing with fiction and poetry, it doesn't have to be flowery or effusive. In our technical context, descriptive writing functions as a kind of amplified definition, verbally portraying an item or a procedure. You don't need a poet's sense of rhythm and rhyme to create an effective technical description. However, you do require some of a poet's tools, such as an attention to detail, a sense of organization, a precise vocabulary; and the ability to encapsulate the unfamiliar by using comparisons to the familiar.

The role of definitions in technical description

Like any other piece of writing, a product description should feature a beginning, a middle, and a conclusion. It's common to begin with a concise definition of the software or hardware. Featuring a definition up front immediately orients your reader. It can also suggest a ready-made structure for you to use in the rest of the description.

Definitions come in different forms, and not every form will suit every situation. Here are the main types:

Formal
A formal definition places an item within a class of items, and then names the quality or qualities that distinguish the particular item from the rest of its class.

- A notebook computer is a portable computer that has a folding screen and is thin enough to fit in a standard briefcase.
- Linux is an operating system written in "open source" code.

Operational
An operational definition names an item's function. Precise verbs constitute the core ingredient here.

- A scroll saw performs fine cuts.
- A web browser enables a user to view web pages.
- A pacemaker artificially regulates an irregular or slow heartbeat.

Metaphorical
A metaphorical definition captures the essence of an item by comparing it to something unlike itself. As we saw in Chapter 2, metaphor is

often the most powerful tool a technical writer can use to "translate" for non-experts.

- A pacemaker is like a battery that controls a heartbeat.
- The web is like a vast library.

Divisional

Just as the name implies, a divisional definition portrays an item in terms of its component parts.

- The human ear is composed of two main parts: the inner and the outer ear.
- A desktop computer consists of three main pieces of hardware: the Central Processing Unit (CPU), the monitor, and the keyboard.

Structuring a technical description

Weak organization undermines the efficacy of many product descriptions. Since the information you're presenting is likely unfamiliar to your reader, you need to take extra pains to create a clear path from one part of your description to the next. You can't assume your readers will simultaneously grasp the detailed and overall perspectives; it's your responsibility to facilitate this task for them.

While there's no standardized format or structure for a product description, for clarity's sake, I suggest you follow two general principles:

1. **Start with the general and move to the specific**
   This may seem an obvious principle, but writers often overlook it. Sometimes it's a matter of no longer being able to see the aerial view of the forest after spending so long among the tree trunks. In my experience, the more intimate knowledge you have of an item or subject, the more difficult it becomes to describe it for a novice audience. The task of writing a clear product description requires a certain amount of distance from the item or process being described.

   To make sure you maintain the necessary perspective, introduce your reader to the product first in general terms and then in progressive levels of detail. For example, if you're describing a router, you might first start by outlining the external physical appearance and dimensions of the hardware and then proceed to describing the internal circuitry. Similarly, if your task is to describe a new email browser, it would probably make sense to begin by explaining the interface before enumerating the program's individual functions.

2. **Start with the old and move to the new**
   Communicating with non-experts is an exercise in bridge-building. IT professionals who successfully reach audiences with limited technical knowledge understand this basic concept: to connect with non-experts,

you need to relate your unfamiliar information to concepts that are familiar to them. Since many non-technical readers are terrified of or hostile toward "techie talk," it's wise to guide them gently from the comfortable world and words they know to the uncomfortable, strange world and language to which you're introducing them.

In practical terms, adopting an old-to-new method of organizing your material means making sure that you define one component or step before advancing to the next. Before you describe the position of the USB 2.0 port on the CPU, for instance, you'd better make sure you've already described at least the general contours of the CPU. Bridges are built one plank at a time. Provide sure footing for your readers all the way across by working from what linguists call the "accessible" information to the "not accessible" (Holloway, p. 207).

Cohesive writing tends to feature old information at the beginning of a sentence, followed by new information, as in this example:

> The taskbar appears in the upper right corner of the screen. On this task bar [old information] appear icons that control input and printing functions [new information].

In context, the second sentence in the example is easy to grasp. Imagine, though, how bewildering it would be to someone who had no idea what a "taskbar" was. You can minimize the risk of creating such confusion by making the old-to-new pattern the norm for structuring information, at the sentence, paragraph, and document level.

Additional advice for creating effective design documents

Here are a few more pointers to keep in mind when you present technical description as the basis of a design document:

1. ***Explicitly state assumptions***
   Eliminate ambiguity about system requirements, equipment specifications, and product versions. If, for instance, you're writing a product description to apply to three different versions of a product, you'll need to indicate which version you're using as the model for your description. If certain features of a software program function only when minimum system requirements are in place, then you'll need to say so when you describe them.

2. ***Use jargon carefully***
   Jargon is not necessarily an evil. It's actually very precise technical language that provides efficient shortcuts when two experts want to communicate with one another. In some circumstances, then, it makes more sense to use jargon—and explain it if necessary—than to substitute an inaccurate word

or phrase. (If you find yourself creating numerous definitions for jargon words, you might want to create a glossary for your document.)

Alan Parslow, a software engineer who specializes in Artificial Intelligence (AI), explains that replacing jargon with a layperson's general terminology can, in fact, jeopardize clarity. For instance, the company for which he works, Deep Vision, has had to strike the word "identity" from all documentation because the word means one thing in ordinary life and something quite different in the AI field. Parslow points out that even communicating with so-called "technical" people can require detailed definitions because "it depends what technical side the technical people are on." Even within the IT world, technical experts can come from discourse communities with subtle differences in vocabulary. When he's having trouble groping for the right word, Parslow turns to a philosophical dictionary to help him define key terms.

3. *Incorporate visual descriptions*
Include diagrams, sketches, screen shots, or photographs to help your readers more clearly "see" your intended product. Sometimes a visual can actually serve as the core of a technical description, with the text consisting of detailed captions or labels.

4. *Bear in mind long-term implications*
Design documents can serve both legal and legacy functions. As you write, contemplate the various roles your document could be recruited to play down the road. Could the language you use be considered legally binding in any sense? Could others rely on your description to design later products or evaluate the product's success? As such questions suggest, your design document may well outlive your involvement with the product or project. The long-term prospect offers additional incentive for grooming your writing to be extra comprehensive and ultra-precise.

5. *Write to facilitate later revision*
Because design documents can endure such a long time, make it easy for others to revise your writing. One way to do this is to structure your information in numbered sections. (Some organizations insist that each paragraph be numbered.) Moreover, be sure your title page clearly indicates the author(s), date, and the version of the document.

6. *Document all references*
The ethics regarding intellectual property apply to design documents just as they apply to any other kind of writing. Make sure you provide complete bibliographical information for all the sources you use and that you follow the citation method that's conventional in your community of practice.

Instructions

If you think the task of writing instructions is child's play, I challenge you to try this simple exercise: construct a set of instructions telling someone how to tie his or her shoelaces. The last time I asked a group of seasoned IT professionals to do this, the class dissolved in laughter. As we looked down at shoes half-laced and cross-laced, we all had to admit that instructions number among the most complex documents an IT worker can be asked to produce.

If you're lucky, your employer will have the funds to hire an experienced technical writer to create user documentation for you. However, many small companies can't afford this, and rely on internal staff instead.

Some guidelines for creating successful instructions

Even if you're never appointed to produce a full-blown user manual, you'll likely create other kinds of instructions quite regularly. Consider the following examples of day-to-day communication tasks that require IT professionals to deliver clear instructions:

- Telling employees how to reset their passwords
- Informing employees of new procedures for accessing the company server
- Providing a client with directions to the office
- Asking employees to log on to a new section of the company website
- Explaining how to prepare a desktop computer for inter-office transfer
- Directing a client how to download a sample software program

Writing even an apparently straightforward set of instructions can be time-consuming. As technical editor Nancy Holland explained to me, crafting manuals that are simple to read requires much painstaking revision. She tells employers, "You're paying me for the words I'm leaving out, not the words I'm putting in." To help you draft—and re-draft—instructions to fit a variety of contexts, I've assembled the following list of suggested best practices. As you decide which of them apply to your writing context, you'll want to conduct additional research into the factors that shape your situation, such as audience needs and budget constraints.

As you decide how to interpret the following suggestions, base your judgments on the purpose of your instructions as well as the intended audience. People who consult instructions "read to do," as opposed to "reading to learn" or "reading to pass the time." However, not everyone reads to do the same thing. You need to be able to predict how the audience will employ your instructions before you decide on such basic matters as length, format, and a table of contents.

For example, a group of readers new to a particular electronic device will want to use instructions to assemble the item and proceed, step by step, through the basic tasks they need it to perform. Another group of more experienced readers, on the other hand, will want to access the documentation for trouble-shooting purposes only. They're content to fiddle with the technology until they encounter a serious difficulty, at which point they want to locate quickly an answer to their problem.

Your grasp of your readers' expectations for *using* (not merely reading) your document will enable you to decide whether you need to create a quick-start brochure, an installation guide, a user guide, a reference manual, a virtual tutorial, or an on-screen help system. Your user analysis may even lead you to create instructions within more than one of these sub-genres of instructions so that you can serve various reader factions.

Use direct commands throughout your document

A reader should immediately be able to identify instructions as such by the direct commands they use.

Rather than describing a process, instructions should tell the reader what to do. Here's an example to show that the distinction isn't just academic:

> *Description:* Once depressed, the switch activates the launching program.

> *Instruction:* To activate the launching program, push down on the switch.

As you can see, if you confuse the two modes of expression, you'll leave your readers bewildered as to what action they actually need to accomplish.

Centre end-user documentation on the user, not the technology being used

Put people ahead of technology and focus on the reader's needs. Organize a user manual according to common questions a user might ask, instead of according to a developer's hierarchy of functions. Depending on the tone of your user manual, you might even consider phrasing your module or section headings as direct questions ("How do I retrieve a deleted file?" rather than "The reverse-delete function").

On the sentence level, consider speaking directly to your readers as "you" in explanatory notes as well as direct commands. It also helps to use active verbs, wherever possible. Here are a few examples of how technology-first language can be turned into user-first language:

Technology-centred	User-centred
At this point, it's recommended that users contact their system administrator.	At this point, you should contact your system administrator. *or* At this point, you're advised to contact your system administrator.
Once the data has been entered, the database is ready to be searched.	Once you've entered the data, you're ready to search the database.

The system will reject any inputs containing an asterisk.	If you make an entry containing an asterisk, the system will not accept it. *or* Avoid inputs containing an asterisk because the system will not accept them
Once the disk is loaded, a green light will appear on the panel.	Once you've loaded the disk, you'll see a green light appear on the panel.

Provide a clear introduction

An accurate title is essential. Forgo poetic touches here. Simple and unmistakably obvious works best, as in "How to install your printer" or "Installing your printer."

Your introduction should provide the reader with the following information (as appropriate):

- Required equipment or functionality
  To install the software, you'll need a computer with Windows XP.

- Assumptions about the tools, equipment, context, and user's existing knowledge
  These instructions assume that the user is already familiar with Version 2.0.

- Length of time needed to perform the task
  It will probably take you two or three hours to assemble the hardware.

- Overall warnings or precautions
  Warning: If you wear a pacemaker, check with your physician before installing this alarm system in your home.

Close with a definite conclusion

Your conclusion should indicate that the task is now complete. Unlike a conclusion to a report or proposal, it shouldn't summarize preceding information. Instead, it should deliver such facts as the following:

- How to recognize that the task has been completed correctly
  You'll know you've properly adjusted the monitor when the Menu screen minimizes.

- Actions to try if the technology does not perform as expected
  See the following chart for help with trouble-shooting.

- Where to obtain additional help
  For further help, call 1-800-987-6548 or visit our web page at www.hotproducts.com.

- How the completed task fits into a larger process, or how the technology interacts with other products

    Now that you've calibrated your equipment, you're ready to start taking measurements outdoors.

    Now that you've installed RecipeWhiz, you may want to try Pocket RecipeWhiz, which enables you to view your recipes conveniently on your handheld computer.

Treat each step as a discrete unit

Thomas Barker (2003), author of *Writing Software Documentation: A Task-Oriented Approach,* maintains that software user manuals work best when they achieve what he calls "modularity" (pp. 361–2); in practice, this means that users should be able to access within a two-page spread all the information they need to perform a particular task, from start to finish.

Even when the two-page module is not practical (perhaps due to budget constraints), you can improve your instructions by adopting certain modular techniques:

- Separate steps. You can do this by means of numbers, headings, or graphical cues (such as indentations or horizontal rules).

- Orient your readers so that they know exactly where they are in the process.

    You've now completed the first phase of the installation.

    Now that you've reconfigured the system, you're ready to verify the program files.

    The next step is to test the cables.

    Make sure, in particular, that you indicate when a task is complete and how to recognize that it's been performed successfully.

- Include cautions and trouble-shooting information immediately before the instruction for a potentially hazardous action (even if the cautions are also listed in a separate section elsewhere). There are four conventional levels of cautions, although individual communities of practice may interpret them slightly differently:

    DANGER flags a serious threat to life or health.

    WARNING flags potential damage to the product or risk of minor injury

    CAUTION flags a risk to proper performance

    NOTE indicates an additional explanation or a description of a possible problem

- Reinforce verbal commands with pictures (line diagrams, photos, screen shots) that demonstrate what needs to be done, how to do it, and how to recognize the desired result. Place charts, tables, and graphics as close as possible to the related text.

Scrutinize your front and back matter for accuracy

Publishers know the painstaking work it takes to prepare an index, but they also realize how crucial such back matter as appendixes, glossaries, and indexes can be to the success of a publication. That's why they contract out indexing to editorial specialists. Few of us workaday writers, however, enjoy the luxury of delegating the detail work to others. Allow yourself plenty of time to create both your back matter and your front matter (title page, table of contents, table of figures). Although word-processing programs can automate some of the work, they can't substitute for diligent cross-checking, editing, and proofreading.

Use simple sentence structures and quantifiable language

Straightforward sentences work best because users can process only small bits of information at a time. Remember, they're doing much more than just reading: they're reading, learning new information, and trying to perform a new activity, all at the same time.

While all instructions benefit from simple *syntax*, not all require simple *language*. An installation manual written for system administrators would, for example, likely feature high-level technical jargon, which would be completely appropriate in that context.

All instruction writers do, however, need to strive for language that is concrete and quantifiable. Avoid ambiguous terms—such as *slightly, a little, short,* or *small*—to describe actions and results. For example, rather than telling users to wait "a few minutes" before plugging in a device, indicate a specific amount of time, such as "ten minutes." Instead of instructing users to strip a "short" piece of tubing from a wire, tell them to strip "two centimetres." When listing equipment needs, make sure you also call a spade a spade, not a general gardening implement. Refer, for instance, to a "jeweller's screwdriver" instead of to a "small screwdriver."

Take design seriously

Donald Norman, one of the fathers of usability design, includes an intriguing sketch in his pioneering book, *The Psychology of Everyday Things.* The sketch, entitled "Coffeepot for Masochists," is by Jacques Carelman (Norman, p. 2). It shows a coffee pot that seems ordinary in all respects but one—its handle appears directly beneath its spout. Thus, anyone who tried to pour a hot cup of java would be painfully scalded. Norman's point is that bad design burns users in a similar way. When consumers complain that a product's manual is hard to read, often their problems are caused by inconsistent document design.

Remember the key design principles from our discussions of other genres:

- Allow plenty of white space
- Construct visible, concise headings
- Use fonts consistently

- Identify different types of information with colour or small graphics (icons)
- Label all figures the same way
- Choose a layout that uses all four quadrants of the page grid

You can learn a lot about effective design by collecting examples of instructions, both good and bad.

Conduct end-user testing (even if you can't afford it)

A set of instructions, we've said, functions as a tool the user employs to accomplish a particular task, step by step. The only way to know if your tool is doing the job is to ask the users.

Of course, in-depth assessment of users' knowledge, needs, equipment, and learning preferences forms part of the homework you do before writing instructions. Once you've crafted your instructions, or perhaps part of them, it's time to test those assumptions you made. As my students experienced when they tried the shoe-tying experiment, wide discrepancies can appear between a writer's intent and a user's understanding.

If you can't afford to hire a consultant to conduct user testing, or to pay users for participating in a focus group, locate free testers who approximately match your user profiles. These might be employees of another department, university students, or your friends. While confidentiality issues can severely hamper such informal testing, be creative with the resources available to you.

! WARNING: releasing instructions without testing them could be highly hazardous to your organization's reputation and your career.

Rhetorical aspects of instruction-writing

Since instructions use the imperative mood (they give direct commands to the reader), you'd think that instruction writers would be naturally attuned to the presence of the intended audience. However, we've all encountered instructions that seem to issue robotic directives into an implied vacuum.

In recognition of this widespread problem, Technical Standards, a California writing company, hosts an annual Worst Manual Contest. For a top prize of a hundred dollars, contestants submit examples of laughably inadequate product documentation. While many entries clearly derive their obscurity from poor translation, there are also plenty of entries authored by writers whose first language is English. Winners for 2005 included instructions for operating a hydraulic jack, a remote control, some desktop publishing software, and a Rubik's cube.

Fortunately, within the IT industry, changes are happening. Following the lead of the popular *For Dummies* series, publishers of consumer user guides, including Microsoft, are realizing that the personal touch brings rewards. The dominant assumption is now that users are more successful and satisfied when instructions take the tone of a friendly conversation with a mentor rather than a set of orders from an inhuman dictator. Increasingly, it's becoming the norm not only to address the reader directly as "you" but also to introduce colloquial language and humour into instructions.

This modern trend points, once again, to the ancient wisdom of rhetoricians, such as Aristotle. As they recognized, there's simply no such thing as perfectly objective communication uninflected by the communicator's personality and attitude. Like it or not, readers will impute a character to the voice behind your instructions. If that voice is anonymous, they'll likely attribute the personal characteristics they infer to the company or organization responsible for the document. What kind of persona do you want your instructions to create for you? For your organization? For your industry?

As an IT insider, it may be difficult to appreciate just how alien your world may appear to outsiders. When you write instructions for novice users, bear in mind that many of them are trembling with nervousness before they even open your document. Many others may feel resentment toward your product or your organization, especially if they're turning to the user documentation because they've just encountered a problem with the technology. You can safely assume that your readers constitute a rather jittery, grumpy lot. Consequently, you need to woo them. The more pleasant, helpful, and human you can make the voice of your instructions, the more likely they are to succeed.

Concluding thoughts

It seems appropriate that we should examine instructions at the conclusion of our journey together. Of all the genres we've explored, instructions require perhaps the highest degree of organizational skill, audience sensitivity, and quality assurance. As you go on to explore the worlds of writing and work, you will encounter additional genres, some of which haven't even developed yet. Keep one eye on documents in the filing cabinet and one eye on the evolving formats and styles in your inbox, and you'll be able to adapt successfully to whatever evolving forms you meet.

Exercises

1. Try out your skills as a writer of instructions by creating step-by-step directions for accomplishing one of the following tasks:

   - tying a necktie
   - making a paper airplane
   - making a favourite food
   - changing a printer cartridge

   Now test your instructions by asking someone else to use them. What about your instructions is unclear? What adjustments would you need to perform to make them foolproof?

2. The following PowerPoint slides breach many of the conventions of effective presentations. Identify as many of these as you can and suggest changes.

What's wrong with this presentation?

COMM 1702
March 2005

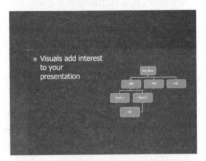

Advantages of using PowerPoint

- By default, PowerPoint requires you to use basic design principles.
- PowerPoint can help you organize your presentation.
- If you're a nervous presenter, PowerPoint can be a comforting prop.
- PowerPoint can make a presentation appear more formal than its meant to be.

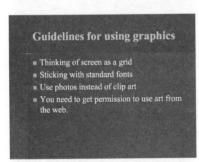

PowerPt guidelines

- A picture tells
A thousand words

- Visuals add interest to your presentation

Guidelines for using graphics

- Thinking of screen as a grid
- Sticking with standard fonts
- Use photos instead of clip art
- You need to get permission to use art from the web.

Some standard fonts

- Arial
- Times New Roman
- Courier

Furthermore...

Use symbols to communicate.

Summary

- Graphics are impt, but not as important as the message you have to presnet
- Always make sure that you put your audience first
- Don't assume that color has universal meaning

- Use sound and animation sparingly
- Avoid reading directly from the screen (this is the number one bad habit of PowerPoint presenters)
- Don't be afraid to present without the aid of PowerPoint
- Make sure that the version of PowerPoint you're using is the same as the version that will be on the machine you'll use to present

3. Practise writing a progress report by imagining you're in charge of creating a user manual for the *Whiz5*, a software package about to be released. Two weeks away from deadline you realize that you are not going to be able to complete the task on time. Last week, you took two days off to recover from the flu. Yesterday, your machine contracted a virus, and you had to spend all day trying to clean it. To make matters worse, you are scheduled to have your wisdom teeth removed next week. (You've been waiting three months for the appointment.)

   Write a brief report to update your supervisor, Flint Grindstone, on your situation. Keep in mind that Flint, who is fifty-two years old and single, is a demanding boss. He works between sixty to seventy hours a week. He has been with the company for only two months.

4. Write an informal proposal for a new course or student service for your college or university. (By "informal," I mean that there is no specified format for you to follow.) Create your proposal as an email of 500–700 words. Address it to the appropriate campus administrator.

5. Create an informal design brief for the home page of new website. (Again, by "informal" I mean that there is no specified format for you to follow.) Imagine you are a freelance consultant serving one of the following clients:

   - a favourite singer or band
   - a charitable organization
   - a campus club
   - a tourist organization
   - a sports team

   Your task is to tell the client your general plans for the page's design and content. (You don't have to provide the content, just indicate what type and amount of information the page will contain.)

6. Rewrite the following instructions so that they are user-centred, rather than technology-centred:

   (i)   The button on the left enables message sending.
   (ii) When the lid has not been locked, the blue light on top of the machine will flash.
   (iii) Users can access the new password by visiting www.companyintranet.com/password
   (iv) Little preparation is required to perform this task.
   (v)   The handle should be grasped firmly to prevent injury.

Where to Go from Here

This book has guided you through the basic processes and principles you'll need to become an effective writer in the IT workplace. However, you won't find any Certificate of Completion at the end of this volume. That's because—let me say it one final time—mastering the art of written communication is an ongoing adventure. A wise colleague once told me, "You never finish a piece of writing; you just abandon it." In a larger sense, you never finish learning how to write; you just learn how to give up the idea of ever nailing down the ultimate template set.

As your career progresses, your ability to keep improving your writing skills will become key to your professional advancement. To help you continue to polish the image you put forward in print, I've assembled a list of books and articles you can consult for further guidance. I invite you to help me grow this list; I would be delighted to hear from you about other resources you've found especially helpful. You can contact me by email through Oxford University Press at editorial.hed.ca@oup.com.

Best wishes as you persevere,

Dawn

Suggested further readings

The writing process

Elbow, P. (1981). *Writing with power: techniques for mastering the writing process.* New York: Oxford University Press.

——— (1998). *Writing without teachers.* 2nd ed. New York: Oxford University Press.

Flower, L. (1981). *Problem-solving strategies for writing.* New York: Harcourt Brace Jovanovich.

Lamott, A. (1994). *Bird by bird: some instructions on writing and life.* New York: Random House.

Murray, D. (2004). *The craft of revision.* 5th ed. Boston: Thomson/Heinle.

Rico, G. (1983). *Writing the natural way: using right-brain techniques to release your expressive powers.* Los Angeles: J.P. Tarcher.

Sharples, M. (1999). *How we write: writing as creative design*. London: Routledge.

Zinsser, W. (1998). *On writing well: the classic guide to writing nonfiction*. New York: HarperCollins.

Zobel, J. (2000). *Writing for computer science: the art of effective communication*. Singapore: Springer.

Web writing

Berners-Lee, T. (1992). *Style guide for online hypertext*. http://www.w3.org/Provider/Style.

Coney, M. and Steehouder, M. (2000). "Role playing on the Web: guidelines for designing and evaluating personas online." *Technical Communication*. 47 (3). 327–35.

Hammerich, I. and Harrison, C. (2002). *Developing online content: the principles of writing and editing for the Web*. New York: Wiley.

Kilian, C. (1999). *Writing for the Web: writers' edition*. North Vancouver, BC: Self-Counsel Press.

Krug, S. (2000). *Don't make me think: a common sense approach to Web usability*. Indianapolis: New Riders Press.

Lynch, P. and Horton, S. *Web style guide*. 2nd ed. http://www.webstyleguide.com.

Zimmerman, B. (1997). Applying Tufte's principles of information design to creating effective web sites. ACM 15th International Conference on Systems Documentation, p.309–17.

Email

Baker, K. and S. Baker (2001). *How to say it online: everything you need to know to master the new language of cyberspace*. Upper Saddle River, NJ: Prentice Hall.

Miller, S. (2001). *E-mail etiquette: do's, don'ts, and disaster tales from* People Magazine*'s Internet manners expert*. New York: Warner Books.

O'Sullivan, P. (2000). What you don't know won't hurt me: impression management functions of communication channels in relationships. *Human Communication Research*. 26 (3). 403–31.

Expression (grammar, punctuation, mechanics, and style)

Dupré, L. (1998). *Bugs in writing: a guide to debugging your prose*. 2nd ed. Boston: Addison-Wesley.

Strunk, W., Jr., E. B. White, and M. Kalman (2005). *The elements of style*. 5th ed. New York: Penguin.

Sun Technical Publications. (2003). *Read me first! A style guide for the computer industry*. 2nd ed. Upper Saddle River, NJ: Prentice Hall.

Truss, L. (2004). *Eats, shoots & leaves: the zero tolerance approach to punctuation*. New York: Gotham Books.

Walsh, B. (2000). *Lapsing into a comma: a curmudgeon's guide to the many things that can go wrong in print—and how to avoid them*. Chicago: Contemporary Books.

Woods, G. (2001). *English grammar for dummies: a reference for the rest of us!* New York: Wiley.

Persuasion

Cialdini, R. G. (1993). *Influence: the psychology of persuasion*. New York: William Morrow.

Lunsford, A., Rusczkiewicz, and K. Walters (2004). *Everything's an argument: with readings*. 3rd ed. Boston: Bedford/St. Martin's.

Document design

Coe, Mariana (1996). *Human factors for technical communicators*. New York: Wiley.

Kostelknick, C. (1988). A systematic approach to visual language in business communication. *Journal of Business Communication*. 25 (3). 29–48.

Schriver, K. (1997). *Dynamics in document design*. New York: Wiley.

IT-specific genres

Barker, T. S. (2003). *Writing software documentation: a task-oriented approach*. 2nd ed. New York: Longman.

Bremer, M. (1999). *The user manual manual: how to research, write, test, edit and produce a software manual*. Concord, CA: UnTechnical Press.

Institute of Electrical and Electronics Engineers (1998). *IEEE recommended practice for software requirements specifications*. New York: IEEE.

Wiegers, K. (2003). *Software requirements: practical techniques for gathering and managing requirements*. Microsoft.

Works Cited

Adkins, M. and Brashers, D. (1995). "The power of language in computer-mediated groups." *Management Communication Quarterly.* 8 (3). 289–322.

Aesop (1880). *Fables.* (G.F. Townsend, Trans.) Retrieved March 26, 2006, from *Electronic Text Center,* University of Virginia Library http://etext.virginia.edu/etcbin/toccer-new2?id=AesFabl.sgm&images=images/modeng&data=/texts/english/modeng/parsed&tag=public&part=232&division=div1.

Aristotle (1991). *On rhetoric: a theory of civic discourse.* (George A. Kennedy, Trans.). New York: Oxford University Press.

Axtell, R.E. ed. (1990). *Do's and taboos around the world: a guide to international behavior.* (2nd ed.). New York: Wiley.

Barker, T. (2003). *Writing software documentation: a task-oriented approach.* Allyn & Bacon Series in Technical Communication. New York: Longman.

Berleant, D. (2000). "Does typography affect proposal assessment?" *Communications of the ACM.* 43 (8). 24–25.

Berthoff, A. (1981). *The making of meaning: metaphors, models and maxims for writing teachers.* Montclair, NJ: Boynton/Cook.

Bonsiepe, G. (1965). "Visual/verbal rhetoric." *Ulm* 14/15/16. 30. Cited in Kinross (1985). 18.

Boyarski, D., Neuwirth, Forlizzi, J., and Regli, S.H. (1998). "A study of fonts designed for screen display." *CHI 98 Proceedings.* pp. 87–84. Cited in Bailey, B. (1999). "Screen fonts & speed reading." Retrieved March 23, 2006, from http://www.webusability.com/article_screen_font_and_speed_reading_3_1999.htm.

Carroll, L. (1969). *Alice's adventures in Wonderland.* In D. Rackin, ed. *Alice's adventures in Wonderland: a critical handbook.* Belmont, CA: Wadsworth. 111–211.

Charvet, S. R. (1997). *Words that change minds: mastering the language of influence.* (2nd ed.). Dubuque, IA: Kendall/Hunt.

Churchill, W. (1945). Speech read in the House of Commons, London, June 4, 1940. In R. Churchill, ed. *Into battle: speeches by the Right Hon. Winston S. Churchill.* (11th ed.). London: Cassell.

Cialdini, R. (1993). *Influence: the psychology of persuasion.* (2nd ed.). New York: William Morrow.

———— (2004). The language of persuasion. *Harvard Management Update.* 2004 (Sept). 10–11.

Clark, H. H. and Brennan, S. E. (1991). Grounding in communication. In L.B. Resnick, J. M. Levine, and S. D. Teasley, eds. *Perspectives on socially shared cognition.* 127–49. Washington, DC: American Psychological Association.

Coe, R. (1988). *Toward a grammar of passages*. Carbondale: Southern Illinois University Press.

Coney, M. and Steehouder, M. (2000). "Role playing on the Web: Guidelines for designing and evaluating personas on line." *Technical Communication*. 47 (3). 3–27.

Cooper, A. (1999). *The inmates are running the asylum: why high-tech products drive us crazy and how to restore the sanity*. Indianapolis: SAMS.

Elbow, P. (1981). *Writing with power: techniques for mastering the writing process*. New York: Oxford University Press.

——— (1998). *Writing without teachers*. 2nd ed. New York: Oxford.

Fahnestock, J. (2003). "Verbal and visual parallelism." *Written Communication*. 20 (2). 123–52.

Faris, K. and Smeltzer, L. (1997). Schema theory compared to text-centred theory as an explanation for the readers' understanding of a business message. *The Journal of Business Communication*. 34 (1). 7–26.

Fernback, J. (1999). "There is a there there: notes toward a definition of cybercommunity." In S. Jones (ed.). *Doing Internet research: critical issues and methods for examining the Net*. Thousand Oaks: Sage.

Flower, L. (1981). *Problem-solving strategies for writing*. New York: Harcourt Brace Jovanovich.

Gardner, E.H. (1915). *Effective business letters*. New York: Ronald Press.

Gardner, E.H. *Effective business letters: their requirements and preparation*. New York: Ronald Press.

Gardner, H. (1993). *Multiple intelligences: the theory in practice*. New York: Basic Books.

Geisler, C. *et al*. IText: future directions for research on the relationship between information technology and writing. *Journal of Business and Technical Communication*. 15 (3). 269–308.

Gilsdorf, J. and Leonard, D. (2001). Big stuff, little stuff: a decennial measurement of executives' and academics' reactions to questionable usage elements. *Journal of Business Communication*. 38 (4). 439–75.

Goffman, E. (1959). *The presentation of self in everyday life*. Garden City, NY: Doubleday.

Goleman, D. (1995). *Emotional intelligence: why it can matter more than IQ*. New York: Bantam.

Gunderson, M., Jacobs, L., and Vaillancourt, F. (2005). *The Information Technology (IT) market in Canada: results from the national survey of IT occupations*. Ottawa: Software Human Resource Council.

Gurak, L. (1997). *Persuasion and privacy in cyberspace: the online protests over Lotus MarketPlace and the clipper chip*. New Haven: Yale University Press.

Hanmerich, I. and Harrison, C. (2002). *Developing online content: the principles of writing and editing for the Web*. New York: Wiley.

Holloway, D. (1981). Semantic grammars: how they can help us teach writing. *College Composition and Communication*. 32 (2). 205–18.

Honeycutt, L. (2001). Comparing e-mail and synchronous conferencing in online peer response. *Written Communication*. 18 (1). 26–60.

Horton, W. (1997). *Secrets of user-seductive documents: wooing and winning the reluctant reader.* (2nd ed.). Arlington, VA: Society for Technical Communication.

Kilian, C. (1999). Writing for the Web. North Vancouver, BC: Self-Counsel Press.

Kinross, R. (1985). The rhetoric of neutrality. *Design Issues.* 2 (2). 18–30.

Knox, R.E. and Inkster, J.A. (1968). Postdecisional dissonance at post time. *Journal of Personality and Social Psychology.* 8. 319–23.

Kress, G. (2002). Colour as a semiotic mode: notes for a grammar of colour. *Visual Communication.* 1 (3). 343–68.

Kress, G. and Leeuwen, T. van. (1996). *Reading images: the grammar of visual design.* New York: Routledge.

Krug, S. (2000). *Don't make me think: a common sense approach to Web usability.* Indianapolis: New Riders.

Langer, E.J. (1978). Rethinking the role of thought in social interaction. In Harvey, Ickes, & Kidd (Eds.). *New directions in attribution research.* Vol. 2. Potomac, MD: Lawrence Erlbaum.

Locker, K., Kaczmarek, S. & Braun, K. (2005). *Business communication: building critical skills.* (2nd Canadian ed.). Toronto: McGraw-Hill.

MacKinnon, J. (1993). Becoming a rhetor: developing writing ability in a mature, writing–intensive organization. In. R. Spilka, ed. *Writing in the workplace: new research perspectives.* Carbondale: Southern Illinois University.

Milgram, S. (1974). *Obedience to authority: an experimental view.* New York: Harper.

Miller, C.R. (1984). Genre as social action. *Quarterly Journal of Speech.* 70. 151–67.

Moody, Fred. (1995). *I sing the body electronic: a year with Microsoft on the multimedia frontier.* New York: Viking.

Morgenstern, J. (1998). *Organizing from the inside out.* New York: Henry Holt.

Morkes, J. & Nielsen, J. (1997). Concise, scannable, and objective: how to write for the Web. Retrieved March 23, 2006, from http://www.useit.com/papers/webwriting/writing.html.

Murray, D. (1987). *Writing to learn.* (2nd ed.). New York: Holt, Rinehart and Winston.

Nielsen, J. (1997). Be succinct! (writing for the Web). *Jakob Nielsen's Alertbox.* Retrieved March 23, 2006, from http://www.useit.com/alertbox/9703b.html.

Norman, D. (1988). *The psychology of everyday things.* New York: Basic Books.

NSERC. (2005). Tips for preparing a successful CGS, PGS or PDF application. Retrieved March 22, 2006, from http://www.nserc.ca/programs/sf/pgs_pdf_tips_e.htm.

Razran, G.H.S. (1938). Conditioning away social bias by the luncheon technique. *Psychological Bulletin.* 35. 693.

Redish, J.C. (2004). Writing for the Web: letting go of the words. *Intercom.* June. 4–10.

Rico, G. (1983). *Writing the natural way: using right-brain techniques to release your expressive powers.* Los Angeles: J.P. Tarcher.

Rifkin, K. (2004). *Recruiting, retaining and developing IT staff: challenges and strategies*. Ottawa: Software Human Resource Council.

Schick, Shane. (2004). [Interview with Eugene Kaluzniacky]. *Computing Canada*. 30 (4). 10.

Sharples, M. (1999). *How we write: writing as creative design*. London: Routledge.

Stauffer, D. (1999). "Can I apologize by e-mail?" *Harvard Management Communication Newsletter*. Nov. 4–6.

Stöckl, H. (2005). Typography: body and dress of a text—a signing mode between language and image. *Visual Communication*. 4 (2). 204–14.

Sztompka, P. (1999). *Trust: a sociological theory*. Cambridge: Cambridge University Press.

Tannen, D. (1994). *Talking from 9 to 5: women and men at work*. New York: William Morrow.

Tiger, L., and Fox, R. (1971). *The imperial animal*. New York: Dell Publishing.

Tufte, E. (2003, Sept.). PowerPoint is evil. *Wired*. Retrieved March 23, 2006, from http://www.wired.com/wired/archive/11.09/ppt2_pr.html.

———— (2003). *The Cognitive Style of PowerPoint*. Cheshire, CT: Graphics Press.

Walther, J.B. (1996). Computer-mediated communication: impersonal, interpersonal, and hyperpersonal interaction. *Communication Research*. 23 (1). 3–43.

Wyllie, A. (1993). *On the road to discovery: a study of the composing strategies of academic writers using the word processor*. Unpublished M.A. thesis. University of Lancaster. Summarized in Sharples (1999, 115–18).

Zervos, C. (1985). Conversation with Picasso. (B. Ghiselin, Trans.). In *The Creative process: a symposium*. Berkeley: University of California Press. 48–53. (Original interview published in *Cahiers d'art*, 1935.)

Interviews

Anderson, Derek. 6 July 2004
Bussey, Wayne and Ron McLeod. 14 July 2004
Cote, Mignona. 18 May 2004
Daniel, Bart. 4 July 2004
Dent, Ann. 29 March 2004
Edwards, Gwyneth. 3 May 2004
Harbarenko, John. 18 May 2004
Heffell, Karen. 30 March 2004
Holland, Nancy. 23 March 2004
Leahy, John. 13 July 2004
Levings, Robert. 15 July 2004
MacCormick, Ron. 29 March 2004
McCurdy, David. 8 April 2004
MacDonald, Allison. 16 April 2004
MacDougall, Bruce. 19 July 2004
Mulle, Jim. 22 March 2004
Musial, Mike. 21 July 2004
Parslow, Alan. 20 July 2004
Pettigrew, Mark. 22 July 2004
Smedley, Garth. 13 July 2004
Spaulding, Karen. 16 July 2004
Taylor, Lysia. 23 March 2004
Thibalt, Sylvie. 20 July 2004
Walsh, Sandy. 24 March 2004
Weeks, Tanya Shaw. 3 Aug 2004
Welsh, Patrick. 2 April 2004
Yeomans, Tommy. 26 March 2004

Index